E<small>LIZA</small> L<small>UCAS</small>

Eliza Lucas Pinckney

Colonial Plantation Manager and Mother of American Patriots, 1722–1793

Margaret F. Pickett

McFarland & Company, Inc., Publishers
Jefferson, North Carolina

LIBRARY OF CONGRESS CATALOGUING-IN-PUBLICATION DATA

Names: Pickett, Margaret F., author.
Title: Eliza Lucas Pinckney : colonial plantation manager and mother of
    American patriots, 1722–1793 / Margaret F. Pickett.
Description: Jefferson, North Carolina : McFarland & Company, Inc.,
    Publishers, 2016. | Includes bibliographical references and index.
Identifiers: LCCN 2016026568 | ISBN 9781476665863 (softcover : acid
    free paper) ∞
Subjects: LCSH: Pinckney, Eliza Lucas, 1723–1793. | Pinckney, Charles,
    –1758. | South Carolina—History—Colonial period, ca. 1600–1775. |
    South Carolina—Politics and government—1775–1783.
Classification: LCC F272 .P65 P53 2016 | DDC 975.7/02092 [B]—dc23
LC record available at https://lccn.loc.gov/2016026568

BRITISH LIBRARY CATALOGUING DATA ARE AVAILABLE

ISBN (print) 978-0-4766-6586-3
ISBN (ebook) 978-1-4766-2528-7

Front cover images © 2016 iStock

Printed in the United States of America

McFarland & Company, Inc., Publishers
    Box 611, Jefferson, North Carolina 28640
    www.mcfarlandpub.com

Table of Contents

Preface and Acknowledgments

Prior to moving to South Carolina in 2010 I had spent 20 years working in museum education in Williamsburg, Virginia—first for the Jamestown/Yorktown Foundation and then for Colonial Williamsburg. It was while working at Colonial Williamsburg that I discovered "living history"—the impersonation of a person from the past. Having done some theater work in high school and college and having an avid interest in history, I was intrigued by the idea of becoming "a person of the past" myself.

I decided to pursue the idea and became a living history interpreter for the National Park Service at Historic Jamestown—the site of the first permanent English settlement in North America. That was in 1999 and I have never looked back. The research I had done on Jamestown led to an interest in all early European settlements in North America and in 2005 my son Dwayne, an historical archaeologist, and I decided to write a book together entitled *The European Struggle to Settle North America: Colonizing Attempts by England, France and Spain 1521–1608*. It was published by McFarland in 2011.

When I moved to South Carolina I planned to give up my living history career since all the characters I had developed were from colonial Virginia—and then I discovered Eliza Lucas Pinckney. I had heard of her, of course, and her well-known sons, but I did not know much about her life and accomplishments. After doing some research on her and reading her letterbook, I was hooked. I had to portray this fascinating and remarkable woman—which I have been doing since December 2011.

At the end of my Eliza programs I return to the 21st century and answer questions from the audience. I soon realized from the nature of the questions I was being asked that the general public has some misconceptions about 18th-century women and their place in society. Eliza is often pictured as a "feminist" who was ahead of her time or a rebel who challenged society and was then ostracized for her accomplishments. None of this was true. Eliza was a quintessential

18th-century woman and everything she did was within the scope of what society at that time considered appropriate for a woman of her class.

In view of these misconceptions, I decided to write a biography of Eliza that places her in the context of her time—that examines both her life and the world in which she lived. It is not a fictional biography, but rather a documented study of the life of a very remarkable woman and the 18th-century world she inhabited. It is my hope that readers will enjoy their journey through this very exciting and interesting time period and will enjoy becoming acquainted with Eliza Lucas Pinckney—a very determined, intelligent and charming lady.

I have relied heavily on Eliza's letters in writing her biography and quoted from them whenever possible. Most of her early letters can be found in *The Letterbook of Eliza Lucas Pinckney 1739–1762* edited by Elise Pinckney and published in 1997. In the 18th century it was customary for people to keep a record of their correspondence in a "letter" or "copy" book. Fortunately for historians, Eliza was not only meticulous in keeping records of her business correspondence but also the letters she sent to friends—some living as close as Charleston just across the Ashley River from the Lucas plantation on Wappoo Creek.

However, there are some letters from that period that are not in the letterbook. Some of them can be found in *Eliza Pinckney*, Harriott Horry Ravenel's biography of her great-great-grandmother published in 1896 and others are in the collections of the South Carolina Historical Society and the Library of Congress. Fortunately for me, Charles Baxley, editor and publisher of the magazine *Southern Campaigns of the American Revolution*, introduced me via email to Connie Schulz, distinguished professor emeritus of history at the University of South Carolina and the editor of *The Papers of Eliza Lucas Pinckney and Harriott Pinckney Horry Digital Edition*, published by the University of Virginia Press, Rotunda in their American Founding Era Collection. Professor Schulz and her staff have done a marvelous job putting together Eliza's and Harriott's papers and including additional information about people, places, events and terms. It is a fantastic resource and has been invaluable to me in writing Eliza's life.

The letters quoted in this book have been modified only to make them intelligible to modern readers. There was no standardized spelling for most of the 18th century. People spelled words phonetically often spelling the same word differently in the same paragraph. There was also no standard form of punctuation or grammar. Many nouns are capitalized in the middle of sentences and verb usage is not always consistent with what is considered proper today. I have chosen to preserve the original spelling and capitalization as much as possible; however, abbreviations in the text such as "wch" for "which" and "ye" for "the," etc., have been written out and elevated letters brought down. Illegible words, words that were left out in the original or an explanation of a word or event have been added and enclosed in brackets [ ] while words in parentheses ( ) are original to the letter writer. Most of the punctuation has been preserved with the exception of the frequent run-on sentences that make passages so difficult to understand—these have been broken up by semi-colons.

Dates can sometimes be confusing for the first half of the 18th century. Until 1752 the new year began on March 25 instead of January 1. Thus an event occurring in February of 1745 would, by our reckoning, have actually taken place in the year 1746. In the book I have advanced the year of all dates before 1752 to correspond with modern usage.

This book covers a long span of time and place names have changed over time. On August 10, 1783, "Charles Town" officially became "Charleston." For the sake of clarity, I have chosen to use the modern name "Charleston" when referring to the city except when quoting from primary source documents. Although ruled by the same monarch starting in 1603, England and Scotland were separate countries until 1707 when the Act of Union was passed. The two countries were then known as Great Britain, however the terms "English" and "British" are often used interchangeably after this time period.

Many people have been helpful to me in writing Eliza's biography. I would especially like to thank Jan Hiester, Curator of Textiles at the Charleston Museum, for taking the time to show me the dress, shoes and valance belonging to Eliza that are in the museum's collection; Dale Purvis, Park Manager at Hampton Plantation State Historic Site, for showing me the beautiful home of Harriott Pinckney Horry where Eliza spent most of her last years; Mary Mikulla, Interpretive Ranger at Hampton Plantation, for patiently answering my many questions; Celia Halley at the South Carolina Historical Society for making Thomas Pinckney's letters to his sister available; J. D. Lewis (www.carolana.com) whose wealth of information on the American Revolution in the south is phenomenal and who is always willing to share; Colin Brooker, architectural historian, for his input on 18th-century dwellings on Antigua; and my friend Gini Holihan for taking the time to read parts of my book and giving me the benefit of her thoughts. Last, but not least, many thanks to my family—my children and grandchildren—for their encouragement and support.

Introduction

In the 18th century, Charleston, South Carolina, was a bustling, thriving city, basking contentedly in the bright Carolina sun. It was known as the richest city in North America. Located on a peninsula at the point where the Ashley and Cooper rivers converge to form a large inlet, Charleston had a spacious, natural harbor and the best and largest port in the south. Because of its location on the southeastern coast of North America, Charleston's port was an important hub on the circular trade route between Europe and the Americas. Ships leaving European ports generally sailed southward down the coast of Europe to the Azores where they caught the trade winds that took them to the West Indies. Then, catching the Gulf Stream, they sailed up the east coast of North America and called at Charleston before veering off to ports in Europe. From November to March as many as a hundred ships could be seen riding at anchor in the gray waters of the harbor. However, in the spring, summer and early fall the number of vessels was not as great—some sea captains being wary of voyaging in the area during the hurricane season.

It was eight o'clock in the morning on April 10, 1793, when five women descended from their carriage and made ready to embark on the *Delaware*—one of the several ships bobbing up and down in the choppy waters along the wharves.[1] The eldest of the women was Eliza Lucas Pinckney and she was accompanied by her daughter, Harriott Horry, and three of her granddaughters. Eliza was suffering from an advanced stage of breast cancer and her companions were escorting her to Philadelphia to consult Dr. Tate, who was known to have had some success in treating the disease. Breast cancer had been recognized for a long time—the first description of it coming from the ancient Egyptians some 3,500 years ago. There were various theories as to what caused it and how to cure it, but it was not until 1757 that doctors began to treat the disease by surgically removing the tumors or the breast—a daunting prospect in an age that had no anesthesia and no knowledge of germs and bacteria.[2]

5

As the women stood on the deck of the ship with the wind whipping at their petticoats, they had an excellent view of the city with the mouth of the Cooper River to the right. The vista was a collection of low, clustered houses on East Bay Street, but, for the five women looking out across the harbor, one house in particular stood out—the large, brick "Mansion House" that Charles Pinckney had built for his new bride, Eliza, in 1745. It was a tall, domineering building as the living quarters were built over a basement which housed the kitchen and offices and was clearly visible from the harbor over the cluster of shops on the wharves and bridges. Harriott, standing next to her mother on the gently rocking deck, had been born in the house as had Charles Cotesworth—Eliza's oldest son—who now lived there with his wife and daughter.

To the left of the Mansion House and also clearly visible from the harbor was the soaring spire of St. Philip's Episcopal Church. Charles Pinckney, "the most amiable, tender and affectionate of husbands,"[3] lay buried in the graveyard there and it was in St. Philip's church that Eliza's daughter Harriott had married Daniel Horry twenty-five years earlier. Up the Cooper River was the site of Belmont, the Pinckney plantation on Charleston Neck. It had been looted and damaged during the War for American Independence and ten years before all that remained of the house had burned. Nothing was left of the beautiful mansion or the lovely pleasure gardens that Eliza had so carefully planted and tended.

It had been fifty-four years since Eliza had stood on the deck of the ship bringing her family from the island of Antigua to their new home in South Carolina. How excited they had all been. Eliza had been impressed by the area. She wrote to a friend in England shortly after her arrival: "I flatter myself it will be a satisfaction to you to hear I like this part of the world, as my lott has fallen here—which I really do. I prefer England to it, 'tis true, but think Carolina greatly preferable to the West Indies. ... Charles Town, the principal one in this province, is a polite, agreeable place. The people live very Gentile and very much in the English taste."[4]

The Ashley River empties into the harbor on the south side of the city and up the river a short distance is Wappoo Creek which connects the Ashley River to the Stono River. It was on her father's plantation on Wappoo Creek that Eliza conducted her experiments with indigo that brought a valuable new crop to Carolina planters. And a little farther up the Ashley is St. Andrew's Church where Eliza had married her beloved Charles in May of 1744.

Now, at the age of seventy, she was leaving the place that held so many memories for her and traveling north to seek treatment for her cancer. As the ship bearing the five women caught the tide and prepared to cross over the sandbar that separated the harbor from the open sea, one cannot help but wonder if Eliza had a premonition that she would not see these shores again.

CHAPTER ONE

The Early Years (1722–1739)

Antigua

In the 15th century Europeans referred to the lands in India and Asia collectively as "the Indies." Therefore, when Columbus landed in the Bahamas in October of 1492 thinking he had reached islands off the coast of Asia, it was quite natural for him to call the area "the Indies" and the inhabitants "Indians." By the time Europeans realized these islands were not located off the coast of Asia, the name had become entrenched. Eventually the word "west" was added in front of Indies in order to distinguish these islands from the ones in Asia.

Thus we have the West Indies—a large group of islands that frame the Caribbean Sea and separate it from the Atlantic Ocean. The islands form a large semi-circle starting off the east coast of Florida and swinging to the east and then southwest toward the coast of South America. The northern group of islands is known as the Bahamas while the center group is called the Greater Antilles and contains the largest islands: Cuba, Puerto Rico, Jamaica and Hispaniola—present-day Haiti/Dominican Republic. To the south forming a wide arc are the smaller islands of the Lesser Antilles—the group known as the Leeward Islands being at the top of the arc while the southwestern part is comprised of the Windward Islands.

The Spanish quickly asserted their dominance in the New World by settling Hispaniola in 1494 and occupying the rest of the Greater Antilles by the early part of the 16th century. They then turned their attention to the mainland and in 1521 conquered Mexico and in 1532 added Peru. After visiting the Lesser Antilles and encountering the fierce and warlike natives, the Caribs, the Spanish decided these smaller islands were not worth considering. Thus the Leeward and Windward Islands remained empty of European settlers for a time.

Spain soon began to reap the rewards of her conquests as gold, silver, pearls and tobacco were loaded on ships for the long voyage back to Spain.

Other European countries, envious of Spain's success, then began to sail into the Caribbean to raid Spanish settlements and attack the treasure ships—challenging the Spanish to stop them if they could. The West Indies soon became a violent and lawless zone frequented by groups of multi-national privateers. The Age of Piracy had begun.

While cruising the Caribbean in search of ships to attack or towns to raid, the privateers sought safe places to anchor and replenish water and food supplies and make repairs on their ships. Since the Lesser Antilles were not inhabited by Europeans, the privateers started to use these islands as places to establish temporary bases.

As time passed, Spain, once the wealthiest and most powerful country in Europe, became overextended and weak. As Spanish power and prestige lessened, Spain's rivals were quick to take advantage by seizing territory in the New World—once the exclusive preserve of Spain. In the Caribbean the focus turned to the Lesser Antilles. Already being used by privateers of all nations, it was only logical that Europeans should start claiming and settling the various islands.

In January of 1624 a group of Englishmen landed on St. Christopher's, one of the Leeward Islands, and founded the first permanent English settlement in the West Indies. Three years later in 1627, Barbados was settled. The colony at St. Kitts, as St. Christopher's was called, was so successful that in a short time the best land had all been taken. Settlers were forced to immigrate to neighboring islands to seek suitable acreage. In 1628 a large group went to neighboring Nevis and in 1632 the first immigrants from St. Kitts reached Montserrat and Antigua.

Since economic gain was the principal reason for establishing colonies in the West Indies, the colonists immediately began to plant tobacco—a lucrative and much sought-after commodity. However, the English were also receiving tobacco from their Chesapeake colonies in North America and, as more and more tobacco was produced, prices started to decline. The island economies began to suffer until a shift was made to the other valuable and sought-after product—sugar.

It was the Spanish and Portuguese who had introduced sugar cane into the New World where the warm climate and rich, moist soil proved highly suitable for its growth. However, it was left to the Portuguese, who had claimed Brazil in 1500, to establish sugar as a lucrative product in the New World. They were so successful with their sugar plantations that by the end of the 16th century Brazil was the wealthiest European colony in the world.[1]

Sugar was introduced into the English colony of Barbados in 1640 by the Dutch and from there sugar production spread to Antigua and the rest of the

Lesser Antilles. Tobacco might be a valuable crop, but sugar was even more valuable. In 1686 England imported £141,600 worth of tobacco from the Chesapeake colonies, but during that same year, the revenue from the importation of sugar was £586,528. In fact, the total value of imports from all of the mainland American colonies combined was only £207,131.[2]

By the middle of the 17th century the English possessed five permanent and promising settlements in the Lesser Antilles: Barbados, the largest at 166 square miles; Antigua, the second largest at 108 square miles; St. Kitts, shared with the French; Nevis; and Montserrat. However, it was Antigua that soon became one of the most important English possessions in the area. Oval in shape, measuring twenty miles at its widest part east to west and extending seventeen miles from north to south, Antigua sat in the middle of the Leeward Islands on the major sailing route to the region. Furthermore, its coastline was indented by creeks and bays forming several excellent harbors—a feature lacking on the neighboring islands. St. John's was the principal town and the administrative center for the island, and as it sat at the head of one of Antigua's extensive, natural harbors on the northwest coast, it was also the chief center for trade and commerce.

English Harbor on the south coast of the island was another of the large, natural harbors. It was well known among mariners for providing excellent shelter from storms, and its position on the southern coast of the island also made it an ideal place to monitor the Caribbean activity of England's greatest rival—France. The Royal Navy soon realized that English Harbor was the only harbor in the East Caribbean large enough to serve as a shipyard to repair naval ships and, therefore, in the 18th century it became the home port for the British Caribbean fleet.

It was in this important British colony that Eliza Lucas was born. Her name appears as Elizabeth on recorded documents—marriage record, husband's will and death notice—but the signature on the letters she copied into her letterbook is Eliza. And while her mother and father called her Betsey, tradition indicates that she was generally known as Eliza.[3] There is no record of her birth at St. John's parish where the baptisms of her younger brothers, George and Thomas, are listed, and the records at St. Paul's church where her younger sister Mary was baptized do not go back to the 1720s. December 28 is her birthday and the year 1722, derived from her obituary in the *Charleston City Gazette*, is generally accepted as her birth year.[4]

Eliza was the oldest child of George Lucas and Anne Mildrum. Eliza's mother remains somewhat of a mystery as very little is known about her or her family. While there are no records of a family by the name of Mildrum living in Antigua, Anne Mildrum had a mother living on the island along with a sister,

Mrs. James Fayerweather, and two nieces, Fanny Fayerweather and Mary Fayer-weather Glover.[5] Anne Lucas did not enjoy good health and apparently suffered from some chronic disorder. "My Mama's bad state of health," wrote Eliza to a friend, "prevents her from going through any fatigue."[6] However, Mrs. Lucas was obviously well educated: her handwriting as seen in a letter she wrote to Charles Pinckney was well formed and flowing and she expressed herself well—both indications of a good education.[7]

While the information about Anne Mildrum is slight, much more is known about the Lucas family. On her father's side Eliza was at least a third generation Antiguan and part of the "plantation society" which prevailed in the sugar-producing colonies in the West Indies. The first mention of the family in Antigua is in 1668 when her grandfather, John Lucas, "son and heir of John Lucas, deceased," received a patent for 25 acres.[8] Whether his father had also lived on the island is not known. The family may have originally come from the Essex area in England as records show that John Lucas used a seal which bore the coat of arms of the Lucas family of Colchester in Essex.[9]

The elite who made up the plantation society of the West Indies were the planters who owned the best sugar-producing land and dominated the political, economic and social life of their colonies. John Lucas was listed as a merchant in 1668 and ten years later began his ascent to the upper echelons of society by acquiring property in earnest.[10] By 1682 he had received grants for over 500 acres of land.[11] At a time when 200 acres was considered sufficient to become a successful sugar planter, John Lucas was poised to become very successful.

The next step toward membership in plantation society was to become part of the political life of the island. Antigua and all the Leeward Islands were governed by a governor general, but each island had its own lieutenant gover-nor. The lieutenant governor was assisted by a council whose members were appointed by the king and an assembly whose members were elected by eligible voters—male freeholders who met strict real property qualifications. In 1683 John Lucas was elected to the assembly representing Willoughby Bay—a dis-trict he continued to represent for many years. He was also chosen several times to be the speaker of the assembly.[12]

According to his will written in 1699 John Lucas had two sons, Thomas and George, who were both listed as being minors at the time.[13] Apparently Thomas died in November of 1707[14] and John Lucas then gave his remaining son George 190 acres of land—his half of an estate which he owned with another man from Antigua.[15] George Lucas was now a landowner and had taken the first step to membership in plantation society. He took the next step in 1710 when he was elected to represent Willoughby Bay in the Antiguan assem-bly.[16]

In August of 1713 George Lucas also began to pursue a military career—he was commissioned a "lieutenant to Captain Grill's" company in the 38th Regiment of Foot in the West Indies. At this time most commissions and promotions were purchased—the price depending on the social status and reputation of the regiment and where it was stationed. Since the West Indies were considered a less favorable location, the price of George Lucas' commission would have been slightly less than usual. The next year he furthered his military career by buying a captaincy in the 38th Regiment. His reputation was good according to a statement made by Governor John Hart in 1724 in which he was described as "a gentleman of a worthy character and heir to one of the best estates in Antigua."[17] In 1726 he was named to the governor's council—a high honor indeed.[18]

Eliza, then, was born into a family that was well-established, respected and prominent in the plantation society of the island. The Lucas family had a house in St. John's and a vast amount of property in the southeastern part of the island, near Willoughby Bay. The main plantation was called Cabbage Tree, after the cabbage palm, and contained some 300 acres. In addition, there were two other plantations: Lucas Junior containing 250 acres and another smaller property known as Lucas Tract near Half Moon Bay.

In those days a sugar plantation was a vast and complex organization—part farm and part manufacturing plant—and Eliza's family was one of the most extensive sugar producers on the island. For this reason, it seems likely that the family lived at Cabbage Tree using the house in St. John's for occasional social and business visits. From this plantation George Lucas could oversee the sugar production on all three of the Lucas plantations and Cabbage Tree seems the most likely place for Eliza to have developed her life-long love of gardening.

Time and hurricanes have destroyed most of the 18th-century buildings on the island of Antigua; however, contemporary references to housing on the islands of Nevis and St. Kitts indicate that most houses in the West Indies at this time were built of timber, painted from top to bottom on the outside, with roofs thatched with palm leaves, containing at least three rooms with a separate building for cooking. The most elaborate house on St. Kitts in the early 18th century measured ninety feet by twenty feet with a porch and an attached pavilion at one end. The house, which was valued at £1,500, had a shingle roof and was "all double boarded clap boarded and painted from top to bottom on the outside and wainscoted within."[19]

The Lucas house, then, was probably a one-story timbered house painted on the outside with either a thatched or shingled roof, containing around 1,200 to 1,400 square feet of living space. The kitchen would have been located in a separate building and nearby there would have been a kitchen garden. There vegetables to supplement the diet of the family were planted along with herbs to make medicines to keep the family in good health. Perhaps it was here that the young Eliza first began to garden, digging in the rich, moist soil to plant her seeds and watching them sprout up from the earth.

Also close by there was probably an area penned off for poultry—ducks, turkeys and chickens—and another penned area for a breeding sow and her young. Other domestic animals—mules, steers and cows—would be kept farther away from the house in an enclosed area to prevent them from destroying the precious fields of sugar. Spreading out from the house as far as the eye could see were fields of sugar cane—their light green stalks pointing upwards to the blue sky. Towering over the fields of cane were enormous stone windmills, their giant blades poised to catch the constant trade winds that fanned the island and powered the huge rollers that crushed the juice from the sugar cane.

As a young girl Eliza's life was filled with the rhythm of the natural world and the cycle of sugar production—planting, weeding, harvesting, processing, packing and loading. Two hundred slaves toiled on the plantation at Cabbage Tree to complete the never-ending chores. Some of the slaves were part of the field gangs that had the back-breaking task of cutting the ripe cane with large curved knives and carting it to the giant mills where the juice was crushed out of it. Other slaves working in the "refining house" boiled the juice over large furnaces in a series of copper kettles until the water evaporated, leaving behind golden-brown crystals. The crystals were then taken to the "curing house" where they were drained of molasses and dried.

The molasses, an interesting by-product of sugar-making, could be packed for sale or, as most planters preferred, the molasses could be taken to the distillery and made into rum—another lucrative product. The light brown sugar then had to be packed in large hogsheads (barrels) and stored in the warehouse until they could be shipped to England. All of these tasks had to be completed in a timely manner—the ripe cane would spoil if it were not crushed a few hours after being cut and the juice would ferment if not boiled soon after it was extracted. Since most of the planter's livelihood depended on his sugar production, any mistake in timing could be catastrophic and constant supervision was needed.

Sugar planters in the West Indies used all their available land to grow sugar, cutting down most of the trees to create fields for planting the all-important cash crop. There was no land left to raise large amounts of food or to graze cattle and few trees to provide timber. Domestic animals were fed on the husks and tops of the sugar cane and some planters grew corn to feed the poultry between their stalks of sugar cane. Timber for buildings and for making barrels was imported from the North American colonies.[20]

In 1724 the population of Antigua was 25,000—5,200 were of European descent and 19,800 were of African descent, the vast majority of whom were enslaved. Since little food was produced on the island, sugar planters were forced to import food from Ireland and the North American colonies to feed their slaves. Some planters tried to defray the cost of these imports by acquiring plantations in the North American colonies to provide provisions and timber for their sugar plantations in Antigua. In 1714 John Lucas bought a small plantation on Wappoo Creek across the Ashley River from Charleston. From his South Carolina plantation his overseer sent oak staves to make barrels, bacon and salted beef and from Antigua came the salt to salt the beef and brown sugar for the bacon.[21]

The provisions and goods needed by the planters themselves came from England. George Lucas had a library—the books came from England as did the wine he and his fellow diners drank in imported crystal goblets to toast the king. The clothes he and his family wore, toys for the children, furniture, china, silverware, linens and other household goods all came from England. The tools needed on the plantation had to be imported and even items as large as carriages were shipped to Antigua from abroad. Under the terms of the Navigation Acts, certain products—tobacco, cotton and sugar—could only be shipped from the colonies to England or other English colonies. Likewise, all European or Asian goods imported by the colonies had to be shipped to England first. Therefore, the goods that George Lucas and other Antiguan planters imported came from all over the world to London and from London to the West Indies—and sugar paid for it all.

London then was the center of the Antiguan planters' world—they sold their sugar in London, acquired the necessities and luxuries of life from London, educated their children in London and, although they lived in Antigua, they considered London home. For a good part of her life, when Eliza mentioned "home" it was London she meant—not Antigua and not South Carolina. In 1742 she wrote to her father, informing him of "the Tyranical Government at Georgia.... There went **home** last year a petition from a great number of sufferers for redress."[22] As late as the year 1775 she wrote: "I cant tell you much Public News, what I have heard is as follows, That the American affairs at **home** wear a more favourable Aspect."[23]

There were no schools in Antigua and people who could afford to do so sent their children back home to attend a London boarding school. Not only would their children receive an education that would enable them to move comfortably in any level of society, but they would also make useful business and social contacts that could give them entrée into every corner of the British Empire. George Lucas was a strong advocate of an English education. All four of his children were educated in London—his two sons as well as his two daughters.

Antiguan girls went off to boarding school in London around the age of nine or ten and remained there for about four or five years, but before they left Antigua, they were given the rudiments of education at home, usually by their mothers. It is likely that Eliza's mother was not as involved in her education as was normal and that it was her father who undertook most of her instruction. Eliza's letters to her father show a close and affectionate relationship—in a letter to him she referred to him as "my best friend." This relationship had to have developed during the first ten years of her life as that was the only period when father and daughter spent any time together.

Eliza and her father were very much alike. They both loved books, valued an English education and had lively, active minds with a penchant for trying out "new schemes." George Lucas was rarely idle, continually devising different ways to improve his fortunes, and Eliza, who once wrote that "an idle man is a burthen to society and to himself,"[24] inherited the need to keep busy from him. Her indigo project is well known, but it was only one of the many "projects" or "schemes," as she called them, which she undertook in her lifetime.

Her father was responsible for Eliza's great interest in gardening for he encouraged her in her gardening projects. "I was very early fond of the vegetable world," Eliza later wrote to one of her children, "my father was pleased with it and encouraged it, he told me the turn I had for those amusements might produce something of real and public utility."[25]

George Lucas might have approved of his daughter's interest in plants, but he did not encourage her to pursue her needlework which in those days was the "fashionable employment for ladies ... declaring ungallantly that he never saw ladies talking over their [needle]work without suspecting that they were hatching mischief."[26] Of course, Eliza did sew, all women at that time out of necessity sewed, but she wrote to a friend after the move to South Carolina that she could never go to her sewing "with a quite easy conscience as I know my father has an aversion to my employing my time in that poreing work."[27]

It was probably in 1732 as she was approaching her tenth birthday, that Eliza left Antigua to embark on the greatest adventure of her young life—sailing home to attend Mrs. Pearson's boarding school. She would not be lonely for two other young ladies from Antigua were going with her—her cousin Fanny Fayerweather and her friend Elizabeth Parry. Since young ladies did not travel alone at this time, the three girls would have sailed under the care of a family, probably well known to them, who were also traveling to England. They would be met as their ship docked in London by either a relative or their fathers' business representative—called a "factor"—who would take them in charge.

London

Presumably Richard Boddicott, George Lucas' factor in London, met Eliza when she arrived in England. As a factor, Richard Boddicott was responsible for overseeing the sale of the hogsheads of sugar from the Lucas estates in Antigua and manage the Lucas' financial affairs in London. Using the profits from the sale of the sugar Boddicott purchased the goods George Lucas requested and shipped them to Antigua, paid the fees for his children's schooling and covered their personal expenses while at school. He was more than an agent—he and his wife were close family friends who served as surrogate parents to the Lucas children when they came to London. That the ten-year-old Eliza formed a close bond with Mrs. Boddicott is evident in this letter written a little over a year after the Lucas family arrived in Charleston: "'Tis one of the greatest pleasures I enjoy to hear from you, for the tenderness I have ever received from my dear friend Mrs. B—especially when a child under her care—entitles her to all the regard I owe an affectionate parent."[28]

Eliza, of course, spent most of her time in London at Mrs. Pearson's Boarding School, but during school holidays she resided with the Boddicotts at their house in Savage Gardens in the City—as the financial center of London was called.[29] Mr. Boddicott was a merchant, an insurer and factor for several Antiguan families and he and his wife undoubtedly socialized with other merchants and men of finance and their families. During dinner or afterward in the drawing room guests at their house would inevitably discuss such topics as the price of sugar or how Spanish harassment of British shipping was disturbing commerce. The young Eliza listening wide-eyed to adult conversations would have gained insight into the London side of the sugar trade—knowledge that would stand her in good stead later for, as an adult, she displayed a good understanding of the business world.

In 18th-century London, boarding schools for young ladies were located for the most part in private homes and were, therefore, small accommodating only ten to twelve boarders plus a few day students. These schools were located in various areas in and around London, but in the late 17th century one area in particular became more popular than others: a small village north of London called Hackney—home to several boarding schools "for the daughters of the City and the landed gentry."[30] Hackney as a location had several advantages: it was close enough to London to provide ease of access and yet rural enough to have open land and clear air—two qualities that also made it a desirable place for nursery gardens. Eliza's little sister Polly attended Mrs. Robert's School in Hackney in 1746[31] and it is quite likely that Mrs. Pearson's school was also located in Hackney, although no record exists of her school or Mrs. Roberts' school or, indeed, any of the other small schools located in the village during that time period.[32]

Eliza arrived in London at an exciting time for someone "fond of the vegetable world"—for a revolution in gardening was taking place in England. In the past English gardens were modeled on formal French gardens, such as the gardens at Versailles, with large planting beds called parterres arranged in symmetrical geometric patterns, lined with stiff rows of hedges dotted with topiaries—shrubs and trees pruned into decorative shapes and animals. Only a few spring and summer flowers were to be found wedged in between the hedges— the English garden of the early 18th century was not known for its diversity of flowers.

However, a movement was gaining momentum to transform the garden from its traditional formal landscape into a more natural one which included a variety of plants from different parts of the world. While plant specimens from all over the world were desired, it was plants from the North American colonies that were preferred as they could be planted outdoors, in the open, unlike the fragile, exotic plants from the tropics which had to be kept in hothouses.

The next step in the horticulture revolution occurred in 1731 just before Eliza left Antigua to attend boarding school. In that year Philip Miller, head gardener of the Chelsea Physic Garden and dedicated botanist, published his *Gardeners Dictionary*. For hundreds of years gardening had been the domain of rich nobles who vied with each other to demonstrate their wealth, power and superior taste by creating, with the assistance of a myriad of professional gardeners, vast parks and gardens.

Miller's *Dictionary*, written in plain English, was intended to "inform the ignorant," he said, rather than the learned and contained instructions so clear anyone could become a successful gardener.[33] In his book Miller listed all the plants in cultivation in England at that time along with their country of origin and offered advice on how to plant and care for them. He also discussed pest control, soil preparation and propagation.

The book was such a huge success that in 1735 Miller published the *Abridgement*, a smaller and less expensive book that contained much of the same information found in the larger edition. Costing only a few shillings, it was affordable and created a group of amateur gardeners that cut through all class divisions—gardening was no longer the preserve of wealthy aristocrats. From both sides of the Atlantic men and women who shared a love of gardening began to correspond exchanging plants and seeds along with information, ideas and advice. Eliza became part of this network of gardeners later in her life sending seeds and plants from South Carolina to her friends in England. In turn she experimented with growing trees from other countries to find those species that could be readily acclimated to South Carolina.

Eliza never mentioned Miller's *Abridgement* as one of the books she owned or read, but it would be hard to believe that she did not have a copy of it or that Mrs. Pearson would not have had it or the *Gardeners Dictionary* in her school. Botany was an extremely suitable subject for young ladies who, when they married, would be expected to manage the kitchen and herb gardens along with the pleasure gardens. Mrs. Pearson may even have taken her young ladies to visit the nursery gardens in Hackney and Thomas Fairchild's nursery in Hoxton located two and a half miles from London. It was reputed to hold the best collection of rare plants to be found in England and was a popular attraction for visiting gardeners.[34]

As marriage was the chief goal for young ladies at this time, the emphasis in female education was on preparing the young lady to become a wife able to manage a large household and skilled in the social graces. English society was very structured with distinct class divisions. At the top of the social hierarchy was the monarch and the royal family followed by the nobles in their ranking order of precedence and then the gentry—made up of those who had inherited land and wealth from their predecessors. The Lucas family was part of the social class known as the "gentry" and as a "gentlewoman" Eliza would have been expected to marry a man with property—either an estate in Great Britain or a plantation in the colonies—and her education was designed to prepare her for that position.

A woman's role in the 18th century was to be a helpmate to her closest male relatives—her father, her brother, her husband. The 18th-century marriage was a partnership between husband and wife with the wife serving as the junior partner. It was considered desirable that the wife understand the business of managing the family property, for she would be expected to take over the running of the estate during her husband's absence or if he were ill or in any way incapacitated.[35]

A wife was also supposed to further her husband's interests by being a charming and gracious hostess and by being able to mix well in society outside the home. To this end Eliza would have been taught the "accomplishments" considered necessary for a gentlewoman—deportment, manners, conversational skills and, of course, in spite of George Lucas' objections, fancy needlework. Mrs. Pearson, who probably taught the "accomplishments" herself, most likely employed a Dancing Master to teach her young ladies the very formal and intricate steps of the minuet—a necessity for all members of the gentry class.

Playing a musical instrument was also a desirable skill for the young lady of Eliza's time and according to her letters Eliza was fond of music and played the harpsichord. Likewise, there was sure to have been a writing master at the school as being able to write in a beautiful, flowing, yet clear hand was a sign of refinement and gentility. While the handwriting itself was important and took much practice before it was perfected, the style of writing was also significant. Connections were of great importance in the 18th-century gentry-world and maintaining connections to family and friends through letters was the wife's responsibility. Social letters, like polite conversation, required a light, civil tone with references to current affairs, art, music and even biblical or classical allusions. Therefore, a knowledge of history, religion, English literature, the arts and "the globes" as geography was called, was helpful as were genteel hobbies that could be discussed with acquaintances.

The writing master also taught reckoning and simple household book-keeping as young ladies would be required to keep household accounts when they married. Whether he also provided guidance on how to write business letters is not known, but somehow or from someone Eliza must have learned how to conduct business correspondence, for at an early age she appears to have been as adept at writing business letters as she was at writing social ones.[36]

In addition, there must have been a French master for Eliza could read, write and speak French. She made this note in the letterbook: "Wrote to my father on business of various sorts desiring he will not insist on putting my sister to school. I will undertake to teach her French."[37] Later she made the following note: "Wrote to my brother George, 27th of October, 1741, desiring him to corrispond with me in French."[38]

Eliza's education was commensurate, then, with her gender and her class. This was the Age of Enlightenment—a time when rational thought and knowledge gathered from observation and experiment were replacing the myths and traditions of the past. The quest was for knowledge that was practical and could be used to improve the human condition. Learning was not gender specific during this time, but more the province of the leisurely and wealthy—the nobility and the members of the gentry class. It was the fashion for the ladies and gentlemen of Eliza's time and class to "amuse" or "entertain" themselves by taking up genteel hobbies that included such diverse subjects as horticulture, history, astronomy, and art. These hobbies not only gave men and women something interesting to discuss with their peers in the drawing room or write about in their letters, but very often brought practical results—like Eliza's work with indigo.[39]

Not all young ladies, however, were as well educated as Eliza and her friends. Some fathers did not place much importance on educating their daughters even though they could well afford to do so. Housewifery skills, which most girls learned from their mothers, and lessons in deportment, dancing and music were all that many considered necessary for girls. Eliza was fortunate that her father was a strong advocate of education for both his sons and daughters. The importance of education was a concept that he passed on to her.

Therefore, as an educated gentlewoman Eliza was able to participate in the intellectual and experimental activities of the time even though she was barred from the scholarly institutions of the day. She would not have been allowed to attend a university, for example, or become a member of the many societies that promoted exchanges of ideas and information—like the Royal Society in London—and her education would not have included Greek and Latin. However, while she could not read the classics in their original language, she could and did read them in translation. She had, moreover, access to books, the desire to learn and moved in a social circle that included men who were learned and belonged to the societies she could not join—she gleaned the knowledge and expertise she lacked from them.[40]

Duty to family was an all-important responsibility in the 18th century—a fact that would have been firmly instilled in Eliza both at school and at home. This obligation was taken seriously by members of society even in families whose members did not particularly like one another. A member of the Pinney family from Dorset in England wrote: "God knows what will become of our whole family, there being no union nor affection left amongst any two or three of them." Yet the family was able to put aside their mutual animosity and, at some risk to themselves, help the youngest member of the family when he was transported to the West Indies.[41]

No one took the responsibility to family more seriously than Eliza. In the late 19th century Eliza's descendants found a series of "Resolutions ... in a little roll of sadly tattered papers, marked, 'papers belonging to myself onely.'" They reflect the tenets Eliza formed in her youth. The first section dealt with her duties to God and the second part to her household responsibilities and the third outlined her duty to her family. After carefully listing her commitments to her husband, children, mother, siblings, servants and friends, she ended by writing: "All these resolutions by God's assistance I will keep to my life's end." She then added a memo to herself to read the resolutions daily "to assist my memory as to every particular contained in this paper."[42]

Eliza emerged from her years at Mrs. Pearson's boarding school an accomplished, intelligent, charming young lady, a good conversationalist with a sense of humor. There is no extant portrait of her, unfortunately; however, she was small—a pair of her shoes which are in the collection of the Charleston Museum measure 8¾ inches by 2½ inches and a gown belonging to her in the same collection shows that she was slim and not very tall. She was most likely a brunette as she preferred to wear colors suited to a woman with dark hair.[43] She was described by her descendants as being very feminine.

Eliza and her cousin Fanny finished their education in London and were ready to return to Antigua by the late spring or early summer of 1737.[44] The Thomas family was also returning to Antigua at that time and it is likely that Eliza and Fanny traveled with them. Mr. and Mrs. Thomas and their daughter were friends and neighbors in Antigua and Mr. Thomas, who was later appointed lieutenant governor of the colony of Pennsylvania, was a member of the Governor's Council in Antigua as was Eliza's father.

At the age of 15, then, Eliza Lucas returned to Antigua—a polished, cultivated young lady ready to take her place as a wife and partner to a successful plantation owner and prepared to manage the affairs of the plantation in her husband's absence. However, it was not a husband who needed her newly acquired knowledge to assist him—it was her father.

Antigua

George Lucas may have inherited one of the finest estates in Antigua, but he also inherited a considerable amount of debt. In 1699 his father had entered into an agreement with five men in London to transport a cargo of goods from London to Antigua. The arrangement among the men was that John Lucas was to sell the cargo in Antigua and send each partner his share of the profits. According to the descendants of his partners Lucas never sent over their full shares, even though they had repeatedly asked him to do so. The business had been dragging on for over twenty years and upon his father's death in January 1729 George Lucas took steps to resolve it. He paid the claim of £1,080 plus £990 in interest by mortgaging Cabbage Tree to the descendants of the partners.[45]

The fortunes of the sugar planter depended on two things: the price of sugar and the amount of sugar produced. In the first part of the 1730s sugar production in Antigua declined due primarily to a drought which lasted for several years, reaching its height in 1736 when Antigua was reportedly "almost burnt up." There are relatively few sources of fresh water on Antigua and in the 18th century the inhabitants dug ponds or built cisterns to collect the torrents of rain that fell during the months of September, October and November. When the rains did not come in sufficient amounts, it caused hardships across the region.

As if the lack of rain was not bad enough, hard on the heels of the drought came an infestation of insects that caused damage to the sugar crop. Referred to as a "blast," a swarm of "myriads of little insects, invisible to the naked eye" descended on the sugar fields and fed on the juice from the sugar cane. The situation was so dire that William Matthew, the governor general, called for a general fast for July 1, 1736, "to deprecate God's Anger from whence this Island has been Afflicted with the blast and Dry Weather."[46]

Sugar planters, like tobacco and rice planters, lived on credit. If the profit of this year's crop was not sufficient to purchase all the necessary commodities or pay the bills, then the planter pledged next year's crop—a practice that if continued for several years, led to a crushing accumulation of debt. George Lucas was no exception. He saw his revenues from sugar dwindling due to the drought and the "blast" and his debts rising. Soon his son George would be joining Eliza in London to attend school, adding to the bills he would be obliged to pay.

As a way out of his difficulties, he sought new lands and new crops to cultivate and since he had inherited a plantation in South Carolina from his father, he decided to add to his holdings there. In 1732 he bought 1,500 acres of land in Colleton County. In May 1734 he bought 1,150 acres in Craven County. Rice was the cash crop grown in South Carolina and George Lucas hoped his new lands and a new crop would give his fortunes a boost. However, it would take time for his affairs to improve. Meanwhile he owed over £30,000 and his property in Antigua was heavily mortgaged. In 1734 he called all his creditors together and offered to "deliver up and sequester" his estates in Antigua until all the debts were paid—reserving for himself the income from his military service and his Carolina estates. His creditors all agreed.[47]

In October of 1736, as if the drought and the "blast" had not caused enough trouble, the island of Antigua was shocked by the discovery of a slave conspiracy. It was said to have been initiated by a group of slaves from Ghana and their intention was to kill all the Europeans on the island. However, the planters became aware of the plot and defused it before any harm could be done. Thirty-six slaves were banished and 88 were executed for their part in the conspiracy—one of the slaves executed on February 18, 1737, belonged to George Lucas who was compensated £70 for his loss.[48]

That same February George Lucas made his first trip to South Carolina where he purchased two more tracts of land in Craven County. He did not stay long; perhaps he feared to be absent from his plantations in Antigua for any length of time. Whatever the reason, he left South Carolina on April 8, 1737.[49] Since the trip from South Carolina to Antigua took about three weeks, George Lucas was home by the end of April—in plenty of time to welcome his daughter when she returned that summer or in the early fall.

What a happy reunion it must have been. Eliza had not seen her mother and father for five years, her little brother Thomas had been only four when she left and there was a new face in the Lucas household—little Mary, or Polly as she was called, just turning two and toddling around the house on wobbly legs. Thomas, who would soon be leaving for school in London, must have inundated Eliza with questions about the trip to England, about life in London and the Boddicott family and, of course, everyone would want to know how twelve-year-old George was faring with school and life in London.

Now that his daughter was back, George Lucas may have felt more comfortable in planning a trip to London in the near future—his youngest son Thomas would soon be ten and it would be time to enroll him in school there and in London he would be able to further his military career by purchasing a commission as a major. In preparation for his trip, it is highly likely that Lucas started instructing Eliza on the management of his sugar plantations so she could supervise them during his absence. That Eliza was familiar with sugar production is evident by a note she made in her letterbook: "Sent him [her father] by the return of the vessel ... 2 keggs Oysters, one of eggs by way of Experiment put up in salt; in case they answere, my scheme is to supply my fathers refineing houses in Antigua with Eggs from Carolina."[50] During the refining or boiling process of sugar production, impurities floated to the surface and had to be skimmed off. Egg whites or lime were frequently added to the mixture to cause the impurities to rise more quickly.[51]

Sometime before September 1738, George Lucas left Antigua, taking his youngest son with him and presumably leaving Eliza in charge of the sugar plantations. Before he left he had some important business to transact—he needed to raise the money to buy his commission and since his Antiguan estates were sequestered, the only property available to provide collateral for a loan was the property in South Carolina. On the fifth of July, he took out his first mortgage on his Carolina property: "The Honorable George Lucas, Esquire to the Honorable Charles Dunbar, Esquire, both of the Island of Antigua, for £350 sterling British, 600 a[cres] on Wappoo Creek.[52] George Lucas arrived in London in November of 1738 and the next month bought a commission as a major in the 38th Regiment of Foot stationed in Antigua.

The idea of moving his family to South Carolina to live probably took shape gradually in George Lucas' mind. The lure of being able to make a fresh start with new lands to cultivate and an opportunity to diversify his crops would have been almost irresistible. There was also the safety factor—the slave conspiracy of 1735–36 had raised fears of further slave insurrections and many Antiguan families were deciding to leave for the relative safety of the North American colonies.

It was not only a slave rebellion that Antiguans feared, it was also the possibility of attack by European enemies. In 1688 Europe was drawn into a series of wars that would not end until the defeat of Napoleon at Waterloo in 1815. These wars were global in scope as they were fought not only on the continent of Europe, but also wherever Europeans had interests: North America, the Caribbean, Africa and Asia. Ten of the islands of the Lesser Antilles lay within a seventy-five-mile radius of the island of Antigua—four of the islands were British, two were French and two were Dutch, one island was shared by Britain and France and one was shared by the French and the Dutch—thus ensuring that the islands would be an area of contention in any European war.

During the interminable wars of the 18th century, European countries often changed alliances with each conflict—there was only one constant: Great Britain and France were always on the opposite sides. The wars in the Caribbean were naval wars and Antigua was always vulnerable to a French blockade of its harbors which would disrupt trade by preventing the sugar fleet from leaving port and would keep ships bringing goods and provisions from entering—a serious matter on an island that depended on imports for most of its provisions. If there was no blockade, there was always the risk that ships carrying sugar or provisions for the island would be captured at sea by the French. In October of 1704 during the War of the Spanish Succession out of the 108 ships that left the Lesser Antilles bound for England only 61 reached their destination—forty-three of the remaining forty-seven were captured and brought into French ports as prizes.[53]

Although the last major European war, the War of the Spanish Succession, had ended in 1713, Great Britain and Spain had continued their hostilities in two minor wars from 1718 to 1720 and again from 1727 to 1729. In the 1730s there was an uneasy peace between the two countries, but the Spanish were becoming increasingly aggressive with British shipping and tensions were high.

George Lucas was still in London in February 1739 when he borrowed money from his friend and factor Richard Boddicott and in March he attended a meeting of the Board of Trade in London. Sometime after March he left for Antigua arriving there in July. Soon after his arrival George Lucas with his wife Anne, his daughters Polly and Eliza and his niece Fanny Fayerweather sailed for Charleston, South Carolina. They were there by August 10 when George Lucas signed a deed with George Starrat. He endorsed another deed on August 29 signing himself "George Lucas late of the Island of Antigua Now of South Carolina."[54]

CHAPTER TWO

The Young Adult Years
(1739–1744)

A Fresh Start

As the ship bringing the Lucas family to Charleston crossed the bar and entered the harbor, those aboard were treated to a panoramic vista of the city that was the capital of "the fairest and most fruitfull Province belonging to Great Britain."[1] Having been founded a mere sixty-nine years before in 1670, South Carolina was young in comparison to the colonies in Virginia, New England and the West Indies. Nevertheless, it was large and prosperous and its capital city was charmingly laid out with streets intersecting at right angles, its skyline dominated by impressive structures: the Council Chamber, the Court House, the Customs House and, of course, the city's landmark—the towering steeple of St. Philip's Church.

The Carolina colony may not have been settled until 1670, but the idea of creating it was conceived in 1629 when Charles I issued Sir Robert Heath a charter for a vast tract of land that stretched from the Virginia border to the present border of Georgia and Florida. At this time England, France and Spain each had colonial territories in North America: the French in Canada, the Spanish in Florida—a vague area comprising most of the southeast—and the English in the land south of Canada all the way to Cape Fear in present-day North Carolina. The three countries were uneasy neighbors who jealously guarded their territory from encroachment by the others. The grant to Sir Robert Heath clearly extended England's colonial territory in North America at the expense of the Spanish—a fact that would cause problems for future English colonists. However, there were no repercussions from the Spanish at this time as the few plans made to settle the area never materialized. Then the English Civil War broke out and diverted all interest in colonization.

It was not until the restoration of the monarchy in 1660 that thought was given again to establishing a colony south of Virginia. There was a renewed interest at this time in opening up new lands for settlement, for land in the older established colonies had become scarce—already settlers from Virginia were spilling over into what is now North Carolina. New Englanders were also looking for new lands to settle as were the colonists in the West Indies, especially on the island of Barbados.

The old grant had expired; therefore, in 1663 Charles II issued a new grant for this territory, which he called "Carolina," to eight of his loyal supporters. These men would be the Lords Proprietors of the colony responsible for governing and protecting the province in return for a chance to enhance their private fortunes with plantations in the New World. It was Anthony Ashley Cooper, one of the proprietors, who organized the expedition to settle Carolina in 1669.

In 1670 the settlers arrived off the Carolina coast and chose a place to plant their settlement. The area they selected had a large, natural harbor formed by the convergence of two rivers, which they promptly named the Ashley and the Cooper in honor of Anthony Ashley Cooper who had organized the expedition. As protection was the main concern, the first settlement was built on high ground on the west side of the Ashely River several miles from its mouth. The colonists surrounded their little settlement with a palisade and called it Charles Towne in honor of the king. They had barely settled in when the Spanish attacked—arriving by ship and accompanied by their Native American allies. Fortunately, after some light skirmishing, a storm arose forcing the Spanish to withdraw.

Ten years later in 1680 "Charles Towne" was moved across the Ashley River to its present location. It was the original idea that the whole Carolina colony would be governed from Charleston. But as the province grew, those in the northernmost regions (what is now North Carolina) found it too difficult to travel to Charleston to participate in the colonial legislature. In 1712 it was decided to officially divide the colony into two parts—North and South Carolina.

Although the South Carolina colony grew and prospered, the colonists did not feel completely secure—always anticipating another attack by the Spanish and/or their Native American allies. Then a new threat appeared from the west. The French, who in 1680 had discovered the Mississippi River, were establishing outposts at Biloxi and Mobile and encouraging their Native American allies to launch attacks on the frontier settlements of western Carolina.

Time and time again the colonists appealed to the proprietors for protection, but the response to colonial appeals was slow and generally ended with the proprietors requesting assistance from the crown. The colonists had long been dissatisfied with the Lords Proprietors and in 1719 the Commons House of Assembly (the Carolina legislature) asked the king to assume control of their province. In 1720 an interim royal governor was sent to Charleston and in 1729 South Carolina officially became a royal colony.

The decade of the 1730s saw an increase in growth and prosperity. Colonists attracted by the promise of land, religious freedom and representative government flocked to South Carolina. They came from the old, established colonies in New England, Virginia, Jamaica and Barbados and they came from Europe. The promise of religious freedom drew dissenters from England and Scotland, also French Huguenots fleeing persecution in France and Sephardic Jews from the Iberian Peninsula. Dutch settlers, whose colony of New Netherland had been taken over by the English in 1674, also made their way to South Carolina.

Rice production flourished during this time period and became the crop of choice for those whose plantations were located in the rich outer coastal plain where the black tidal rivers, swamps and savannahs provided the ideal setting for its cultivation. As an added inducement to plant rice, the British government had partially removed it from the enumeration list—the list of crops that could be sold only to Great Britain. Carolina rice planters could now sell their crop directly to any country south of Cape Finisterre—that is, south of Spain.

Charleston also saw a spike in growth during the 1730s—the sight of a British man-of-war anchored in the Cooper River lessened the sense of insecurity the town had felt in the past. In 1733 Carolinians were to feel even more secure for Georgia, the last of the British colonies in North America, was established. The new colony provided a buffer between South Carolina and Spanish Florida and, even better, was home to a regiment of British soldiers.

The Lucas family arrived in Charleston, then, to find an active, thriving city and one that was, as Eliza put it, "a polite and agreeable place." Later she was to describe the colony in a letter to her brother Thomas, then at school in London.

> I am now set down, my Dear Brother, to obey your commands and give you a short discription of the part of the world I now inhabit. South Carolina then is a large and Extensive Country Near the Sea. Most of the settled parts of it is upon a flatt—the soil near Charles Town sandy, but further distant clay and swamplands. It abounds with fine navigable rivers, and great quantities of fine timber. The Country at a great distance, that is to say about a hundred or a hundred and fifty mile from Charles Town, very hilly.
>
> The Soil in general very fertile, and there is very few European or American fruits or grain but what grow here. The Country abounds with wild fowl, Venison and fish. Beef, veal and motton are here in much greater perfection than in the Islands, tho' not equal to that in

England; but their pork exceeds any I ever tasted any where. The Turkeys extreamly fine, especially the wild, and indeed all their poultry is exceeding good; and peaches, Nectrons and mellons of all sorts extreamly fine and in profusion, and their Oranges exceed any I ever tasted in the West Indies or from Spain or Portugal.

The people in general hospitable and honest, and the better sort add to these a polite gentile behaviour. The poorer sort are the most indolent people in the world or they could never be wretched in so plentiful a country as this. The winters here are very fine and pleasant, but 4 months in the year is extreamly disagreeable, excessive hott, much thunder and lightening, and muskatoes and sand flies in abundance.

Charles Town, the Metropolis, is a neat pretty place. The inhabitants polite and live in a very gentile manner; the streets and houses regularly built; the ladies and gentlemen gay in their dress. Upon the whole you will find as many agreeable people of both sexes for the size of the place as almost any where. St. Phillips church in Charles Town is a very Eligant one, and much frequented. There are several more places of publick worship in this town and the generallity of people of a religious turn of mind.

I began in haste and have observed no method or I should have told you before I came to Summer that we have a most charming spring in this country, especially for those who travel through the Country for the scent of the young mirtle and Yellow Jesamin with which the woods abound is delightful.

The staple comodity here is rice and the only thing they export to Europe. Beef, pork and lumber they send to the West Indias.[2]

George Lucas owned two houses in Charleston: one was "next door to Mr. Harvey near White Point" and the other "near Conselliere's at the upper end of Tradd Street."[3] The family probably stayed in one of the houses for a few weeks after they arrived—resting and recovering from the voyage. Eliza and her cousin Fanny would have been especially anxious to explore the town and see the sights. Perhaps they visited the shops and old market on Middle Bridge—the largest of the wharves or bridges, as they were called, that jutted out into the Cooper River from East Bay Street. And they would have entertained visitors—members of Charleston society—who came to call on them. There would have been many people in town for the family to meet for most of the planters in the low country came to Charleston to spend the summer months. They came for health reasons—trying to avoid "country fever" (malaria) which was rampant in the country during the summer.

At this time Carolinians did not know that malaria is caused by a tiny parasite injected into a person by the bite of an infected mosquito. Nor did they know that mosquitoes liked to breed in the still, fresh water ponds and swamps found on their low country plantations. They also did not understand why Charleston, surrounded by salt water and fanned by ocean breezes, thereby attracting fewer mosquitoes, was healthier—they just knew from experience that it was and so they flocked to town.

George Lucas probably moved his family across the Ashley River to his 600-acre plantation on Wappoo Creek in the fall. While the ladies of the family tackled the job of making the house comfortable and suitable for their use, George Lucas, no doubt, was busy looking over his property—taking stock of his land, outbuildings and domestic animals and, given his penchant for new projects, devising plans for the future. As in Charleston, the family would have received visits from their neighbors. The closest plantation to theirs was only three miles away and was owned by Mrs. Woodward, a widow, who lived there with her young, widowed daughter Mary Chardon. Another neighbor was Andrew Deveaux, an elderly Huguenot planter.

As the family settled down to life in South Carolina disturbing rumors of escalating tensions with Spain were reaching the colony. For a decade, ever since the end of the last Anglo-Spanish War in 1729, British merchant ships trading with Spanish colonies in the New World had been subjected to search by the Spanish guarda-costas, patrol boats used to deter smugglers. Under the terms of the treaty ending the last war, the Spanish had been given the right to board British merchant ships to ensure that British merchants were complying with the asiento, a contract signed by both countries in 1713 that allowed the British to bring an unlimited number of slaves and 500 tons of goods per year to Spanish colonies for trade. As the decade progressed Spanish sea captains became more and more aggressive, not only boarding and searching merchant ships, but also abusing the crew and confiscating the cargo. The list of indignities to British seamen grew as did tensions between the two countries. Spain and Great Britain tried to reconcile their differences at the Convention of Pardo in August of 1739, but to no avail and on August 14 the British left the conference recalling their ambassador to Spain.

The first indication in South Carolina of the seriousness of the situation came when an announcement appeared in the *South Carolina Gazette* of September 8–15 that Lieutenant Governor William Bull was awarding letters of marque for "fitting out private Ships of War" for the purpose of seizing ships belonging to the king of Spain. Events moved quickly from that point: Admiral Edward Vernon was sent from England to the West Indies with a fleet of nine ships; on September 18 General James Oglethorpe's regiment in Georgia, moved to the Georgia-Florida border; then on October 23 Great Britain officially declared war on Spain; the next month the *South Carolina Gazette* of November 10–17 and November 17–24 carried the announcement that all officers must return to their regiments "on pain of being cashiered."

The war with Spain came at a very inconvenient time for the Lucas family. Major George Lucas had no choice but to return to Antigua and report to his regiment—the prospect of being dishonorably discharged from the army being unacceptable. He would have to leave his family in South Carolina and put his ideas for developing his new lands on hold for a while. He would also have to leave his oldest daughter in charge of all his property while he was gone—the 600-acre plantation on Wappoo Creek, a 1,500-acre plantation called Garden Hill on the Combahee River and 3,000 acres of rice growing land along the Waccamaw River. It was a tremendous responsibility for a young woman just a month shy of her seventeenth birthday; however, it would not be for long. George Lucas planned to seek an exchange with an officer in the British regiment stationed in Georgia—from there he would be able to supervise his Carolina property and the family would be together again.

On November 2 and 3 George Lucas undertook two important pieces of business involving grants for lands he had recently purchased. These lands were to act as security for the loan he had received the previous February from Richard Boddicott in London. In the early part of November, he had signed the papers as George Lucas "late of the Island of Antigua now in the province of South Carolina."[4] He was gone by December 13 when Lieutenant Governor William Bull signed the two grants over to him—neither George Lucas' location nor his signature is on the papers.[5]

As Eliza, her mother, sister and cousin strived to adjust to life at Wappoo without the head of the family, they found support among the many friends they had made during the few months they had been in South Carolina. Major George Lucas had gone off to fight the Spanish, Great Britain's enemy—an enemy, incidentally, that had long plagued South Carolinians—and plantation society was more than willing to assist his family during his absence. It is even possible that George Lucas received assurances of their support before he left for Antigua. There would have been much sympathy among their friends and neighbors for the young Eliza, left in charge of three plantations, an ailing mother and a four-year-old sister with only another young lady, her cousin Fanny, for company.

Fanny, however, had not intended to remain long in Charleston. In July of 1740 she left for Boston to stay with her uncle, John Fayerweather, and settle some property that she had inherited from her father who died in 1726.[6] The business of settling her inheritance took several years to complete and it was not until 1745 that she was able to leave and return to Antigua. She was greatly missed by the ladies at Wappoo. Eliza lost a close and longtime friend when her cousin left, but fortunately she found a replacement in Mary Chardon, the widowed daughter of Mrs. Woodward, the Lucases' closest neighbor. Mary, though widowed with a child, was close to Eliza in age and the two young women became good friends visiting each other as often as once a week.

South Carolina presented a different environment for Eliza—it was not like Antigua or England the only two places she had ever lived. While the social setting, being very English, was familiar to her, the political, business and agricultural practices were not. Rice was grown on all three of the Lucas plantations, but the plantations also supplied pitch, tar, lime, lumber, beef and pork for export. Eliza knew nothing about rice cultivation or the production of pitch, tar and lime nor did she understand the particular business and political problems confronting planters in the colony. She had a lot to learn.

Fortunately, two of her father's plantations—Garden Hill and the rice-producing lands along the Waccamaw River—had competent resident overseers. The accounts of William Murray at Garden Hill show that he planted on shares with George Lucas[7] and while there is no matching account for George Starrat at Waccamaw it is possible that he had some kind of arrangement with George Lucas also—he was the previous owner of the land and had worked it for several years. The day-to-day management of these two plantations, therefore, would have not have fallen to Eliza. She did, however, need to correspond frequently with both Murray and Starrat and keep up to date on the situation at both plantations.

Eliza was responsible, then, for the daily running of only one plantation—the one on Wappoo Creek. Since rice was the main crop grown on the plantation, Eliza's first task was to learn the process of rice cultivation and how it was conducted at Wappoo. It is likely that she got that information from her neighbors and by observing the slaves at work. It is very possible that she also received assistance from an enslaved man called "Mulatto Quash" (Christian name John Williams) listed as a carpenter and the most valuable of Wappoo's twenty slaves. He may have also helped her to run the plantation which would explain why Eliza seemed to take an extraordinary interest in his welfare.

The Spanish were in the habit of encouraging slaves in South Carolina to flee to Florida by promising them freedom once they were there. In January of 1743 several slaves were overheard planning to escape and make their way to the Spanish fort at St. Augustine—Mulatto Quash was accused of being one of the group. Eliza was present in court when he was tried and reported proudly to her father that Quash "proved him self quite Innocent."[8] Several years later, after Eliza's marriage, Charles Pinckney, most likely at her request, freed Quash "in consideration of the good and faithful service of the said John Williams." Eliza was present at his manumission.[9]

Eliza was further aided in her endeavors by the fact that she had a good understanding of plantation management in general and some experience in running a plantation. She was also more than willing to seek support and accept advice. Among the family's acquaintances were men like Charles Pinckney and John Cleland who were successful planters, businessmen and prominent in colonial government. These men were able to give Eliza legal advice and assistance in business matters while keeping her up to date on political happenings in the colony.

The ladies were not behind their husbands in offering support. Mrs. Cleland and Mrs. Pinckney were determined that Eliza should have some respite from her duties and responsibilities and enjoy activities suitable for her time of life. Eliza explained her situation in a letter to Mrs. Boddicott:

> I flatter myself it will be a satisfaction to you to hear I like this part of the world, as my lott has fallen here—which I really do. I prefer England to it, 'tis true, but think Carolina greatly preferable to the West Indias, and was my Papa here I should be very happy.
>
> We have a very good acquaintance from whom we have received much friendship and Civility.... My Papa and Mama's great indulgence to me leaves it to me to chose our place of residence either in town or Country, but I think it more prudent as well as most agreeable to my Mama and self to be in the Country during my Father's absence. We are 17 mile by land and 6 by water from Charles Town—where we have about 6 agreeable families around us with whom we live in great harmony.
>
> I have a little library well furnished (for my papa has left me most of his books) in which I spend part of my time. My Musick and the Garden, which I am very fond of, take up the rest of my time that is not imployed in business, of which my father has left me a pretty good share—and indeed, 'twas inavoidable as my Mama's bad state of health prevents her going through any fatigue.
>
> I have the business of 3 plantations to transact, which requires much writing and more business and fatigue of other sorts than you can imagine. But least you should imagine it too burthensom to a girl at my early time of life, give me leave to answer you: I assure you I think myself happy that I can be useful to so good a father, and by rising very early I find I can go through much business. But least you should think I shall be quite moaped with this way of life I am to inform you there is two worthy Ladies in Charles Town, Mrs. Pinckney and Mrs. Cleland, who are partial enough to me to be always pleased to have me with them, and insist upon my making their houses my home when in town and press me to relax a little much oftener than 'tis in my honor to accept of their obliging intreaties. But I some times am with one or the other for 3 weeks or a month at a time, and then enjoy all the pleasures Charles Town affords.[10]

Meanwhile George Lucas was actively seeking an exchange of commissions with an officer in the 42nd Regiment of Foot stationed in Georgia. In the spring of 1740 he found a potential candidate in Alexander Heron who had been commissioned a major in the regiment in April. Major Heron indicated that he was willing to exchange but wanted £1,000—more than George Lucas was willing to pay. Negotiations for the exchange would continue for another two years and Eliza was always hopeful that her papa would soon be with them again.

While waiting for his exchange George Lucas was thinking of another way to help his daughter—he wrote to her proposing two candidates for marriage. Eliza was a dutiful daughter and treated her papa with the greatest respect, but she was also a very determined young lady who did not hesitate to make her feelings known—in the most courteous way possible, of course. This is her answer to his proposals:

As you propose Mr. L. to me I am sorry I can't have Sentiments favourable enough of him to take time to think on the Subject, as your Indulgence to me will ever add weight to the duty that obliges me to consult what best pleases you, for so much Generosity on your part claims all my Obedience, but as I know 'tis my happiness you consult [I] must beg the favour of you to pay my thanks to the old Gentleman for his Generosity and favourable sentiments of me and let him know my thoughts on the affair in such civil terms as you know much better than any I can dictate; and beg leave to say to you that the riches of Peru and Chili if he had them put together could not purchase a sufficient Esteem for him to make him my husband.

As to the other Gentleman you mention, Mr. Walsh, you know, Sir, I have so slight a knowledge of him I can form no judgment of him, and a Case of such consiquence requires the Nicest distinction of humours and Sentiments. But give me leave to assure you, my dear Sir, that a single life is my only Choice and if it were not as I am yet but Eighteen, hope that you will [put] aside the thoughts of my marrying yet these 2 or 3 years at least.

You are so good to say you have too great an Opinion of my prudence to think I would entertain an indiscreet passion for any one, and I hope heaven will always direct me that I may never disappoint you; and what indeed could induce me to make a secret of my Inclination to my best friend, as I am well aware you would not disapprove it to make me a Sacrifice to Wealth, and I am as certain I would indulge no passion that had not your approbation.[11]

There were no more prospective husbands put forth by George Lucas for his daughter.

Eliza's father was always looking for ways to improve his financial situation and diversification on his land was a top priority. When he returned to the West Indies he wrote Eliza that he thought she "might produce something of real and public utility" if she "could bring to perfection the plants of other Countries."[12] Accordingly he sent her different kinds of seeds to experiment with—to discover what would grow best in South Carolina. Since Eliza was ignorant about growing conditions in the area when she began her experiments, she was extremely grateful to her neighbor Andrew Deveaux, who, she wrote to her father, was "very kind in instructing me in planting affairs."[13] Eliza was patient and determined and though she made mistakes in planting, she learned from those mistakes and moved forward—a trait that remained with her throughout her life.

While Eliza struggled to manage her father's plantations and begin her experiments with "the plants of other Countries" the war with Spain was gaining momentum in Florida and the West Indies. Eliza tried her best to shield her mother from any unpleasantness or undue stress, but the war and George Lucas' involvement in it hung over their heads—like a dark shadow.

In the Shadow of War

The colony of Georgia had been founded by a group of twenty-one men called trustees who envisioned it as a haven for London's poor. In June of 1732

George II granted the trustees a charter for all the land between the Altamaha and Savannah Rivers—an area that had long been contested by both England and Spain. It was James Oglethorpe, one of the trustees, who brought the first group of colonists over in 1733 settling them on a bluff seventeen miles inland on the south side of the Savannah River—a good defensive site. Defense would be important for this vulnerable new colony for Georgia may have been established to serve as a refuge for the poor, but it was also designed to serve as a buffer to protect South Carolina and the other southern colonies from invasion by the Spanish in Florida.

In the spring of 1739 with tensions growing between England and Spain James Oglethorpe was named commander-in-chief of all British forces in Georgia and South Carolina. In September General Oglethorpe ordered his regiment to the Florida-Georgia border in anticipation of a declaration of war between Great Britain and Spain. In January of 1740 he made several passes into Spanish territory capturing two Spanish forts along the St. John's River.

However, it was in May of 1740 that he began his major invasion of Florida with the capture of the fort at St. Augustine as his goal. As he crossed the border on May 9 he had under his command a large but diverse force and his intention was to launch a surprise attack on the fort. However, disagreements among the commanders of the different forces delayed his progress and caused him to lose the advantage of surprise. Instead of attacking the fort he opted for a siege. Unfortunately, Oglethorpe could not coordinate his land and naval forces and the Spanish were able to re-supply the fort. By July, heat and disease had taken its toll on the army and Oglethorpe was forced to break off the siege and retreat to Georgia leaving all his artillery behind.

Eliza, like most South Carolinians, was caught up in the St. Augustine Expedition and followed it very closely. General Oglethorpe bore the blame for the failure of the mission and was highly criticized by many of the men who took part in the campaign—one of his officers even going to the length of filing serious allegations of moral and military misconduct against him. The trustees in London and many of the colonists in Georgia were not particularly happy with Oglethorpe's administrative style and complaints about his government mounted. Rumors of dissatisfaction with Oglethorpe were prevalent in Charleston and Eliza duly reported them to her father.

While Georgians and South Carolinians were fighting the Spanish in Florida, the Royal Navy was seeing action in the Caribbean. Admiral Edward Vernon had arrived in Antigua in the latter part of October and had immediately set his sights on Portobello on the coast of Panama. He captured it in twenty-four hours. Emboldened by his victory, Vernon decided to try his luck at Cartagena on the coast of present-day Colombia. However, when, after twenty-one days, Cartagena had not fallen, Vernon was forced to withdraw and leave the area. He went on to attack and destroy the fortress of San Lorenzo el Real Chagres near Portobello and then decided to take on Cartagena again in May. Unfortunately, Spanish ships blocked the harbor preventing him from attacking. So far the British had not been entirely successful in their efforts against Spain—either in the West Indies or in Florida.

South Carolina planters had an intense interest in the progress of the war in the West Indies as their livelihoods depended on their ability to get their goods to market and naval action in the Caribbean seriously affected that ability. Eliza was also following events in the West Indies with great concern, but her concern was mainly for the safety of her father. However, on November 18, 1740, an event took place in Charleston that obliterated everyone's interest in the war for a time.

It was two o'clock in the afternoon and in a hatter's shop located on the corner of Broad and Church streets a small blaze flared up catching nearby objects on fire before engulfing the entire shop in flames.[14] Once started, the fire, aided by a brisk fall breeze, spread quickly through Charleston's wooden buildings. The *South Carolina Gazette* of November 13–20 reported "the wind blowing pretty fresh at northwest carried the flakes of fire so far, and by that means set houses on fire at such a distance, that it was not possible to prevent the spreading of it."

All in all, some 300 buildings were burned including warehouses along the docks containing valuable stores of rice, deerskins and timber. It was a catastrophe. Many people were left homeless, businesses were ruined and the governor put out a call for charitable contributions to help support the victims of the disaster. Eliza and her mother at Wappoo would have seen the billowing clouds of smoke rising above Charleston that November day and been concerned for their friends and acquaintances in the city.[15]

While Carolinians were coping with the aftermath of the fire, Eliza was trying to cope with a physical ailment that was causing her some discomfort. She had been suffering from prolonged headaches and in November had written to Mrs. Boddicott requesting that she ask Dr. Meade, a well-known London physician, to send her a prescription for the headaches. She received the medicine in February and in May wrote Mrs. Boddicott:

> I received Doctor Meads prescription with the meddicines made up accordingly—have not
> yet begun upon them as my head has been something better, but as the hott weather advances
> I know it will increase and then I shall do the Doctor's prescription justice. I have had all the
> advice I could in this part of the world and generally found relief for a time. To comply with
> your obliging request and give you as particular an account of it as I can, I am to inform you
> 'tis by no means periodical. I find it rather worse in hott weather than cold and have it some

times for 6 months together without a days' intermission—tho' not to a violent degree but now and then. I remember I had in England once the same acute pain for one week before I had the small pox—as I some times have here. When 'tis very violent 'tis attended with a sickness at my stomach.[16]

Eliza tried different remedies for her headaches—she reported having a "blister to my Neck and one to each temple for a pain in my head, and from which I have found some benefit."[17] In the 18th century illness and disease were thought to be an indication of an imbalance in the body's humors or bodily fluids and treatment was centered on restoring balance by removing the excess—such as blood-letting, purging the body through an emetic, diuretic, laxative, excessive sweating or raising a therapeutic blister by applying a poultice or a heated blistering iron. The "blister" was not Eliza's only option as she found a more appealing treatment: "keeping my feet a little while every night before I go to bed in hott water."[18]

Charles Pinckney and his wife Elizabeth had another remedy for Eliza's headaches—that she come to visit them in town. Eliza replied to Charles Pinckney's letter:

> I received yesterday the favour of your advice as a phisician and want no arguments to convince me I should be much better for both my good friends' company—a much pleasanter prescription yours is, I am sure, than Dr. Meads, which I have just received. To follow my inclination at this time I must endeavour to forget I have a Sister to instruct and a parcel of little Negroes whom I have undertaken to teach to read, and instead of writing an answer bring it myself. And indeed gratitude as well as inclination obliges me to wait on Mrs. Pinckney as soon as I can, but it will not be in my power till a month or two hence.[19]

Eliza's sister Polly had turned five in November and George Lucas thought it was time for her education to begin and told Eliza to enroll Polly in school in Charleston. Mrs. Lucas was a very indulgent and anxious mother and Eliza knew it would cause her a great deal of stress to send her youngest child away to school. Therefore, she persuaded her father to allow her to teach her sister at home.

Eliza, like her father, was fond of projects and she had heard that the Rev. Alexander Garden, a commissary of the bishop of London, was advocating the education of slaves. A great proponent of uplifting the Africans in South Carolina, he proposed that each large plantation train an enslaved person as a schoolmaster to teach the other slaves.[20] It was an idea that appealed to Eliza and she set about educating a few of the slaves at the same time she was instructing her sister.

As indicated in her letter to Charles Pinckney, Eliza was not always available to visit her friends as much as she would have liked. In a letter to her father she wrote: "I am greatly obliged to good Mr. and Mrs. Pinckney for their partiality

to me, and was it not on account of leaving my Mama too much alone and
neglecting some affairs that require my attention at home, the friendly and
pressing invitation they continually give me to give them as much of my company as I can would induce me to be much oftener in town than I am."[21]

Eliza had now settled into a comfortable routine at Wappoo and wrote
this account of her weekly schedule to satisfy the repeated demands of a friend
in Charleston who wanted to know how she spent her time:

> In general then I rise at five o'Clock in the morning, read till Seven, then take a walk in the
> garden or field, see that the Servants are at their respective business, then to breakfast. The
> first hour after breakfast is spent at my musick, the next is constantly employed in recolecting
> something I have learned least, for want of practise it should be quite lost, such as French and
> short hand.[22] After that I devote the rest of the time till I dress for dinner [eaten in the early
> afternoon] to our little Polly and two black girls who I teach to read, and if I have my papa's
> approbation (my Mamas I have got) I intend [them] for school mistres's for the rest of the
> Negroe children—another scheme you see. But to proceed, the first hour after dinner as the
> first after breakfast at musick, the rest of the afternoon in Needle work till candle light, and
> from that time to bed time read or write. 'Tis the fashion here to carry our work [needlework]
> abroad with us so that having company, without they are great strangers, is no interruption
> to that affair; but I have particular matters for particular days, which is an interruption to
> mine. Mondays my musick Master is here. Tuesdays my friend Mrs. Chardon (about 3 mile
> distant) and I are constantly engaged to each other, she at our house one Tuesday—I at hers
> the next and this is one of the happiest days I spend at Woppoe. Thursday the whole day
> except what the necessary affairs of the family take up is spent in writing, either on the business
> of the plantations, or letters to my friends, Every other Friday, if no company, we go a vizeting
> so that I go abroad once a week and no oftener.[23]

Eliza's schedule drew some comments from one of her neighbors: "An old lady
in our Neighbourhood is often querrelin with me for riseing so early as 5 o'Clock
in the morning, and is in great pain for me least it should spoil my marriage,
for she says it will make me look old long before I am so." This same lady also
disapproved of the fact that Eliza read so many books. However, reading was
one of Eliza's greatest pleasures and in addition to the library at Wappoo she
had access to Charles Pinckney's extensive collection. She wrote: "I cant help
runing a parallel between the above lady and my valueable and worthy friend
Mrs. Woodward who ... incourages me in every laudable pursuit."[24]

While following her familiar routine on the plantation, the war and her
father's safety were never far from Eliza's mind. Mail from the West Indies was
erratic in arriving in the best of times, but during war times it was even more
sporadic. When Eliza had not heard from her father for several months, she
started to fear the worst. Then four letters arrived very closely together. In great
relief Eliza wrote her father, "Never were letters more welcome than yours of
Feb. 19th and 20th and March the 15th and 21st, which came almost together.
It was near 6 months since we had the pleasure of a line from you."[25] So far

Major George Lucas had not been involved in any military action—a circumstance that greatly irritated him but brought comfort to his wife and daughter.

Eliza was still following events in Savannah regarding General Oglethorpe whom she seems to have taken in dislike. In the late spring of 1742, Lieuteant Colonel William Cook, one of Oglethorpe's officers, and his family stopped in Charleston for several weeks before embarking for England. It was Colonel Cook who had filed charges of misconduct against General Oglethorpe and he was now returning home on leave. The colonel with his son and two daughters called upon Eliza and her mother and the daughters were quick to tell Eliza how greatly General Oglethorpe had mistreated their father. "They sail from hence in about ten days for London," Eliza wrote to her father. "I hope Colo. Cooks representation of his [Oglethorpe's] conduct ... will produce some good effects, and from the expected alterations at Georgia we draw some hopes of seeing my dear papa settled with us once again."[26]

The "expected alterations at Georgia" that Eliza mentioned were the dismissal of General Oglethorpe as governor and the appointment of her father in his place. The negotiations for an exchange with Major Heron were producing no results and Eliza was hoping that her father would soon be governor of the adjoining colony of Georgia. She was to be disappointed. The charges against General Oglethorpe were not heard until 1744 and by that time George Lucas' situation had changed.[27]

There was soon another added worry for Eliza and her mother. The previous spring both of Eliza's brothers had been stricken with smallpox in England. Mrs. Boddicott, who took care of the boys while they were sick, reported that George had made a swift recovery from the disease but that Thomas had not yet regained his strength or his health. The young teenager's condition continued to deteriorate over the next ten months and by June of 1742 Mrs. Boddicott wrote to tell Eliza that Thomas was very seriously ill and that he had been "given over by the Phisicians."[28]

It was devastating news. "The meloncholy contents of our letters from England," Eliza wrote to Mary Chardon, "deprives us of the pleasure of waiting on you this morning as we promised. The languishing condition my brother Tommy is in is almost insupportable to so tender and indulgent a mother as my poor Mama." Everyone, including Tommy, expected that he would not live. Eliza wrote he "assures us he is intirely resigned to that Almighty Being in whoos hands are life and death."[29]

On top of that news George Lucas wrote to inform them that George Lucas, Jr., who had received his commission as an ensign in his father's regiment the previous summer, was soon to go on active duty in Antigua. Eliza wrote to her brother that "the meloncholy consideration of a beloved father and brother being in great danger depresses me to the greatest degree and prevents my proceeding any farther—."[30]

Eliza, though, could not resist the opportunity later to give her brother some advice as he entered military service. Her advice was influenced by the philosophy of the Enlightenment with its emphasis on the importance of reason in governing human passions or emotions. Perhaps being aware that her brother might not relish advice from his sister, she concluded by writing: "Pardon my dear brother the liberty I take with you. I am a little older than you are and therefore assume on that account, or advise rather from the tenderest regard for your happiness."[31]

The next letter to her brother was over three pages long and contained more advice. When she wrote it, Eliza was reading or had just read the works of Robert Boyle, a 17th-century natural philosopher, chemist and inventor, who was well known for his writings in theology—tracts on the limits of reason and the role of the philosopher as a Christian. Eliza, afraid that her young brother would become a follower of the nonreligious movement that was fashionable among young men of the time, urged him to "live agreeably to the dictates of reason and religion"[32] and gave him several examples from the writings of Boyle that proved there was no conflict between the two.

Eliza's concerns were soon diverted from the plight of her brothers by a threat closer to home—the long expected invasion of Georgia by the Spanish. At the end of June 3,000 troops from Havana and St. Augustine landed on St. Simon's Island in Georgia and were met and defeated by General Oglethorpe's forces at Bloody Marsh and again at Gully Hole Creek.

Rumors of the Spanish landing reached Charleston very quickly. Eliza was concerned and took steps to protect her father's slaves: "July 2nd, 1742. Wrote my father ... informed him that the 30th of June an express arrived from Georgia that 12 hundred Spainyards were landed at a small Island near Friderica ... wrote to Murray [overseer at Garden Hill] upon the least alarm or apprehension of danger imediately to bring down the Negroes."[33]

Eliza gave her father a more complete report in September. South Carolinians were relieved when they heard that the Spanish had been repulsed in Georgia, but the worry that they would return in the future always lurked in the back of their minds. Therefore, they were greatly heartened when the fleet from Jamaica arrived in Charleston in November of 1742. Eliza and all the young ladies in town were excited also for they were "told there is fifty officers" with the fleet. Later in November she wrote to her father:

> Since my last [letter] the fleet is returned to Jamaica. Their orders were such that, if the Spain-
> yards were gone and we under no apprehensions of their returning, to return to Jamaica with

the whole detachment. They were very desirous to stay longer, and the Carolinians as desireous to have them stay. They were very well received here and took great pleasure in acknowledging it upon all occations. They are quite enamoured with Carolina; nor is it to be wondered at after coming from Jamaica, a place of which they give a most horrible character. The character they give of the women there must, I think, be exaggerated and therefore I wont enlarge on that head.

The Governor gave the Gentlemen a very gentile entertainment at noon and a ball at night for the ladies on the Kings birthday at which was a Crowded Audience of Gentlemen and ladies. I danced a minuet with your old acquaintance Capt. Brodrick, who was extreamly glad to see one so nearly related to his old friend. I promised to pay his compliments to you and asure you how extreamly glad he would be to see you. A Mr. Snell (a very talkative man) desires his best respects and says many obliging things of you for which I think my self obliged to him and therefore punish my self to hear a great deal of flashy nonsense from him for an hour together.[34]

Meanwhile trouble was brewing in Europe. In 1740 Charles VI (Holy Roman Emperor, king of Bohemia, Hungary and Croatia and archduke of Austria) died leaving his empire to his twenty-three-year-old daughter Maria Theresa. Under ancient Salic Law Maria Theresa, as a woman, could not become the ruler of the Holy Roman Empire. The ensuing war known as the War of the Austrian Succession was ostensibly fought over the right of Maria Theresa to assume all her father's domains—but in reality it was fought to maintain the balance of power in Europe.

Frederick the Great of Prussia struck quickly before the young and inexperienced Maria Theresa had settled in to her new role. He invaded and conquered Silesia—a wealthy Austrian province now part of Poland. Not wanting to see Prussia expand its borders, Great Britain and the Dutch Republic along with the Kingdoms of Sardinia and Saxony allied themselves with Austria. France, Prussia and the Electorate of Bavaria were joined by Spain who wanted to re-assert her influence in northern Italy—now controlled by Austria. In 1742 the war with Spain merged into the War of the Austrian Succession which was contested in Europe, India, the West Indies and the American colonies where it was called King George's War. By the end of 1742 the focus of the fighting was beginning to move away from the West Indies; however, there were still campaigns being conducted in the area and enemy privateers cruised the waters waiting to pounce on unsuspecting ships.

Wars were prevalent during Eliza's lifetime and often those she loved were involved in the fighting—causing her great anxiety and concern. She also witnessed firsthand the havoc caused by wars on people's lives and their economic interests and she was dismayed by it. "Do they say," she wrote to a friend, "whether the Warr is likely to continue or not? I was going to say I wish all the men were as great cowards as my self, it would make them more peaceably inclined. Now could I moralize for half an hour on the wickedness and folly of war and bloodshed, but my letter is of a convenient length."[35]

The people of Charleston were adversely affected by the wars of the 18th century for they were dependent on ships. Ships carried their goods to market and brought goods from Europe back to them and also carried their correspondence to friends, business associates and relatives in Europe and the West Indies and brought letters and news from abroad back to Charleston. During times of war merchant ships had to be escorted by a warship to ensure their safe arrival in port. If escorts were not available and enemy ships were active in the area an embargo was placed on the port and no ships were allowed to leave. Eliza complained: "We have not heard from England for more than three months. What can keep the shipping? We conjecture 'tis an imbargo."[36]

George Lucas, trying to recoup his fortunes with his property in South Carolina, was also a victim of the war. He had acquired his South Carolina plantations in the 1730s when the price of rice was high. However, in the 1740s the price began to fall, caused in part by overproduction, but mostly caused by the war which disrupted markets in Europe and the West Indies and caused freight costs to rise. Rice was a bulky product to ship and plantation owners depended on low shipping rates to transport their product to market. But the dangers of ocean travel in times of war drove up insurance rates and consequently drove down the price of rice. Eliza reported to her father: "The [rice] crop at Garden Hill turned out ill, but a hundred and sixty barrels; and at Wappo only 43. The price is so very low as thirty shillings per hundred. We have sent very little to town yet for that reason."[37]

Many planters in South Carolina relied solely on their rice crop for their income and were content to allow their fortunes to rise and fall with its price. There were others, though, who diversified by engaging in outside ventures—such as owning a mill or a fleet of boats to transport their neighbors' crops to town. However, few, if any, outside of George Lucas, considered the possibility of cultivating a second cash crop on their plantations to off-set the vagaries of the market. But as the war dragged on and trade continued to be interrupted and the price of rice kept falling, the idea of a second crop became more and more appealing to many planters. The time was right for the introduction of indigo.

Indigo and Other Projects

George Lucas had never intended to just cultivate rice on his plantations—he wanted to diversify, but first he needed to determine what other viable crops would grow on his land. For that reason, he sent Eliza several different kinds of seeds and asked her to use her expertise with plants to determine their potential. She began her experiments in the spring of 1740 by planting indigo, ginger, cotton, lucerne (a form of alfalfa), and cassava, a plant whose edible starchy root was a food staple in the West Indies.

Ginger and cassava are both tropical plants and Eliza found the climate in South Carolina was not suitable for their cultivation. As for the alfalfa, Eliza reported to her father that the "lucerne is yet but dwindleing, but Mr. Hunt tells me 'tis always so here the first year."[38] She continued to cultivate alfalfa, but with mixed results. She was more successful with cotton and it was grown at Garden Hill for many years, but for domestic use only. At that time there was not much demand for cotton in England—the textile mills there could only process so much raw cotton and they were being supplied with all they needed from the West Indies.

Indigo was also a success. Eliza reported to her father she "had greater hopes from the Indigo ... than any of the rest of the things I had tried."[39] Indigo, the name of both the plant and the blue dye made from it, was in high demand in Great Britain. While the textile mills in the country needed dyes of all colors, they were especially interested in obtaining good blue dye to dye the wool for the uniforms of the Royal Navy.

The indigo plant originally came from India and was mentioned in Indian manuscripts dating back to the 4th century BC. Early European explorers in the Far East realized that the plant was the source of a valuable blue dye, but it was Arab traders who first introduced indigo into Southern Europe. It was not until the 16th century, however, that indigo began to be widely cultivated in India and it was not until the middle of the 17th century that the East India Company began to import indigo to England. Indigo produced a rich blue dye and quickly replaced the weak blue dye made from woad—a plant native to most of Western Europe.

While there are over 700 species of the indigo plant, only two varieties were commonly used in making dye: *Indigofera tinctoria*, native to Asia, and *Indigofera suffruticosa*, native to Central and South America. Although many people thought the Asian variety produced a better dye, the New World species was used exclusively by planters in the Americas. Indigo was grown on many of the French and Spanish islands in the West Indies and on at least one British island, Montserrat, during the first part of the 18th century. Most of the indigo exported to Great Britain at this time came from the West Indies—much of it from the French islands.

Eliza had demonstrated that the soil and climate in South Carolina were suitable for the cultivation of indigo, but that was just the beginning. She had to produce a sizable crop and then produce a creditable dye and, as it turned out, those two tasks were not easy to accomplish. One of the difficulties she faced was getting the seeds for her plantings—the indigo plant being an annual which must be re-sown each year. At first Eliza relied on her father to send seeds from the West Indies, but her goal was to be able to obtain the seeds she needed from her own plants.

The indigo plant forms a seed pod which in the fall of the year splits, spilling the seed upon the ground. The seed must be left there to dry and then gathered and saved to plant in the spring. That first fall Eliza received a slight setback. She wrote to her father in June of 1741:

> I wrote you in [a] former letter we had a fine Crop of Indigo Seed upon the ground, and since informed you the frost took it before it was dry. I picked out the best of it and had it planted, but there is not more than a hundred bushes of it come up—which proves the more unluckey as you have sent a man to make it. I make no doubt Indigo will prove a very valuable Commodity in time if we could have the seed from the West Indies [in] time enough to plant the latter end of March, that the seed might be dry enough to gather before our frost.[40]

Indigo had been one of the first crops the early settlers planted in South Carolina, but it was soon abandoned in favor of rice. Rice might be difficult to cultivate, but required only muscle power to prepare it for market. The indigo plant, on the other hand, was relatively easy to cultivate, but processing the leaves to make the dye was a very precise process that took skill and careful timing. An "indigo maker"—a man skilled in making the dye—was needed to supervise the process.

As soon as George Lucas knew that indigo could be grown in South Carolina, he hired an "indigo maker" for Wappoo. His name was Nicholas Cromwell and he was from the island of Montserrat where large quantities of indigo were produced. Cromwell arrived at Wappoo in the summer of 1741 to find a very small amount of indigo growing on the plantation. However, he started to work at once to build the vats needed for the production of the dye.

The problems with the seed and the cultivation of the plant were not over, however. Eliza saved the seeds from her small crop and used those seeds along with seeds her father sent her to plant her next crop in the spring of 1742. However, there was a problem. Eliza wrote: "The last Indigo seed sent not good. None of it came up. We shall save enough of our own to make a Crop next year."[41] Unfortunately, the next year's crop was "cut down by a worm."[42] Finally, in the summer of 1744—five years after she had first planted the indigo—Eliza had a successful crop.

While she was struggling to successfully cultivate the plant, Eliza was also having some experiments done with making small amounts of the dye. The first step in this process was to cut the leaves and stalks from the bushes. This had to be done at just the right time—too early and the quality of the dye would be poor and too late both the quality and quantity of the dye would be affected. The bushes were generally cut to within two inches of the ground in order to ensure a second cutting later in the season. In Carolina planters got only two cuttings per season while farther south in Florida and the West Indies the average was three or four.

The stalks and leaves were then gathered into bundles and placed in the first of a series of three large vats. The vats were built on platforms and each vat was lower than the one before—like three giant steps. When the bundles of stalks and leaves were placed in the first vat, called the "steeper," they were covered with a mixture of water and urine and large flat boards were placed on top of the bundles to keep them completely submerged. Indigo is insoluble in water; therefore, a chemical must be added to the liquid to ensure its absorption. In the past urine was used—most particularly the urine of pre-adolescent boys (mostly likely slave boys) collected first thing in the morning. The bundles of leaves and stalks were left to soak in this mixture for eighteen to twenty-four hours during which time the leaves began to decay and release their blue color into the surrounding liquid.

After a time, the entire mixture began to ferment and bubble. Slowly at first blue bubbles rose to the surface, then they came faster and faster and a blue froth began to collect in the corners of the vat. This was a critical time in the process and the indigo maker had to keep a constant watch on the mixture and when, in his opinion, the bubbles were rising to the surface rapidly enough, the color of the froth in the corners was just right and the odor of the liquid mixture had reached a certain point, he knew it was time for the next step in the process to be taken.

The liquid from the steeper was drained into the second and lower vat, called the "beater," and the rotting stalks and leaves were removed from the steeper and taken away in an attempt to lessen somewhat the noxious smell. The liquid in the beater was then stirred by workers who beat it with wooden paddles to introduce oxygen into the mixture—a process that caused the dye to separate from the liquid. The beating continued for twenty to twenty-five minutes or until the mixture turned a deep green in color and there appeared to be small pebbles of a mud-like substance floating in it. At this point lime water, made by mixing burnt and crushed oyster shells with water, was added and the mixture was beaten again.

Slowly a clear liquid began to rise to the top and a mud-like substance, which contained the dye, sank to the bottom. The clear liquid was drained off and the mud was transferred to the third and lowest vat and allowed to drain. The drained mud was worked by hand until it was smooth and then pressed into boxes and cut into small one and a half inch squares called indigo bricks. The bricks were placed on open shelves in the drying house—a building with a roof but no walls—to dry. Slave children waved palm fronds over the drying bricks to keep flies, attracted by the smell, from laying eggs on the indigo. It took about three weeks from the time the leaves and stalks were placed in the steeper vat until the indigo bricks were dry enough to be packed into barrels for shipment.[43]

Cromwell was able to make a small amount of the dye in the fall of 1741, just after his arrival. However, the indigo bricks that he produced were, as Eliza put it, "very indifferent." Cromwell had built the vats out of brick, which was unusual as they were generally made of wood, and Eliza wrote her father: "The works being new and not dry enough in time the Indigo stood until many of the leaves dropped"—a situation that undoubtedly had a negative impact on the quality of the dye.[44] Eliza was left to hope that next year's batch of indigo would be better.

However, Cromwell's indigo continued to be indifferent. Eliza and her mother, examining some linen dyed with Cromwell's indigo, were dismayed at the results—his dye "gave linnen a red cast," Anne Lucas reported to her husband.[45] When confronted, Cromwell blamed the climate in South Carolina for the poor quality of the dye. However, Eliza was not satisfied with his explanation and was becoming more and more frustrated with him. Cromwell was being paid a high wage for his services which included explaining to Eliza how the process worked, but, according to Eliza, "he made a great mistery of it." Later he was heard to say "he repented coming as he should ruin his own country by it."[46] Clearly Cromwell did not want indigo from Carolina to compete with indigo from his native country.

The production of indigo was a smelly and unpleasant business. The stench from the liquid in the vats was foul and attracted a myriad of disease-carrying, biting insects. For that reason, vats were typically located as far from the dwelling houses of the planters as possible. Nevertheless, Eliza braved the smell and the bugs to go down to the production site to watch and learn as much as she could. In a letter years later Eliza recalled:

> I observed him [Cromwell] as carefully as I could and informed Mr. Deveaux an old Gentleman a neighbor of ours of the little knowledge I had gained and gave him notice when the Indigo was to be beat; he saw and afterwards improved upon it, not withstanding the churlishness of Cromwell who wished to deceive him, and threw in so large a quantity of Lime water as to spoil the color."[47]

Adding lime water to the mixture in the beater vat to speed up the process of separation was controversial. Many planters thought that lime spoiled the color of the dye and that the separation was best achieved by continued beating.

Since Cromwell's vats were made of brick, it is also possible that the lime in the mortar leached into the mixture adding to the amount of lime present. Cromwell had been contracted to work for three years at Wappoo and in June of 1744 his time of service was over and he was replaced as "indigo maker" by his brother Patrick who was more successful and produced seventeen pounds of good dye.

Eliza worked on the indigo project from 1740 to 1744 but, although it was important and she devoted a good amount of time to it, it was seasonal work. There was time enough for her to do other things. Besides instructing her sister and several of the slave children, she took time to engage in one of her favorite activities—gardening. In the spring of 1741 there was a chance that the exchange with Major Heron would take place and Major Lucas would be with them again. In anticipation of this event Eliza planned and laid out a pleasure garden at Wappoo. The garden was completed, but Major Lucas was not there to appreciate it as the exchange with Major Heron did not take place.

In January of 1742 a young lady, who was to prove a lively addition to Eliza's social circle, arrived in Charleston on a visit from England. Her name was Mary Bartlett and she was Mrs. Pinckney's niece—the daughter of Mrs. Pinckney's sister who lived in London—and she had come to spend a year with her aunt and uncle in Charleston. Mrs. Pinckney, who was very fond of Eliza, lost no time in introducing the two young ladies to each other. They became very good friends visiting each other frequently and engaging in a lengthy correspondence.

In our modern age of instant communication, when news and pictures from all over the world are transmitted instantly and connecting with family and friends is only a touch or a click away, it is difficult to appreciate the importance of letters to the people of Eliza's time. Letters brought news and descriptions of events taking place in other parts of the world as well as information about the health and welfare of family and friends. This was also a time when the ability to expound on diverse subjects with wit, cleverness or originality was highly valued both in written and verbal forms. Witty, clever or very descriptive and newsworthy letters were viewed as entertainment and 18th-century people often shared these letters with family and friends reading all or parts of them aloud to an assembled audience.

For example, when King George III married Charlotte of Mecklenburg-Strelitz in September of 1761, Mrs. King, Eliza's friend in England, wrote her an account of the subsequent coronation and a description of Queen Charlotte. A grateful Eliza wrote her: "You cant think how many people you have gratified by your obliging me with so particular a discription of the Queen. We had no picture of her Majesty nor discription that could be depended upon till I received your favour [letter]."[48] Eliza obviously read the letter again and again to all her friends and acquaintances.

Eliza knew that Mary Bartlett would read all or part of her letters aloud to her aunt and uncle—two people whom Eliza admired and respected—and she wanted her letters to be worthy; therefore, she expended time and thought on their composition. As a result, the letters are a delightful display of her wit, eclectic interests and powers of observation and thought—it is not surprising that she kept copies of them.

In her first letter to her new friend Eliza confided that she might not be able to find enough to write about as she lived in "solatary retirement" at Wappoo. However, she assured Miss Bartlett that "rather than not scribble you shall know both my waking and sleeping dreams, as well as how the spring comes on, when the trees bud and inanimate nature grows gay to chear the rational mind with delight."[49] And true to her word Eliza did write Mary, a city girl, about the delights of spring in the country—the fresh green of the pine trees, the fragrance of the myrtle and the jasmine and "a thousand nameless beauties of the woods [that] invite you to partake the pleasures the country affords."[50] She told her when her particular favorite, the mocking bird, began to sing and even sent her a poem she had composed one morning as she was getting dressed.

That spring a comet appeared in the sky above Charleston and Eliza could not resist the opportunity to observe it, even though it meant rising early to do so. Apparently Miss Bartlett was able to resist the urge as Eliza had to describe it to her.

> By your enquiry after the Comett I find your curiosity has not been strong enough to raise you out of your bed so much before your usual time as mine has been. But to answer your querie: The Comett had the appearance of a very large starr with a tail and to my sight about 5 or 6 foot long—its real magnitude must then be prodigious. The Tale was much paler than the Commet it self and not unlike the milkey way. 'Twas about a fortnight ago that I see it.
>
> The brightness of the Committ was too dazleing for me to give you the information you require. I could not see whether it had petticoats on or not, but I am inclined to think by its modest appearance so early in the morning, it wont permit every Idle gazer to behold its splendor, a favour it will only grant to such as take pains for it—from hence I conclude if I could have discovered any clothing it would have been the female garb. Besides if it is any mortal transformed to this glorious luminary, why not a woman.
>
> The light of the Comitt to my unphilosophical Eyes seems to be natural and all its own. How much it may really borrow from the sun I am not astronomer enough to tell.[51]

Mary Bartlett, the younger of the two young ladies by two years, obviously admired Eliza. "But I must beg it as a favour for the future," wrote Eliza, "that you treat me less in the stile of Compliments or the consequence will be that

I shall be very vain, when I know a good judge—one of my own sex, too—has so high an oppinion of my trifleing attainments."[52] Perhaps for this reason Eliza made Mary her confidant telling her friend about the schemes or projects, as she liked to call them, which she undertook.

One of these schemes was the planting of a large grove of oak trees. Oak was the preferred wood used in ship building and Eliza thought the trees would prove to be a good investment when, in the future, people began to build ships in the colony. "I am making a large plantation of oaks," she informed Mary, "which I look upon as my own property, whether my father gives me the land or not." She had a plan for the eventual profits from the oaks—two thirds would go to a charity and the other third "for those that shall have the trouble of putting my design in Execution." She continued:

> I sopose according to your custom you will show this to your Uncle and Aunt. "She is [a] good girl," says Mrs. Pinckney. "She is never Idle and means well." "Tell the little Visionary," says your Uncle, "come to town and partake of some of the amusements suitable to her time of life." Pray tell him I think these so, and what he may now think whims and projects may turn out well by and by. Out of many surely one may hit.[53]

Eliza had another gardening scheme to relate to Miss Bartlett: she had planted a large orchard of fig trees—her plan was to dry the figs and then export them. "Your good Uncle," wrote Eliza. "I know has long thought I have a fertile brain at scheming. I only confirm him in his opinion; but I own I love the vegitable world extremly. I think it an innocent and useful amusement."[54] In addition to the fig orchard, Eliza planted a cedar grove in which she connected the solemnity of summer or autumn with the cheerfulness and pleasures of spring by filling it with all kinds of flowers—garden flowers as well as wild flowers. Unfortunately, she did not name the flowers she planted—only mentioning that there were seats of chamomile and "here and there a fruit tree."[55]

However, not all of her schemes were centered on the "vegetable world." Eliza liked to read and there was a library at Wappoo containing several of George Lucas' books—one of which was Dr. Wood's *Institute of the Laws of England*—a book designed to instruct non-lawyers in the basics of English common law. Eliza knew nothing about the rudiments of the law, but was drawn to reading the book in an effort to help some of her poor neighbors "who," she told Mary, "have a little Land and few slaves and Cattle to give their children that never think of making a will till they come upon a sick bed and find it too expensive to send to town for a Lawyer." Eliza struggled with the book, many of the words and phrases were unfamiliar to her and she had to look them up in the dictionary. However, she was determined to apply herself and did not grudge the effort if, she said, it would make her useful to any of her poor neighbors. She confided to Mary:

If You will not laugh too immoderately at me I'll Trust you with a secrett. I have made two wills already. I know I have done no harm for I coned [learned] my lesson very perfect and know how to convey by will Estates real and personal and never forget in its proper place, him and his heirs for Ever, nor that 'tis to be signed by 3 Witnesses in presence of one another. But the most comfortable remembrance of all is that Doctor Wood says the Law makes great allowance for last Wills and Testaments presumeing the Testator could not have council learned in the law. But after all what can I do if a poor creature lies a dying and their family takes it in to their head that I can serve them. I cant refuse; but when they are well and able to employ a lawyer, I always shall.[56]

Eliza's letters to Mary Bartlett are light and cheerful and must have served as a welcome break from the more serious business correspondence that took up so much of her time—just as being entertained at the Pinckney house in Charleston was a reprieve from the responsibilities that pressed on her at Wappoo. She was struggling at this time with the challenges of indigo production, which included dealing with the uncooperative Nicholas Cromwell, and the many other concerns of plantation management and as welcome as these sojourns with the Pinckneys might have been, she was not always able to socialize as much as she would have liked. "I am sorry I cant wait on Dear Miss Bartlett on Monday," Eliza wrote. "I have so much business on my hands at present I hardly know which to turn my self to first, and most of it such as cant be deferred."[57]

Eliza engaged in many different projects, but not all of them were successful. Apparently she was not able to teach her little sister Polly to read—not through any lack of effort on Eliza's part, but perhaps through a lack of enthusiasm on the part of Polly and a lack of support from Mrs. Lucas. "Mama's indulgence," Eliza wrote her father in April of 1742, "now makes her [Polly] going to school necessary."[58] In September she was able to report to her father that she had "prevailed on Mama to send Polly to school." Polly was then duly enrolled in a boarding school in Charleston—at Mrs. Hext's establishment.[59]

It had always been expected that George Lucas would return to South Carolina; indeed, for over two years Eliza had been eagerly anticipating his arrival. It was also assumed that South Carolina would continue to be their place of residence. However, at the end of 1742 something happened to put these plans on hold for a while—George Lucas was appointed lieutenant governor of the island of Antigua. For the immediate future it appeared that instead of George Lucas returning to South Carolina the family would all return to Antigua.

Eliza must have received this news with mixed feelings. On the one hand, she wanted very much to be reunited with her father, but on the other hand she liked living in South Carolina and would be leaving some of her projects there unfinished—always a problem for Eliza who hated "to undertake any thing and not go thro' with it."[60] She expressed her feelings in a letter to Miss Dunbar in Antigua in February of 1743: "The hopes of seeing you is an additional pleasure to what I promise my self in haveing again my Papa and brothers company, and indeed nothing but this satisfaction can atone for the regret with which I shall leave Carolina, a country for which I shall always have the greatest regard."[61]

However, George Lucas' administrative and military duties (at the end of 1742 he had been promoted to lieutenant colonel[62]) were heavy and would not allow him time to come to Charleston to escort his wife and daughters back to Antigua. Their return would have to be delayed until Ensign George Lucas could be spared to make the journey in his place. The uncertainty surrounding the date of their departure did not deter Eliza from continuing her agricultural pursuits, especially with indigo, and, since George Lucas was still determined to improve his Carolina property, she continued to be much involved in implementing plans for expanding his interests.

In January of 1743 Mary Bartlett's visit to her aunt and uncle came to an end and she returned to London. However, Mary and Eliza continued to correspond and Eliza was able to give her friend a glowing description of a "tour" she had taken that spring. Charles and Elizabeth Pinckney, always striving to make Eliza's life more pleasant, had proposed a tour of the area around Goose Creek—to the northwest of Charleston. The tour included stops at several handsome plantations in the region where the Pinckneys and Eliza were made welcome and "entertained with the most friendly politeness." One of the most beautiful estates they visited was Crowfield, the home of William Middleton, where they "spent a most agreeable week." Eliza, as might be expected, was very impressed with the grounds which were elaborate and quite extensive and she sent Mary a detailed description of them.[63]

The tour with Mr. and Mrs. Pinckney, which took place in April, was a delightful diversion for Eliza as she had been worried about her father. Lieutenant Colonel George Lucas had finally had his desire to see action fulfilled and had taken part in the British attack on La Guaira—a Spanish stronghold off the coast of Venezuela—in March of 1743. The "unfortunate and ill conserted" attack was an overwhelming defeat for the British. Commodore Charles Knowles, in charge of the operation, was forced to withdraw in order to re-fit his ships and prepare for another attack along the coast in April.

Eliza knew that her father had taken part in that ill-fated expedition, but his present whereabouts and his next destination were unknown—a situation that caused her some anxiety. She acknowledged as much in her letter to Mary Bartlett: "Thus I have given you," she apologized, "a very languid discription of a delightful place [Crowfield]; the Laguire [La Guaira] Expedition has damped every gay Idea and faded every flowery expression; nor would the sylan [sylvan] scenes or even Arcadia it self charm till my dear fathers safe return."[64]

Meanwhile, the British fleet carrying the 38th Regiment of Foot and its commander, Lieutenant Colonel George Lucas, was preparing to attack Puerto Cabello off the coast of Venezuela. After bombarding the batteries defending the harbor castle, the landing force led by Colonel Lucas disembarked. It was night and one of the advance guard while trying to overpower a sentry fired off his musket. The rest of the landing party then fired in the dark on their own men thinking they were being attacked by the enemy. The Spanish in the castle then opened fire whereupon the British forces made a rush for the beach—"the officers being unable to rally their men," George Lucas reported.[65]

When Eliza left on her travels with the Pinckneys, it is likely that the news of the April assault on Puerto Cabello had not yet reached Charleston. Eliza was, therefore, spared, for the time being, the knowledge of the ill-starred attack led by her father on the batteries guarding the harbor. She probably learned the results of the expedition after she returned to Wappoo and while she was certainly relieved to learn that her father had returned unharmed, she was distressed by the outcome of his mission.

Back at Wappoo after her tour Eliza settled into her familiar routine managing the affairs of the plantations, hoping the next batch of indigo would be creditable and wondering how much longer they would be able to stay in South Carolina. As the long days of summer slowly passed, there was still no word from her father to indicate when Ensign Lucas would arrive to escort them back to Antigua. Meanwhile in Antigua George Lucas was trying to find time between his military duties and his responsibilities as lieutenant governor to make arrangements to bring his whole family together again.

His major problem was persuading his youngest son Tommy to return to Antigua. The fifteen-year-old was still ill and in a weakened condition in England and was not anxious to board a ship for the long voyage back to Antigua—a sentiment that had the support of both Mr. and Mrs. Boddicott with whom the boy was living. George Lucas decided to leave Tommy in England a little while longer, hoping his health would improve enough for him to make the voyage the next year. He then turned his attention to making arrangements for his son George to travel to South Carolina to escort his mother and sisters back to Antigua—possibly in the late fall. It appeared that at last George Lucas was making progress towards having his family together for the first time in many years.

At the same time Eliza's good friends, Mr. and Mrs. Pinckney, were facing a crisis of their own. Mrs. Pinckney, whose health had been declining for several years, was now very unwell. In the fall of 1743 Charles Pinckney rented his town house in Charleston and gave notice in the *South Carolina Gazette* that his law office would, for the foreseeable future, be located at his mother's house on Queen Street. He then moved with his wife to Belmont, his plantation on Charleston Neck, where he hoped the country air would bring about some improvement in her health.

Eliza was a frequent visitor at Belmont and spent a good deal of time with Mrs. Pinckney during her illness. In the course of her visits, she would have relayed some sad news to her friends—she would soon be leaving South Carolina. Ensign George Lucas was to come in January to make arrangements for his mother and sisters to return to Antigua.

Sadly, all of Mr. Pinckney's hopes for his wife's recovery were in vain. Her condition continued to deteriorate and on January 23, 1744, Mrs. Pinckney, who had been such a kind and affectionate friend to Eliza, died. Pinckney family tradition maintains that just before her death Mrs. Pinckney urged her husband to remarry and suggested a young wife who would be able to give him the children he had always wanted.

The death of his wife left Charles Pinckney in a dilemma. He had been sincerely devoted to her and it had been difficult for him to watch her suffering during her final weeks. He knew that now she was at peace and, for a man of his religious principles, it was a sign of God's goodness that He had ended her pain. He needed time, though, to mourn her passing, but he also did not want Eliza to return to Antigua. Ocean travel was risky at the best of times and even more so in times of war. He might never see her again. A month after his wife's death, Charles Pinckney made a decision—he rode to Wappoo Plantation and asked Eliza to be his wife.

CHAPTER THREE

The Married Years
(1744–1758)

South Carolina

Charles Pinckney, the middle son of Thomas Pinckney and his second wife Mary Cotesworth Pinckney, was born in Charleston on August 13 in either the year 1699 or 1700.[1] His father, originally from the small coal mining town of Bishop Auckland in the north of England, had left home as a young man to seek his fortune in Jamaica. In 1692 after having spent three years in the West Indies as a privateer, Thomas had come to Charleston, married Grace Bedon and using the money he had made from privateering established himself as a merchant.

He bought property on the waterfront in Charleston and his house, which faced the Bay, served as both a residence and a place for Thomas to carry on his thriving business. He was soon able to buy more property in town plus a 480-acre tract of land on the east side of the Ashley River. Thomas and Grace had no children, and after her death in 1697, Thomas decided to return to England to visit his family. There he met Mary Cotesworth. The two were married on January 19, 1698, and sailed to Charleston soon after.

Thomas and Mary had two sons in addition to Charles: Thomas, the oldest, was born in 1698, and the youngest, William, in 1704. Unfortunately, a yellow fever epidemic swept through Charleston in early 1705 claiming many victims—one of whom was Thomas Pinckney, Sr. He left his young widow well provided for, but he also left her with three small boys to raise. Wanting to do the best she could for her sons, Mary made sure they had a good education. She was an attractive woman and married two more times—her last husband William Betson died in 1723 leaving her a tidy fortune.

Thomas, the oldest son, became master of a ship and was engaged in trade in the Bahamas. He apparently never married and died on a voyage to Nassau in 1733. The youngest son William followed in his father's footsteps and became a merchant in Charleston, while Charles decided on a career in the law. In order to pursue his career, Charles took his inheritance and went to London—the preeminent place to obtain professional legal training. Not being able to afford to study at one of the Inns of Court, Charles read law with a prominent barrister concentrating on English common law, the constitution and the Acts of Parliament. He learned shorthand so that he could take notes quickly and accurately while he was attending sessions of the House of Commons or watching trials in London's courts.

On September 15, 1726, in St. Paul's Cathedral Charles Pinckney married the twenty-one-year-old Elizabeth Lamb. The next year the young couple sailed for Charleston, arriving there in December of 1727. Charles Pinckney's legal training was exceptional and he was soon admitted to the South Carolina bar arguing his first case in January 1728. Three years later, having established a prosperous legal career, he was elected to the Commons House of the General Assembly.

By 1734 Charles Pinckney was one of the most prominent lawyers in South Carolina. He had served as the interim attorney general of the colony in 1733 and was an advocate general in the Vice Admiralty Court. As a result of his older brother's death in 1733, Charles had become the owner of some properties in England that had been left to his brother by their uncle Richard Pinckney of Bishop Auckland. The next year he was able to buy his first plantation in South Carolina—Espalainga Island in Port Royal Sound located 60 miles southeast of Charleston and lying between Hilton Head Island and the mainland. Today it is known as Pinckney Island.

One of Charles Pinckney's most significant accomplishments as a lawmaker occurred in 1735. During that year the Commons House of the General Assembly passed a tax bill that did not provide money for the salary of the chief justice—a man whom they intensely disliked. The Council, the upper house, instead of passing on the bill amended it to include a tax to be used for the payment of the salary. The lower house was outraged over this usurpation of one of their prerogatives—the right to initiate tax bills. They appointed a committee to draw up resolutions of protest and Charles Pinckney was chosen to draft them. He wrote:

> Resolved, That it is the Opinion of this House that it is the inherent right and privilege of every Englishman not to be charged with any taxes or aids of money but what are given and granted by his Representative in Parliament.
> Resolved, that his Majesty's subjects of the Province are entitled to all the liberties and privileges of Englishmen.[2]

Thirty years before Patrick Henry stood up in the Hall of the House of Burgesses in Williamsburg, Virginia, and uttered the immortal words "Taxation without representation is tyranny," Charles Pinckney had laid the foundation for the protests against Great Britain that would lead to the American Revolution. The members of the Commons were loud in their praise and Charles was elected speaker of the House.

By the time Eliza and her family came to South Carolina Charles Pinckney had become a large land owner. He had acquired several properties in Charleston in addition to his house on Union Street and several more plantations in addition to his island plantation in Port Royal Sound. Charles and Elizabeth had no children, but in 1740 they had taken their eight-year-old nephew, Charles Pinckney, II, to live with them.

Five years earlier Charles and his brother William, along with several other prominent men in Charleston, had started and financed America's first fire insurance company—the Friendly Society. Unfortunately, many of the buildings destroyed in the fire of 1740 had been insured by the company and the financial loss to the owners was great. Charles was able to absorb the costs, but his brother William, although a successful merchant, had a large family and was financially hampered by his share of the company's loss. In order to help his brother, Charles offered to raise William's son, Charles Pinckney, II, and pay for his education in London.[3]

Charles was already an important man in colonial affairs, but there was another honor in store for him in the summer of 1741—George II signed the commission making Charles Pinckney a member of the Governor's Council. He was sworn in on October 26. The man, then, who rode to Wappoo Plantation at the end of February in 1744 was a prominent man in colonial government, an outstanding lawyer and a wealthy land owner. He was 43 or 44 years of age with "a charming temper and disposition, gay and courteous manners, was well looking, well-educated and of high religious principles."[4]

The lady whose hand he was soliciting was twenty-one years old—petite, charming, lively and intelligent with a good sense of humor and also with high religious principles. Eliza, who promised her father that she "would indulge no passion that had not your approbation," accepted Charles Pinckney's offer with no hesitation, knowing that her father could have no objection to her choice. Her acceptance, of course, was conditioned on the approval of her family. Ensign George Lucas and Mrs. Lucas readily gave their consent and all that was left to be done was for the prospective bridegroom to pen a letter to Colonel Lucas and formally ask his permission to marry his daughter.

Eliza's father must have received Charles Pinckney's letter informing him first of the death of his wife and then of his desire to marry his daughter with mixed feelings. On the one hand, he could not have conceived of a better husband for his daughter, but on the other hand, his financial situation was such that he could not provide a suitable dowry. He was obliged to explain in a letter to Charles that his estates in Antigua were encumbered by the debts left him by his father, and that his property in South Carolina was hampered in part by the debts he had incurred in traveling to London to further his military career by purchasing a commission.

He could give Eliza £500 sterling, but not in ready money. Instead he proposed to settle on her the plantation at Wappoo with its twenty working slaves. However, since it was mortgaged the plantation would have to be sold, the debt paid and the remainder of the dowry would have to be raised from his other Carolina properties. George Lucas concluded his letter by writing: "[I am] sensible Sir how unequal this sum is to your Fortune and Figure, [but] as it is not in my power at present to do more without leaving [my other] children destitute, I thought proper to lay the naked facts before [you] ... and if as your letter speaks, you think fit to [marry my daughter] I shall think my self extremely happy in your alliance."[5]

Colonel Lucas had also written to his daughter to explain the status of her dowry. She replied:

> Honored Sir, I received your indulgent letter of the 26th of March and take the earliest opportunity to express my Thanks for that and for the fortune you are pleased to promise me. I have had too many instances of your paternal affection and tenderness to doubt your doing all in your power to make me happy, and I beg leave here to acknowledge particularly my obligations to you for the pains and money you laid out in my Education, which I esteem a more valuable fortune than any you could now have given me, as I hope it will tend to make me happy in my future life, and those in whom I am most nearly concerned.... Mr. P. has told my mama that he is fully satisfied with what you intend him, and desires me to tell you so, and that if it will embarrass your affairs he will readily resign it.[6]

Charles Pinckney and Eliza Lucas were married on May 27, 1744, at St. Andrew's Church. The wedding took place just four months after the death of his first wife—not an uncommon occurrence in the 18th century, especially in the colonies where people tended to remarry more quickly than in England. After the wedding Charles and Eliza returned to the Wappoo plantation where they were to remain until Ensign Lucas, Mrs. Lucas and little Polly sailed for Antigua.

That Eliza was radiantly happy can be seen in the letters she wrote to her friends telling them of her marriage. Her father was the first to know that she had, indeed, married Charles Pinckney. She wrote to him on June 2:

> Since I last payd my duty to you, I have pursuant to your advice as well as my own inclination, entered into a new state of Life; it gives me all imaginable satisfaction to know that I have the

approbation of the tenderest of Parents, and that of all my friends and acquaintances, of my choice. I do assure you Sir that tho I think Mr. Pinckney's character and merit are sufficient to engage the esteem of any lady acquainted with him, the leaving you at such a distance was an objection I could not easily get over; but when I considered that Providence might by some means or other bring us together again, and that it must be a great satisfaction to you as well as to myself, to know that I have put myself into the hands of a man of honour, whose good sense and sweetness of disposition gives me a prospect of a happy life, I thought it prudent, as well as intirely agreeable to mee, to accept the offer; and I shall make it the whole Study of my Life to fix that esteem and affection Mr. Pinckney has professed for me and consequently be more worthily your daughter.[7]

Eliza wrote also to her good friend Mrs. Boddicott about her marriage. "I have now dear Madam," she wrote, "some prospect of seeing you again; if the pain in my head continues, which I have been so long troubled with, Mr. Pinckney intends to bring me to bath [Bath, a spa town in England] next spring."[8] Eliza had not mentioned her headaches in her letters for some time, but she was still suffering from them. While Charles and Eliza were still at Wappoo, Mary Betson, Charles' mother, became very ill and Charles went down to Charleston to visit her. In a note to him inquiring after Mrs. Betson Eliza wrote: "Instead of sending to know how my Mother [mother-in-law] does I should have come myself, but am so much disordered with the headache, I am not able to come down in the heat of the day; if she is not better please send me word and I will be down early in the morning."[9]

It must have given Eliza great pleasure to be able to write to her cousin Fanny Fayerweather in Boston:

I am sure you will pardon me my dear Cousin, tho I have not acknowledged the receipt of your letter by Mr. Symons before and thanked you for the barberrys (which were very good), when you consider I have had so weighty a matter upon my hands as that of matrimony; I see you smile and wonder, that difficult girl (that's your phrase) ever married; that filled her own head, and was always preaching up to you the great importance of a matter of which the generality of the world make so light; nay you did not scruple telling me I should never get a man to answer my plan, and must therefore dye an old maid; but you are quite mistaken; I am married and the Gentleman: I have made Choice of comes up to my plan in every title.... When I tell you 'tis Mr. Pinckney I have married, you will think I do him barely justice when I say his good Sence and Judgement, his extraordinary good nature and evenness of temper joyned to a most agreeable conversation and many valuable qualifications, gives me the most agreeable prospect in the world.[10]

Charles and Eliza had planned on staying at Wappoo until Mrs. Lucas, her son and daughter embarked for Antigua which was scheduled for the middle of June. However, fearing an invasion—the War of the Austrian Succession was still in progress—an embargo was laid on the shipping. The Lucas family was not able to sail until the second of July. Then, at last, Charles was able to take his new wife to Belmont and the couple had some time to themselves.

A glowingly happy Eliza wrote to her mother:

> Two days after you sailed we came to Belmont, where we often wished to enjoy your Company, in a state of tranquillity, a state we so long before had been almost strangers to. We have spent the summer here very agreeably without being (what you seemed to apprehend) at all lonesome, for my dear Mr. Pinckney (whose humanity none can be a stranger to that know him) has never left me but one day in the week since I have been here.[11]

Belmont, Charles Pinckney's country seat, was located approximately five miles from Charleston in an area known as Charleston Neck. It was described by Eliza's great-great-granddaughter as "a delightful residence, a large brick house, standing, as most of the country houses did, a few hundred yards from the water's edge, on a semicircular headland making out into a bold creek, a branch of the Cooper River."[12]

Mrs. Lucas and the rest of the family arrived safely in Antigua after a very rough voyage and were joined soon afterward by Tommy who arrived from England "in a very low and weak Condition." With his family safely settled, Colonel Lucas was then able to take the time to give Eliza some advice on her marriage. Evidently George Lucas felt that his daughter, a very capable and determined young lady, might try to take more control in the marriage than was seemly. His letter to Eliza has not survived, but much can be inferred from her reply:

> I am greatly obliged to you for your good advice in my present happy relation, I think it intirely reasonable and tis with great truth that I assure you 'tis not more my duty than my inclination to follow it; for making it the business of my life to please a man of Mr. Pinckneys merit even in triffles I esteem a pleasing task and I am well assured the acting out of my proper province and invading his would be an inexcusable breach of prudence, as his superior understanding, without any other consideration, would point him to dictate; and leave me nothing but the easy task of obeying.[13]

He need not have worried. In many ways Charles Pinckney was the perfect husband for Eliza. He was an older man—successful, well-educated and cultured. Before their marriage he had been her mentor—lending her books, discussing them with her and patiently answering her many questions. He taught her shorthand and teased her about her schemes and projects. It is easy to imagine him sitting in the drawing room of his Charleston house with his wife, smiling and shaking his head as Mary Bartlett related another of Eliza's schemes to them. A younger, less experienced man may have been intimidated by such a determined and competent wife, but Charles Pinckney was not a man to feel threatened by his wife's accomplishments.

It is very evident from her letters that Eliza admired and respected Charles Pinckney more than any person she had ever met and that she was very much in love with him. "I can indeed tell you," Eliza wrote to Charles soon after their marriage, "I have the greatest esteem and affection imaginable for you; that next to Him that formed it, my heart is intirely at your disposal, but this you knew the day I gave you my hand."[14]

One person Eliza was very anxious to inform about her marriage was Mrs. Bartlett, Mrs. Pinckney's sister, in London. She wrote to her in March of 1745:

> As I have succeeded your good Sister, with whom I had the happiness of an intimate acquaintance for some years and I flatter myself a very great degree of her affection and friendship, I take the liberty to pay my respects to you though I have not the pleasure to be personally acquainted with you; I am conscious Madam how unworthy I am to supply the place of so good a wife as your sister was, but at the same time I must beg leave to assure you that however I may come short of her in other matters, in one thing I shall equal her, vizt in preserving a due regard to her relations and a readiness to do everything in my power to serve them. I shall be very glad of a correspondence with one so nearly related to my deceased friend as Mrs. Bartlett and shall look upon it as a particular obligation done me if agreeable to you.[15]

At the same time Eliza enclosed a letter for Mary Bartlett in which she staunchly defended her husband against a scandalous story that was being circulated in London—Mrs. Gregory, a Charleston lady visiting in England, had been telling people there that the first Mrs. Pinckney had been sadly neglected during her last illness and "could not have what she wanted" because her husband was about his business and the enslaved servants out of call. Eliza replied:

> I am a good deal surprised at the ridiculous story you mention from Mrs. Gregory as it has so little appearance of probability; indeed she was in the right, if she had any view of telling such a story, to do it out of Carolina and to people quite unacquainted with Mr. Pinckney's character. Had I not known him to have made the best of husbands I had not been in the relation I now am to him.

Eliza pointed out to Mary that Mrs. Pinckney could hardly have been neglected during her illness when, in addition to a number of enslaved servants, she had her cousin, Mrs. Beesly, with her along with Mrs. Fiddling, her housekeeper, and a young woman from town hired expressly to help take care of her. "Besides," Eliza wrote, "I think I may be confident had any thing laid upon her mind there was such an intimacy between us that she would have communicated to me," for "I my self was a great part of the time she was Ill with her." She continued:

> I am sorry Mrs. Gregory has given herself any unbecoming airs about you, but am more so to hear you express so much concern at it; for you can never think people of sence and penetration can ever regard what such a tatling woman says, that seems to study and love mischief for no other reason but to gratify an envious malicious temper or a tatling gossiping one, I would charitably hope the latter; I confess my self at a loss to find out what could induce her (if not what I have mentioned) ... to insinuate any thing to Mr. Pinckney's prejudice who has been always a friend to her; but I thank God his character is too well and too deservedly established to receive any hurt from her.[16]

Mrs. Bartlett did indeed choose to correspond with Eliza. Neither she nor her daughter paid any more attention to the story and their relationship with both Eliza and Charles remained warm and cordial.

Eliza and Charles may have been spending an idyllic summer together at Belmont but they were still very much involved in the business of looking after George Lucas' Carolina property. They would soon be even more involved. Shortly after her wedding Eliza informed her father that the man who had long held his power of attorney was no longer able to act for him. However, Eliza was able to offer her father an excellent replacement—her husband. Eliza assured him, "You may depend on his best endeavors as well as on mine to promote your interest."[17]

Their first item of business was the Wappoo Plantation which George Lucas had wanted to be sold. "These precarious times," wrote Eliza to her father, "makes the sale of land very difficult, that we can hardly hope to sell wappoe soon; Mr. Harvey offers to rent it imediately which we think better than having the house quite empty till 'tis sold; the rent will be upwards of 200£ which will pay the interest of Mr Dunbars Mortgage."[18] Mr. Harvey took over Wappoo plantation with the "stock of cattle and the Cropp (the indigo excepted)."[19] The indigo crop at Wappoo was part of Eliza's dowry.

In early June Nicholas Cromwell's contract as indigo maker was over and he returned to Montserrat. He was replaced by his brother Patrick who was more successful at making the dye. At the end of July Eliza was happy to report to her father:

> We hear from Garden Hill they have a prospect of a very good crop; we gave particular charge to Murray about the Indigo seed which I am still in hopes will prove a valuable commodity. Out of a little patch of Indigo growing at Wappoo (a present from Mama to Mr. P.) the Brother of Nicholass Cromwell, besides saving a quantity of seed, made us 17 [pounds] of very good Indigo, [so] different from NC [Nicholas Cromwell] that we are convinced he was a mere bunglar at it. Mr. Deveaux has made some likewise and the people in general very sanguine about it. Mr. P. sent to England by the last man of war 6 pound to try how it is approved of there; if it is I hope we shall [have] a bounty from home [England]; we have already a bounty of 5s. currency per Pound from the province upon it. We please ourselves with the prospect of exporting in a few years a good quantity from hence and supplying our Mother Country with a manufacture for which she has so great a demand and which she is now supplied with from the French Colony and many thousand pounds per annum thereby lost to the nation, which she might be as well supplied here if the matter was applied to in earnest.[20]

James Crokatt, the South Carolina agent in London, received the six pounds of indigo sent to him by Charles Pinckney and, as requested, took it to an expert to determine its quality. The report was very encouraging: "I have shown your INDIGO to one of our most noted Brokers in that Way, who tried it against some of the Best FRENCH, and in his opinion it is as GOOD.... When you can in some measure supply the British Demand, we are persuaded, that on proper Application to Parliament, a Duty will be laid on Foreign Growth, for I am informed that we pay for INDIGO to the French £200,000 per annum."[21]

In order to encourage the cultivation of indigo, Charles Pinckney, with his wife's concurrence, distributed small amounts of the seeds from the 1744 crop to anyone who would agree to plant them. Charles kept a portion of the seeds for himself and had them planted the next year at Auckland, his plantation on the Ashepoo River. He used his indigo crop only to produce seed which he and others who had followed his example were able to sell the next spring. Eliza had been quite correct in assuming that the seed itself would become a valuable commodity.

It was difficult to obtain indigo seeds from the West Indies—the sources were unreliable and the seeds subject to all the hazards of ocean travel during war time. It would be easier for planters if they could buy the seed locally and soon advertisements for the sale of indigo seed began to appear in the *South Carolina Gazette*. It would become increasingly important in the next few years that South Carolina have a local supply of seed, because once indigo was established in the province, the French, fearing the competition, made the exportation of indigo seeds from their island colonies a "Capital Crime."

Charles Pinckney, acting for his wife, gathered all the information he could about the production of indigo, even questioning French prisoners of war brought to Charleston, and published the results in the *South Carolina Gazette* for the "information of the people at large."[22] As a married woman Eliza had no separate legal identity—her existence was merged with that of her husband's and she had very few individual rights. As the great British jurist Blackstone wrote: "husband and wife are one, and the husband is that one."[23] And as "that one" it was the husband's duty to represent his wife in her dealings with the outside world. Therefore, when Charles Pinckney undertook any actions involving indigo, he was doing so on behalf of his wife. That these acts were done in his name and not hers did not in any way diminish her role in the indigo enterprise, for everyone in South Carolina and many people in England knew that it was Eliza who had developed indigo on her father's plantation,

When Eliza's indigo made its debut in London in 1744, it created much excitement both in England and in the province of South Carolina where many planters were quick to grasp the potential indigo presented as a second cash crop. There was a sudden scramble for seed and for information on the process of making the dye.

Indigo was the perfect second crop for low country planters. It could be grown on the high ground between rice fields and since its cultivation and processing occurred during the down times of rice cultivation, the same labor force could be used for both products. However, the low country was not the only place where indigo was planted—it was also grown in the backcountry and on the Sea Islands where the salt marshes made the cultivation of rice difficult. The production of valuable indigo bricks spread quickly. Since indigo was less bulky to ship than rice, planters were not faced with high freight rates and soon fortunes were being made.

In the year 1747 Carolina planters exported 135,000 pounds of indigo to Great Britain—by the time of the American Revolution the amount had risen to over one million pounds.[24] In 1748 Parliament authorized a bounty of 6 pence per pound on indigo produced in British America and exported directly to Great Britain. During this time it was said that indigo planters doubled their capital every three or four years. In 1745 George Lucas was finally able to realize some profit from the years of indigo experiments. His overseer at Garden Hill reported indigo worth over £225 was sent to Richard Boddicott in London.[25]

There was a native indigo plant that grew in South Carolina and in 1745 Mr. Cattel, a fellow Carolina planter, made Eliza a present of "a couple of large plants of the wild indigo which he had just discovered."[26] Experimental batches of dye were made from the plants and although the plants produced a good dye, they did not produce the same quantity of indigo as the imported plant. For that reason, Carolina planters continued to use the imported plant rather than the native one.

For most women in the 18th century marriage brought responsibilities and obligations that signaled an end to their previous carefree existence, but for Eliza it was just the opposite. Marriage freed her from the burdens of managing three plantations and conducting a vast amount of correspondence and left her with the pleasant task of being mistress of Belmont and the house on Union Street in Charleston. Finally she had time to thoroughly indulge her love of "the vegetable world" and to lay out pleasure gardens at both the country estate and the house in town.

One of her new responsibilities was looking after their nephew Charles and in the spring she was busy seeing that he was properly outfitted for school in London. Eliza still had letters to write, but they were now confined to the usual social correspondence with friends and family. It was Charles who took care of letters dealing with plantation business—which must have been a great relief to her. Charles and Eliza also enjoyed an extensive social life and no longer would Eliza have to excuse herself from a pleasurable outing because of "plantation business that could not be deferred." Her married years were the happiest and most carefree of her adult life.

Eliza was still involved in looking after her father's property, but since Charles held George Lucas' power of attorney, he took care of much of the business for her. There was really only the 1,500-acre plantation at Garden Hill that required their attention—Wappoo had been rented and George Starrat was overseeing the rice-producing lands along the Waccamaw River. George Lucas had big plans for his Garden Hill plantation and with the changes he had in mind in addition to some shrewd suggestions offered by his son-in-law, he was beginning to have hopes of improving his financial situation—but it was not easy as times were difficult for everyone.

The War of the Austrian Succession was causing great hardships in both Antigua and South Carolina. Great Britain was at war with both France and Spain and ships from both nations plus privateers in large numbers lurked in the waters off the southeastern coast of North America and in the Caribbean and played havoc with trade. Prices in Charleston were high and many goods were simply not available. "I am obliged to you for the sugar," Eliza wrote to her father, "what we have now in town is bad and dear and if it will not be intruding too much I shall be obliged to you for some white powdered sugar a thing that cant be purchased here at this time."[27] Eliza trying to gather clothing together for her nephew Charles when he was leaving for school in London wrote to Mary Bartlett whose family Charles would be staying with: "I send an account of Charles's things: I have made him up but little new linning [linen—shirts most likely] as everything here is excessive dear; and he may be supplyd with what more is necessary when he comes to London."[28]

George Lucas had always intended to make his home permanently in South Carolina and even though events so far had interfered with his plans to live in Carolina, he had not given up hope. He decided not to sell his plantation on Wappoo Creek as he considered its proximity to Charleston to be an advantage. He was certain rice cultivation would have to be curtailed in the future and alternatives developed. "Many useful things," he wrote to Charles, "might be done at a place so near the Metropolis." The lease on the Wappoo plantation was for two years and George Lucas requested that in the future Charles rent the plantation only from year to year as "I look upon Wappoo as the most convenient place to retire, whenever I could bring my Affairs to bear, So as to spend the remainder of my Days in Carolina."[29] There was soon another reason for George Lucas and his wife to wish to be in South Carolina—by the summer of 1745 Eliza was expecting a child.

Motherhood

Sometime in 1745 Charles Pinckney decided to build a large, elegant house for his new wife on a prime lot he owned in Charleston. The lot was located on the western side of East Bay Street and covered the entire square from Market Street to Guignard Street. The house, which was to be situated in the center of the property, was designed to face east with an unobstructed view of the water and poised to catch the prevailing breeze. Plans were drawn up and building had begun on the house when Charles decided to pen a sketch of it and send it to his brother-in-law for his perusal and comments. A very flattered George Lucas, Jr., replied: "in my humble opinion 'tis planned out in a very pretty Genteel taste & all the apartments prettily laid out. I hope you have room enough behind the house for a Small Garden as I know yourself & my Sister are Extremely fond of that amusement."[30]

In the same letter George warned his brother-in-law that he had not been able to keep the news that Eliza was expecting a child from his mother as she "never suffers any letters from Carolina to escape her."[31] Childbirth in the 18th century was a very risky affair and being aware of Mrs. Lucas' tendency to worry, Charles had instructed his brother-in-law to conceal the news from his mother.

Later Charles wrote to his father-in-law telling him that he would send him news about Eliza in his next letter if that was acceptable. He then added, "but I think my good mama [Mrs. Lucas] laid me under Some restraint in point of giving her any information concerning that matter [Eliza's pregnancy] 'till the business was happily over; So I must not Say a word of my apprehention about it."[32]

Charles Pinckney was perhaps justified in his "apprehention about it" for Eliza was still suffering from headaches and, in fact, did not feel well during the entire term of her pregnancy. After the birth of the baby, she confided to Mary Bartlett: "I have been a good deal confind of late for this child has so reduced and weakened me that you would be surprised to see me if you did not know how much out of order I was all the time I was with child with him."[33] It was most likely that at this time Charles Pinckney took over the complete management of the Lucas property. In the past letters from Murray concerning Garden Hill affairs had always been addressed to Eliza, but there was a change beginning in the summer of 1745. All of Murray's letters from that time forward were addressed to Charles.

Sometime before the birth of their child, the couple was able to move into the new house in Charleston. The house, which Charles Pinckney always called his "Mansion House," was built of English brick with stone copings and stood over a basement which contained wine and lumber (storage) rooms along with the kitchens and offices—the laundry, the scullery and other rooms where housekeeping activities took place. Unfortunately the house was destroyed in the fire of 1861, but Harriott Horry Ravenel, Eliza's great-great-granddaughter, left a description of it.

According to her description there were four rooms on the first floor opening off a large center hallway: the dining room and a bedroom on one side and the library and housekeeper's room on the other. The staircase was located between the two latter rooms. The window on the staircase was reputed to be one of the most remarkable features of the house and had three arches with heavily carved frames. There were five rooms on the second floor: the large and small drawing rooms occupying the whole eastern front of the house and three bedrooms at the back. The entire house was wainscoted in the heaviest paneling and the mantel pieces were high and narrow—the fronts beautifully carved with shepherds, shepherdesses and cupids. There was a vegetable garden out back and grass plats with flower beds on the south side of the lot—one of the largest in town.[34]

The house was apparently built under the supervision of Quash, the enslaved carpenter who had been of such assistance to Eliza at Wappoo, and it is possible that he was also responsible for the beautiful woodwork in the house. Charles Pinckney thought highly of Quash's ability and paid him for his work. Pinckney's accounts show that Quash received a yearly allowance of £200 for over three years and was also given fees at different times "to encourage him in his carving work."[35]

After Charles and Eliza settled in their new house, they began making preparations for the birth of their first child. The anxious grandmother-to-be wrote to Charles:

> By Captain Fowle I Received your very kind letter wherein you mention in so Exact a manner the Expected time of my Dear Daughter lying in [giving birth]; the Extream care and tenderness you Express towards her will in some measure alleviate the uneasiness I must needs labour under at being at this distance from her in so dangerous a time; but rest persuaded that no care or conveniency will be wanting on your part to make her lying in as Easy and agreeable as possible, & dont in the least doubt but that that same merciful God who has hitherto guided & assisted her will continue his favour in her time of danger. Very many & melancholy hours have I had on this Subject & which are daily Encreased as Febryary draws nigh; I cant but acknowledge my self Exceedingly happy as I find good Mrs. Woodward has promised to be with her and am persuaded than any Service She can be off will be readily offered. I am thankful to you for her letter that you sent me & shall Write her very Soon....
>
> I shall now conclude with wishing you & my Dear [Betsey] all the joys & comfort of a Safe Delivery.[36]

The baby so anxiously awaited was born on February 14, 1746—a fine, healthy boy. Eliza was delighted to have been able to present her husband with the son he had always wanted. The little boy was christened Charles Cotesworth Pinckney,[37] and though the family called him Charles, he was generally known as Charles Cotesworth to distinguish him from his cousin Charles Pinckney II. A very tired, but happy Eliza wrote to Mary Bartlett:

Since my last [letter] Heaven has blessd us with a fine little boy and would you think I could flatter my self so much as to believe I can discover all his papas virtues already dawning in him or would you imagine I could really be so fond a Mama so soon of a little babe of 3 months old that I could go on to describe his fine black Eyes with a thousand beauties more till I filled my paper and tired you, but I will not indulge it least you think me vain.... I have no disorder but weakness and I hope the country air into which I am going will be a remedy for that.[38]

In 1693 the eminent English philosopher John Locke published an essay entitled "Some Thoughts Concerning Education" in which he extolled the virtue of play in educating children. Locke's essay profoundly influenced educational practices in the 18th century and sent hundreds of parents in search of "toys that would educate as well as amuse"—Eliza and Charles were of that number. Eliza wrote to Mrs. Boddicott for her assistance:

Since Mr. Pinckney's last [letter] to Mr. Boddicott Heaven has blest us with a son and a fine boy it is ... shall I give you the trouble my Dear Madam to buy him the new toy (a discription of which I enclose) to teach him according to Mr. Locks method (which I have carefully studied) to play him self into learning. Mr. Pinckney himself has been contriving a set of toys to teach him his letters by the time he can speak; you perceive we begin by times [early] for he is not yet 4 months old.[39]

Evidently the toys were a success because Eliza wrote to her sister Polly, then at school in London, that her nephew Charles asked her to tell "his aunt Polly if she don't take care and a great deal of pains in her learning, he will soon be the best scholar, for he can tell all his letters in any book without hesitation and begins to spell before he is two year old."[40] The family legend states that as an adult Charles Cotesworth "always declared this early teaching to have been sad stuff, and that by haste to make him a clever fellow he had nearly become a very stupid one ... and that he never allowed his own children to be taught until they had attained a reasonable age."[41] It is interesting to note that there is no mention of "early teaching" in connection with the other children born to Eliza and Charles.

In the early part of 1746 George Lucas had reason to be happy. He had a fine grandson and his son-in-law reported that his plantation at Garden Hill was clear of debt. He had reasonable hopes before very long of being able to pay off the mortgages held on his other properties. Indigo seed was proving to be a valuable commodity and being sold locally there were very few expenses attached to it.

Things were progressing nicely and in the spring George Lucas asked the king's permission to travel to London "in order to be relieved from Some hardships attending my Service here."[42] George Lucas had been obliged to spend some of his own money during his tenure as lieutenant governor and, not being able to get a settlement from the General Assembly in Antigua, was hoping to recoup his expenses by appealing to the British government in London. Sometime in the fall he must have received permission to journey to England, because he left Antigua late in 1746.

Sailing was always hazardous even in times of peace, but during wartime it was even more dangerous. George Lucas, as lieutenant governor of Antigua, had complained bitterly to the British government that French privateers were preying on Antiguan shipping and had asked for protection from the Royal Navy, but had received no satisfactory response. Consequently privateers continued to lurk unchecked in the waters of the Caribbean to pounce on any passing vessel. The ship he was traveling on, unfortunately, was captured by a French privateer. He was taken prisoner and held in Brest, France, where all his dreams of spending the remainder of his days in Carolina ended. He died in Brest in January of 1747.

Eliza was in the early stages of her second pregnancy when news of George Lucas' death reached his family in Antigua. It is not clear who made the decision not to tell Eliza at that time about her father's death, but the entire Lucas family in addition to Charles Pinckney must have agreed to keep it a secret or the plan would not have succeeded. Just how Eliza finally discovered the truth was never revealed and the following letter contains the only mention of the incident found in her surviving papers. The letter was written to Mary Bartlett in December of 1747:

> Upon looking over a packet indorsed letters not yet answerd I am quite ashamd to find 3 from you, or till I consider the great interruptions to an Epsitolary intercourse which I have lately had and which I know will be readily admited by you as just excuses. The first was the loss of my dear father, a very affecting one indeed it was to me, not only on my own account as he was a most tender parent, but on my poor Mothers, my brothers and Sister, such a loss was extreamly great to his family on all accounts; as I was with child it was long conceald from me and I at last discovered it by accident, which indeed might have been fatal to me, for in a few hours after, I was taken ill and early next morning was deliverd of as fine a boy as ever was born, but the dear babe lived but 15 days. Young as it was, the pain was sharp we found at parting with it; it was a most lovely infant, but I dare not complain of the Devine dispensations, for God knows best what is best for us. And infinite Wisdome and goodness are his indispenseable attributes and when I consider the many mercies and blessings I still enjoy, I must be forever dumb to any complaint and adore in silence that great and good Being who is above all my praise. I thank God My dear Mr. Pinckney and little Charles both have a good state of health which is a blessing I can never be sufficiently thankful for. My little boy is at my knee, the picture of peace and plenty and as rosey as a cherubim; he desires me to pay his compliments to you, and tell you he is a very good boy and his mama will add as promising a child as ever parents were blessd with.[43]

Eliza was distraught by the death of her father. They had been very close and were, in a matter of speaking, kindred spirits. She had not seen him in over seven years, ever since he left Charleston in the late fall of 1739 to assume his military duties in Antigua. However, she had corresponded regularly with him and always had the hope and expectation of seeing him again. That hope was still very much alive after her marriage when she looked forward to either visiting her family in Antigua or better yet having her family move permanently to Carolina. Now all those hopes and dreams were gone. It was a very difficult time for her as she mourned the loss of both her father and the little baby who had lost his struggle to survive.

However, Eliza had her husband to comfort and console her and a darling baby boy to bring a smile to her face. By the time she wrote to Mary Bartlett in December of 1747, she had put these sad events behind her and was looking forward to the future and the birth of another child. The baby, a little girl, was born on August 7, 1748, and christened Harriott Pinckney. And a little over two years later on October 23, 1750, Eliza's last child was born—a little boy who was named Thomas after his paternal grandfather and in memory of his father's deceased older brother.

It would not have been like Eliza to let childbirth, child rearing and her duties as the wife of a prominent member of government stop her from undertaking projects. Consequently, she decided to take-up silk cultivation at Belmont. It, like indigo, had been one of the early industries attempted by the first colonists and at one time a large number of mulberry trees had been planted, silk worm eggs had been imported and, in fact, a fair amount of silk had been produced in the province. However, like indigo, it had been abandoned in favor of rice.

When Eliza decided to introduce silk cultivation at Belmont, she made a thorough study of it, learning the proper procedures, especially the correct method for drying the cocoons and then sent for the silk worm eggs. Eliza organized the slave children into groups to gather the mulberry leaves and feed the worms and then she and the house maids "reeled" the silk. She continued silk cultivation for many years at Belmont and was able to produce a fair amount of raw silk.

Despite her father's objection to fancy needlework, Eliza was accomplished with a needle and thread and in between her other activities she took some time to create a beautiful wrap or shawl for herself. The wrap was a long, rectangular-shaped piece of white cloth, the fashionable color for wraps at that time, and on both ends of the cloth, she painstaking embroidered the foliage of the indigo plant—light, delicate leaves sprouting from slender stalks.[44] Eliza was proud of her work with indigo, proud of the letters she wrote and the ones she received from other women and proud of the fact that women were competent in business affairs. Years later she received some letters from a female friend in England that had obviously been opened before coming into Eliza's possession. She responded that it was of no consequence if a curious third party had read the letters for they were "prettily and obligingly" written and "show how capable women are both of friendship and business" and, she added, "whatever raises the reputation of my particular [female] friends or my sex in general gives me a great deal of pleasure."[45] Eliza decorated her wrap with indigo leaves and wore it with great delight as a reminder to society that women were capable of important achievements.

Sometime before the fall of 1752 Charles decided to rent the Mansion House on East Bay Street to Royal Governor James Glen and move his family to a house he owned on Colleton Square. Thus it was that the family was not living in the brick Mansion House, but a wooden house when a natural disaster of enormous magnitude hit Charleston—the hurricane of 1752 thought to be one of the most severe ever to hit the city. The Pinckneys decided to evacuate the house when the water reached a depth of four feet in the downstairs rooms and escaped by boat to the house of a friend who lived on higher ground.[46]

It was probably one of the most frightening events in Eliza's life and one that she was never to forget. Later in her life Eliza made a list of days that were to be "sett apart to be remembered with the utmost Gratitude and Thankfulness to Almighty God." The "day of the great Hurricane in 1752 when our whole family was mercifully preserved from the great danger we were then in" was one of the days to be commemorated.[47]

In early September about a week before the great hurricane, James Graeme, the chief justice of South Carolina, died, leaving a docket of important cases scheduled for October. A replacement was needed as soon as possible and Governor Glen, after looking over a list of potential candidates, very quickly chose Charles Pinckney, one of the most distinguished lawyers in the province, for the post. Having no doubt that the appointment would be approved by the king, the governor had Charles promptly sworn in so he could begin hearing cases immediately.

However, as chance would have it, in London the king was looking for a post for Peter Leigh, the high bailiff of Westminster, who was in the middle of an embarrassing controversy. Leigh, a member of the king's party, was accused of incorrectly proclaiming a king's man the winner in a closely contested race for a seat in the House of Commons. The government wanted to remove Leigh from England in order to put the matter to rest and sending him to South Carolina to fill the office of chief justice seemed like a perfect solution to their problem. Sometime in March Charles Pinckney received a private report that the king had appointed Peter Leigh in his place.

When the news of Peter Leigh's appointment was printed in the *South Carolina Gazette* in April, there was a great deal of indignation felt in South

Carolina. The office of chief justice was the second most powerful in the province and many people were outraged that a native Carolinian, who happened also to be an outstanding lawyer, had been replaced in this important post by a "king's man" for pure political expediency.[48] Charles Pinckney must have also felt the sting of that appointment. A week after the notice appeared in the newspaper, Charles Pinckney, his wife, children and several enslaved servants set sail from Charleston for London. The *South Carolina Gazette* of April 11 reported Charles Pinckney's departure: "We cannot omit saying he was a true Father of the Country, that his absence is loss to Carolina and that her sons mourn that loss."

England

Charles and Eliza had not made the decision to travel to England at the last moment, but had, in fact, been planning the trip for several months before Peter Leigh's appointment was made known to them. There were several factors involved in their decision to go to England—for one thing, little Charles was almost seven years old and it was time to enroll him in school. Both Charles and Eliza were strong advocates of an English education and Charles, in particular, was adamant that both his sons be educated in London. And a trip to England would also give Charles an opportunity to inspect the estate in Durham that he had inherited upon the death of his older brother.

It also appeared that now would be a propitious time to leave South Carolina. Native Americans, incited by the French, were harassing settlements on the western frontier and there was a widespread fear that the colony would soon be involved in another Indian war. The War of the Austrian Succession had finally ground to a halt in 1748 and peace had reigned for five years—people and goods were moving smoothly across the ocean unhampered by the prospect of attack. Consequently, Charles began to make plans for the management of his Carolina property while he was away and by January 24 had drawn up a "Rent Roll.... For raising Funds For the Support of myself and my Family in England."[49]

Having decided to make the trip, the only detail left to be determined was the date of their departure and that decision was made for them when they learned the date of Peter Leigh's arrival in Charleston, for Charles Pinckney was determined not to be in the province when Leigh arrived. Quickly putting his plans to rent his property in South Carolina into action, he and Eliza were soon ready to leave. On April 4, 1753, the *Edinburgh* sailed out of Charleston harbor. On board were Charles and Eliza with their three children: Charles aged seven, Harriott four and a half, and Thomas, just a toddler, only two and a half years old. Traveling with them to attend school in London were ten-year old William Henry Drayton and his nine-year-old brother Charles—the grandsons of Lieutenant Governor William Bull. The family was also accompanied by several of their enslaved household servants.

Eliza, who still thought of London as home in spite of having lived fourteen years in South Carolina, was probably elated with the prospect of returning to England, but the departure was most likely bittersweet for Charles. He was very attached to his homeland and proud of its progress and undoubtedly felt a twinge of sorrow at leaving.

They had a swift and uneventful crossing arriving in Portsmouth, England on the 29th of April—a voyage of only twenty-five days. However, for Eliza the voyage was not short enough. "Never poor wretch," she wrote, "suffered more that escaped with life than I, notwithstanding we had so fine a passage."[50] Perhaps the small, cramped space on board ship or the supervision of five young children under the age of eleven contributed to her feeling of unease during the voyage. Whatever the reason she was greatly relieved to be on solid ground again.

They had intended to spend ten to twelve days in Portsmouth, before traveling up to London, but they arrived in port only to discover that a smallpox epidemic had broken out in the area. Instead of landing at Portsmouth they went directly to London where Charles was able to rent a house for them in the London suburb of Richmond in Surrey. Arrangements were then made for the children to be inoculated—a controversial and sometimes dangerous procedure that at the time was gaining support throughout Europe and the American colonies.

The procedure, which had been practiced for centuries in Asia and Africa, involved deliberately injecting fluid from a healing smallpox lesion into the body of a healthy person giving that person a mild form of the disease and immunity from future attacks. However, it was not without risk as it was not unheard of for people to catch a virulent form of smallpox from the inoculation and die from it. Many people were willing to take the risk, however, as the death rate from smallpox contracted the natural way was 20 to 40 percent and many survivors were left with disfiguring facial scars or were left blind.

Since smallpox was contagious, the inoculation process required that the patients remain isolated until the disease had run its course, usually a little over two weeks. It was not unusual for several people to be inoculated at the same time and stay together in the same house. Most people were only mildly affected during the procedure and it was desirable to have other people to play cards or other games with or just to chat with during the recovery process. Therefore, the Pinckney children and presumably the two Drayton boys were all inoculated at the same time and would have had each other for company during their period of isolation.

Eliza indicated in one of her letters that she had already had smallpox when she was a child in England and presumably Charles had also had it, as almost anyone who survived to adulthood had to have been exposed at one time or other to the disease. Eliza and Charles, then, were able to attend to business in town and socialize with friends and acquaintances while the children were recovering.

Peter Manigault, whose parents Gabriel and Anne Manigault were friends of the Pinckney's in Charleston, was a young law student in London when Charles and Eliza first arrived and was frequently in company with them. He wrote to his mother in the middle of May: "Last night I had the Pleasure of Mr. & Mrs. Pinckney, Mr. Corbett, Mr. & Mrs. Freeman to spend in the Evening with me.... Mr. Pinckney was just returned from seeing the Ceremony of Inoculation performed upon the Children."[51] Fortunately everything went well with the inoculation and all the children emerged unscathed.

While Eliza adjusted quickly to life in England, Charles, or so it seemed to their friends, was not adjusting as well as his wife. Peter Manigault reported to his mother:

> Colonel Pinckney has taken a House at Richmond. He already seems to have some desire to return to Carolina, & I daresay he will, sooner than he at first talked of: but this is only my private Opinion, I would not have you depend much upon it. His wife is an excellent Woman, & I venture to say would chuse to pass her days in England; however she is too good a Wife, ever to thwart her Husband's Inclinations. When I see this happy Couple, enjoying all the Sweets of an agreeable Life, in uninterrupted Union, I am in Raptures with [the] married State.[52]

Peter Manigault's next report on the Pinckneys showed that Charles appeared to be more acclimated to life in London. "I was two days ago at Colonel Pinckney's at Richmond," wrote Peter. "He seems a little better reconciled to England, but can't yet bring himself to play Whist for Crowns [a British coin worth 5 shillings]."[53]

Charles Pinckney came to England for private, personal reasons and had no official tasks to perform. However, he was a member of His Majesty's Council for South Carolina and as such was received by the king who "honoured him with a Conference."[54] Charles Pinckney may have been a colonial, but he was part of a political circle that included men of importance and power. That summer he was able to use his political influence to obtain an audience for himself, Eliza and their daughter Harriott with Princess Augusta, Dowager Princess of Wales—the widow of Frederick, Prince of Wales, and mother of the future King George III.

Charles had sought the audience in order for his daughter to present the princess with some birds from Carolina, and not being sure whether they would be allowed to accompany the almost five-year-old Harriott to present the gift, Charles and Eliza had provided her with a card explaining the circumstances of the visit. The card read:

> "Miss Harriott Pinckney, daughter of Charles Pinckney, Esquire, one of His Majesty's Council of South Carolina, pays her duty to her Highness and humbly begs leave to present her with an Indigo bird, a Nonpareil, and a yellow bird, which she has brought from Carolina for her Highness."[55]

They had been told that Princess Augusta would see them at eleven o'clock any day the next week, and after selecting a day, the three of them with the three caged birds set forth on the short journey to Kew Palace on the banks of the Thames—just up-river from London. They were a little late in arriving and discovered that the princess and her children were walking in the gardens and the servants were not sure when they would return. The Pinckneys were given the choice of waiting there or leaving the birds and the card being assured that the princess would be presented with both. Charles and Eliza, disappointed at not being able to see the royal family, decided to leave the birds and return home. They were surprised and pleased that evening to receive a message from Kew Palace that Princess Augusta would be pleased to see them the next afternoon at one o'clock. Eliza wrote a long, detailed description of the audience in a letter to an unidentified person—some parts of which, unfortunately, are missing.

> We accordingly went in full dress, and were desired to sit in a parlour where we were received by an old lady, a foreigner, till the Princess should know we were there.... After we had sett some minutes a Gentleman came in and desired we would follow him, we went through 3 or 4 grand rooms of the Princess of Wales apartment till we arrived at her dressing room, where we were received in a manner that surprised us, for tho' we had heard how good a woman the Princess of Wales was, and how very affable and easy, her behaviour exceeded every thing I had heard or could imagine.

The princess, who had four of her children with her, received them personally at the door and, according to Eliza, "mett us with all the chearfulness and pleasure of a friend who was extreamly glad to see us." The Pinckneys stood—no one being allowed to sit in the presence of royalty—for two hours talking with the princess and answering her many questions about Carolina. During the audience ten-year-old Prince William took Charles aside to ask him his own questions about South Carolina and about his sons and what "he designed to bring them up to" and where little Charles was going to school.[56]

The Prince of Wales, then 15 years old, was sent for and introduced to the Pinckney family. Unfortunately, the page containing the interview with the future George III did not survive so there is no indication of the impact he made upon the family. Eliza was certainly impressed with the audience and her first introduction to royalty. She wrote to her unidentified friend: "This, you'll imagine must seem pretty extraordinary to an American."[57] It was the first time in any of her letters that Eliza had referred to herself as "American."

When she came to England, Eliza brought with her the raw silk she had produced at Belmont and at some point arranged to have it woven into cloth. Surprisingly, the raw silk made enough cloth for three beautiful gowns. One of the gowns she presented to Princess Augusta, another she gave to Lord Chesterfield who had been a good friend to the Carolina colony and the third, a lustrous gold brocade, she kept for herself.[58]

Soon after Charles arrived in London he met with James Crokatt, the agent representing South Carolina in England. After their meeting Crokatt told Charles that he was going to tender his resignation as agent and recommend to the Committee of Correspondence in South Carolina that they appoint Charles Pinckney in his place. Crokatt felt that Charles was the better qualified of the two to hold the post. Both he and Charles then settled down to await the reply from South Carolina.

In the meantime, having settled little Charles in school, Charles and Eliza decided to go on a tour of England which included a sojourn of three months in Bath, a fashionable spa town in the southwest of England known since Roman times for its hot springs. Bath attracted many 18th-century visitors—some came to cure their various ailments by bathing in the springs or drinking the waters while others came to take advantage of the many social activities offered in the Lower Assembly Rooms. Bath was the place to be during the "season" as it was called—the months of September, October and November.

Eliza thoroughly enjoyed herself and at the end of 1753 was able to report to her friend Anne Manigault back in Carolina that they had had a busy but exciting and interesting first six months in England:

> We have traveled about seven hundred mile by land this summer. 'Tis a very pleasant but expensive way of spending time.
> We spent the last Season at Bath where we were so Luck'y to meet with several of our acquaintance…. We spent some time most agreeably at two Gentlemans Seats in Wiltshire— one of Major Luttrells relations, a very ancient and Rich family. They treated us with great friendship and politeness and showed us every thing that was curious and Elegant in that County, of which there is not a few.
> We go to London next week for good. We have been at a great loss for a house there, and— would you think it—have not been able to get a tolerable unfurnished house from Temple Barr to Charing Cross so that we are obliged to take a furnished one. 'Tis however a very handsome one and gentilely furnished in a very good street and in the Center of every thing. With these conveniences and an Extensive good acquaintance I hope Mr. P. will be quite reconciled to England for the time he proposes to stay here. At present he is not quite satisfied with it and has many [y]earnings after his native land, tho' I believe never strangers had more reason to like a place, every thing considered, than we have.[59]

In the late fall of 1753 Charles and Eliza moved into the furnished house she had described in her letter to Anne Manigault. The house was located on Craven Street and was, as Eliza had written, "in the center of every thing"— within easy reach of all the amusements London had to offer and close to the Board of Trade headquarters at Whitehall. Word had finally arrived from South Carolina regarding the position of agent for South Carolina—the Commons House had not appointed Charles as the agent, but had, instead, persuaded James Crokatt to continue in the office for the present time. However, Charles had received a letter from Governor Glen in the fall authorizing him to represent the governor and the Council of South Carolina at the meetings of the Board—it was not an official position but there was a precedence for such a representative. Henceforth, Charles attended as many of the meetings as he could, sometimes in addition to James Crokatt and at other times on his own.[60]

Charles and Eliza were satisfied with the house on Craven Street, but after learning that he was not to be appointed the agent for South Carolina and need not be in constant attendance in town, Charles felt free to pursue an idea that had been forming in his mind. He had for a long time been interested in a property in Ripley—a prosperous and bustling town located in Surrey County in the southeast of England. Located on the main post road to London it offered easy access to both the attractions of town and to the offices of the Board of Trade.

The property, a villa known as Ripley House, had been owned by Henry Pawley the barrister at Clifford's Inn with whom Charles had studied law as a young man. Pawley was now deceased and when Charles discovered that his heirs were interested in selling Ripley House, he purchased the villa in late 1753 or early 1754. He then made plans for extensive additions and renovations to be made.

Charles Pinckney's accounts show that he had several additional buildings erected on the property: a coach house, a granary, a laundry, a dove cote and a hen-house. There was repair work done on the house itself, a new cistern and pump built and the rooms were either freshly painted or wallpapered. There were gardens at Ripley House and Charles ordered everything that Eliza needed to engage in her favorite activity—from bell glasses and glazed frames for hot beds to flower pots, wheel barrows and dung to fertilize the soil. Young peach and apricot trees were bought to be espaliered on the garden walls along with grape vines and cedar trees to be planted about the property. Ripley House still stands today although much altered and added to since the mid–18th century and local tradition has it that the cedar tree now standing in the garden was planted by Eliza.[61]

When the house was repaired to satisfaction, it was time to furnish it in a style that reflected the status of the Pinckney family. Mahogany seemed to have been the favorite wood for the furniture as there were two or three chests of drawers, a three-leaved breakfast table, bottle stands, small tables and half a dozen claw footed chairs—all made of mahogany. A Turkish carpet covered the floor in the drawing room and looking glasses mounted on the walls reflected light from the candles in the wall sconces or placed about the room in silver or pewter candlestick holders. Fine china and silverware was ordered to adorn the dining table where guests would be entertained at elegant dinner parties.[62]

In July 1754 the Pinckney family moved into their new home and Charles and Eliza were immediately swept up into the social life of the little town of Ripley. There were several families within walking distance of Ripley House for the Pinckneys to exchange visits with and Ripley had a further social attraction for Eliza—it was just twelve miles from Beddington, the home of Sir Nicholas and Lady Carew. Lady Carew, the former Miss Katherine Martin, had been at Mrs. Pearson's Boarding School with Eliza and the two girls had been good friends. They had lost touch with one another after Eliza returned to Antigua, but a chance mention of Lady Carew's asking after Eliza in one of Mrs. Pearson's letters rekindled the friendship. The two families made the twelve-mile trip frequently to exchange visits.

The Pinckneys soon settled down to the routine of English country life. Little Charles was in school and was only with the family during holidays and the two younger children were most likely under the care of a governess. While there is no record of a governess being hired by Charles Pinckney for his younger children, it is difficult to believe that there was not such a person in the household to provide them with the rudiments of education. Harriott, in 1754, was almost six years old and, if her education had not already begun, it was definitely time for it to start and Thomas at the age of four would have to begin preparing for his entrance into school in two or three years. Although governesses were usually associated with the education of young ladies, they also taught the basics to young boys; however, when the time grew near for Thomas to be enrolled in school, a separate tutor was most likely hired to make sure he was well prepared.

The Pinckney children were always close throughout their lives, but there was a special bond between Thomas and Harriott that was probably formed during their stay in England. Charles, four years older than Thomas and two years older than Harriott, was away at school during most of that time leaving the two younger ones together. They would have played together, had lessons together and Thomas, no doubt, looked to his big sister—two years his senior—for assistance and comfort.

Eliza's days would have been full of making calls upon her neighbors, sharing recipes and gossip and working in her garden. There would be trips to London to attend the theater, visit galleries and exhibitions and long vacations in Bath. Eliza was thoroughly enjoying her stay in England and fond memories of that time remained with her throughout her life. Her granddaughter recalled that her grandmother "always spoke with pleasure of the gayeties in which she had participated during her second visit to England, of the celebrated actors and actresses she had seen, and that she never missed a single play when [David] Garrick was to act."[63] Eliza loved it all—the social scene, the theater and the gossip. "I was a few days ago to see Mrs. Pinckney," wrote Peter Manigault to his mother. "She is certainly a mighty good Sort of a Lady, though with all her Virtues, she is a little addicted to Scandel."[64]

Charles Pinckney spent much of his time attending meetings of the Board of Trade where his primary goal was to convince its members that Native Americans, encouraged and armed by the French, presented a serious threat to the Carolina frontier. His arguments were compelling and, as a result, the Board voted to increase funding for the defense of the colony. Charles also liked to attend trials in Westminster Hall and, according to Peter Manigault, "seems very fond at passing his time among the Gentlemen of his own Profession."[65]

Meanwhile in Charleston, the Commons House of Assembly was debating whether to appoint Charles Pinckney as the agent for South Carolina. Charles Pinckney, like many men in public office, had made enemies in the course of his career. He had been the hero of the Commons House when he drafted the resolutions certifying the right of the lower house to initiate tax bills. The members of the lower house were generally at odds with the governor's council and they felt that the resolutions put the upper house in its place and they, therefore, chose the author of the resolutions as their speaker. Then in 1741 when their champion accepted a place on the council, instead of being glad that there was now at least one voice on the council to represent their point of view, some in the legislature thought Charles had betrayed them by accepting the seat. These men were now determined to keep him from being appointed as agent for the colony. The debate lasted for three years until finally in January of 1757 James Wright was appointed.

The years passed quickly, but events taking place in other parts of the world began to intrude on their lives. The War of the Austrian Succession may have ended in Europe, but hostilities between the French and the British colonists on the western frontier in North America had not ceased. The British colonies in North America were hemmed in by the Spanish to the south and the French to the north and west. The French seeking to expand the limits of their territory to the east came into conflict with the British settlers who were wanting to expand to the west—the major point of contention being the Ohio Country—and in 1754 trouble broke out between French and British settlers over control of this territory.

The French had built a line of forts in what is now western Pennsylvania in the early part of the 1750s to prevent the colonies of Pennsylvania and Virginia from extending their borders into the Ohio Country. In May of 1754 the British sent a Virginia Regiment of colonial militia led by a young and inexperienced George Washington to tell the French to leave Fort Duquesne at the Forks of the Ohio—the site of present-day Pittsburgh. Fighting broke out and Washington was forced to surrender his hastily built fort, which he had called Fort Necessity. The French and Indian War or as it was also called in North America, the Great War for Empire, had begun.

The next year the British under General Braddock were thoroughly defeated by the French and their Native American allies in a raging battle during which Braddock lost his life. Subsequent British campaigns in the frontier areas of Pennsylvania and New York during 1755, 1756 and 1757 resulted in more failures. Eliza and Charles in England followed the developments in North America very closely. In the late summer of 1755 Eliza wrote to her good friend Lady Carew:

> Instead of this [letter] We intended to have done our selves the pleasure of Breakfasting with your Ladyship this week at Beddington, but Mr. Pinckneys time has been wholly ingaged in prepareing papers and attending on the Lords Commissioners for Trade and Plantations on the late alarming accounts of the strides the French are making on the backs of the English Colonys in North America—and which may too soon very materially affect that province to which we are so neerly related.[66]

The Pinckneys continued to monitor the news from America and as one British defeat followed another they became seriously alarmed. It appeared that the French might soon be in control of much of North America. Then in 1756 the fragile peace that had ended the War of the Austrian Succession in Europe was shattered by the outbreak of fighting. The ensuing war—the Seven Year's War— was in reality a continuation of the previous war in which Austria had lost Silesia to Prussia and suffered humiliating defeats.

Empress Maria Theresa of Austria had signed the Treaty of Aix-la-Chapelle in 1748 ending the war only to gain time to rebuild her military forces and to forge new alliances—goals which she attained with remarkable success. Not satisfied with the aid she had been given by the British during the last war, Maria Theresa abandoned Austria's twenty-five-year-old alliance with Great Britain and formed a new alliance with Austria's centuries-old enemy France— the only country Maria Theresa felt could help Austria re-take Silesia and check Prussian expansion. This re-alignment of alliances saw Austria, France and Russia forming a single alliance against Prussia with the help of Sweden, Saxony and later Spain. Prussia's only major assistance came from Great Britain.

Once again conflicts between European powers spread over the rest of the world with fighting taking place in Europe, Africa, India, the Philippines, North America, the Caribbean and South America. And once again planters in South Carolina faced disruption of trade, high freight rates and the embargos that limited travel and the exchange of correspondence. Anxiety was high among British subjects the world over for the years 1756–1757 brought nothing but bad news. First the British lost Calcutta in India then both the British and Prussians suffered humiliating defeats in Europe and the news from North America continued to be bad. The experts were predicting that Prussia and Great Britain would soon be forced to make peace and that the French would be left in control of all of North America west of the Alleghenies.

For Charles and Eliza there was more bad news. In the early part of 1757 they learned that William, Charles's brother, had suffered a stroke and was not able to look after the two properties that he had agreed to manage for his brother during his stay in England. The income from these properties was essential for their financial support during their sojourn abroad. Charles decided to return to South Carolina for two to three years to put his affairs in order and then the family would return to live in England. Charles and Eliza had intended to spend the winter in Bath with Sir Nicholas and Lady Carew. In February Eliza wrote her friend a hasty note explaining why they would not be able to join them there.

> For upon our continual alarms from abroad Mr. Pinckney came to a resolution to return to Carolina for two Year and wait an opportunity to dispose of the greatest part of what he has there and fix it in a more secure tho' less improvable part of the world. And as I can by no means think of staying behind him, you can judge, My dear Madam, what I have suffered and do still suffer in the expectation of parting with all my dear children for 2 or 3 year—and considering the uncertainty of life, perhaps for ever?
>
> We first had thoughts of carrying our little girl with us, but considering the danger to which she must be exposed have thought better of it and leave her as well as her brothers.
>
> We think of letting [renting] our house at Ripley with the furniture standing till our return and shall be some time in London before we Embark, as we intend to wait for a man of War if there should be any prospect of one in the Summer or fall of the year going that way.[67]

Charles and Eliza had to wait for over a year—until March 12, 1758—before they were able to depart. They left twelve-year-old Charles and seven-year-old Thomas at Wilson's Grammar School at Camberwell near London, but decided at the last minute to take their nine-year-old daughter Harriott with them. John Chatfield, their friend and neighbor in Ripley, agreed to manage their villa for them while they were in South Carolina. They reached Charleston in the middle of May.

Charles Pinckney was anxious to see to his neglected plantations and immediately set out on a tour of his property. He was discouraged by the conditions he found while inspecting his plantations and bothered by the swarms of mosquitoes that seemed to be everywhere. Five years spent in the cool, cloudy climate of England had caused him to forget the heat and humidity of a Carolina summer. He had also forgotten why planters came to town during the summer months. After a month of traveling around the countryside, he was forced to return to Charleston—he had contracted "country fever" or malaria.

Charles had not taken time to recover from the long ocean voyage and the fever took its toll. Their good friends Mr. and Mrs. Motte invited Eliza to bring her husband to their home across the harbor in Mt. Pleasant in the hopes that the ocean breezes would improve his condition. Eliza was tireless in her care of him. She wrote to Lady Mary Drayton, the wife of Thomas Drayton, at the end of June:

> I have long intended my self the pleasure of writing to Your Ladyship since your going into the Country but a Succession of intervening circumstances has from time to time prevented me, and now sleepless nights and an aching heart occationed by poor Mr. Pinckneys severe illness makes me very unfit for this employment as I have such a tremor upon my nerves I can but just hold my pen.[68]

Charles Pinckney's condition grew worse and he died at Mt. Pleasant on July 12, 1758. He was buried the next day in the graveyard at St. Philip's Church in Charleston. The church was full and there were many speeches made in his praise—even his critics acknowledged that he had worked not for himself but for the good of South Carolina.[69]

CHAPTER FOUR

The Middle Years
(1758–1776)

Dealing with Grief

Eliza was overwhelmed by the death of her husband. Having an optimistic nature it had not occurred to her during the days she tended him that he would die. If her friends were not as optimistic about Charles's recovery as Eliza, they did not share their feelings with her. Even the physicians attending Charles kept their fears and doubts to themselves and that, coupled with Eliza's belief that he would recover, made "the stroak sudden and unexpected." Not being prepared for her husband's death, Eliza was stunned by the enormity of it and incapable of action. "Such a union as ours," Eliza wrote, "could not be dissolved with a less shock than I sustained, and such a one as disabled me from doing any thing as I ought."[1]

Not being able to bear the thought of living in the house that she and Charles had intended to occupy when he recovered from his illness, Eliza accepted the invitation of her good friend Mary Butler Golightly to stay with her in the country at her plantation in St. Andrew's Parish on the Ashley River. It was an ideal situation for Eliza and her daughter. Mary Golightly was a widow with two daughters who were close in age to the ten-year-old Harriott and who were able to provide companionship and some semblance of normalcy to the little girl who had lost her father, was separated from her brothers and whose mother was distraught with grief. And at the Golightly plantation Eliza was able to live in relative seclusion while she tried to deal with her grief and begin to forge a new life for herself and her daughter.

However, as little as she might relish the task, there were people in England who needed to be informed of Charles Pinckney's death. In August Eliza was finally able to relate the sad news to them and turn her attention to some urgent business. She wrote four letters to England—one was to Mrs. Evance the wife of Branfill Evance—a Charleston merchant who had owned a plantation on Charleston Neck close to the Pinckney plantation at Belmont. Mr. and Mrs. Evance and their family had moved to London in 1758 just before Charles and Eliza returned to South Carolina. Since the two families had been close friends as well as neighbors, Charles had asked Mr. and Mrs. Evance to act as guardians to his two sons while he and Eliza were in South Carolina. Mr. and Mrs. Evance, then, were surrogate parents to the two Pinckney boys just as Mr. and Mrs. Boddicott had been for the Lucas children when they came to London to attend school.

> I never wrote to you with reluctance, My dear friend, till now for I surely was the happiest of mortals till the last dismal, fatal month. Oh! dreadful reverse of what I was. Think if you can what is my distress when I tell you the beloved of my soul! all that was valueable and aimable in man! my dear, dear Mr. Pinckney is no more. Great God soport me in this terrible affliction! For 'tis heavy indeed!
>
> I beg you, my dear Mrs. Evance, to take care of my dear fatherless babes, to comfort their tender hearts; and let them be a little while at home with you upon this meloncholy occasion.... Poor dear creatures! What an example, what a Councellor, what a father have they lost!
>
> Adieu, my dear friend. I can say no more. My soul is oppressed with bitter Anguish beyond the power of words to utter.[2]

It was difficult for Eliza to write letters about her husband's death as each accounting of the sad facts re-emphasized the extent of her loss. Therefore writing four letters was trial enough, but she had to copy each letter twice—once for the letterbook and a second copy to send on a separate ship. The Seven Years' War or the French and Indian War as it was known in North America was still being fought and ships were subject to capture or being sunk. "When I am able I will write to you again," Eliza wrote at the end of her letter to Mrs. Evance, "'Tis a painful task to have these dismal letters to coppy, but it seems there is a necessity for it—'tis so uncertain whether you will get this."[3]

Her next letter was to Mr. George Morley, the Pinckney's man-of-business in London:

> You have known me (My friend Mr. Morley) the happiest woman upon Earth! Can you then possibly guess at the distress I now write to you in when I tell you my dear husband, your friend, my dear, dear Mr. Pinckney is no more! The 12th of last month deprived me of the best and most valueable of husbands and of men!

It is possible that Charles Pinckney had not been entirely well when he boarded ship in England for the voyage back to South Carolina for Eliza continued in her letter to George Morley:

> How much happiness did I promise my self, when I found he grew so much better at sea? and was very well for the first month after his arrival here. But my happiness was of short duration.

He was soon after taken sick and continued upwards of 3 weeks ill—an example to all about
him of the greatest resolution, patience and perfect resignation to the Will of God that ever
was known.

It had been difficult for Charles and Eliza to leave their two sons in London
and return to Charleston. Consequently, they were greatly relieved when they
received a letter from George Morley a month after their return telling them
that the two boys were well and although greatly saddened by the departure
of their parents and sister, were coping with it thanks to the kind attention
given them by Mr. and Mrs. Middleton. William Middleton, a member of His
Majesty's Council in South Carolina and owner of Crowfield Plantation, had
moved with his family to England in 1754 and he and his wife were good friends
of the Pinckneys. Eliza related to George Morley how much his letter and its
good news about the boys had meant to her husband. She continued:

When you see Mr. and Mrs. Middleton, pray thank them, and tell them, their notice of our
poor little boys upon our leaving them gave great comfort to the tender heart of their dear
affectionate father, the tenderest and best of parents…

I intend to write to Mrs. Middleton but 'tis too much for me now. I know I need not beg
of you good Sir to be kind to my dear fatherless children and to supply Mrs. Evance with what
ever money is wanted for them—which shall be repayed with speed and gratitude. I am not
able to write to you now upon business but my nephew [Charles Pinckney II] will do it by
this convoy.[4]

Eliza's most pressing concern was reimbursing George Morley as quickly as
possible for any money he would need to give Mrs. Evance for the boys. However, sending money to England was a complicated affair for someone living
in the colonies. There was no common currency in British North America at
this time. South Carolina planters or merchants doing business in England
were always paid in British pounds, but since British money was not allowed
to leave the country, this money had to be deposited in a bank in London and
a credit established in their names. This credit could then be sold in the form
of a "bill of exchange" to someone in the colony who needed to send money
to England.

Eliza, then, needed to find someone in Charleston who had established
credit with a bank in England and was willing to sell it. However, she did not
feel able to make the necessary inquiries and arrangements herself; therefore,
Charles Pinckney, II, the nephew whom Charles Pinckney had raised and educated and who was now a successful attorney in Charleston, offered to do it
for her.

Another piece of business Eliza needed to take care of was the delivery
of several turtles and game birds that Charles had ordered sent to various
friends in England. Turtles were a great delicacy in the 18th century and it was

a common practice for people in the colonies to send live turtles and/or game birds to friends and relatives in England. Since the turtles and birds did not always arrive alive, Eliza had to be very explicit in her letter to Mr. Morley as to who had priority for the turtles and birds that did survive the voyage.

Enclosed in the letter to Mr. Morley was one for Mr. Gerrard, the headmaster at her sons' school. The letter to Mr. Gerrard also contained one for the boys. To Mr. Gerrard she wrote:

> This informs you of the greatest misfortune that could have happened to me and my dear children on this side Eternity! I am to tell you hard as that task is, that my dear Mr. Pinckney, the best of men, of husbands and of fathers is no more! Comfort, good Sir, Comfort the tender hearts of my dear children. God Almighty bless them, and if he has any more blessings for me in this world may He give it me in them and their sister.
>
> The enclosed [letter] for the dear boys be so good to give them when you think it a proper time. What anguish do I and shall I feel for my poor Infants [youngsters][5] when they hear the most afflicting sound that could ever reach them!
>
> I remember poor Tommy, upon the first talk of our coming to Carolina early one morning as he lay abed, and I alone with him, without any discourse leading to it, told me he had a favour to beg of me, which was: If we went to Carolina and his dear papa should dye there that he might never know it, and that he would ask his papa the same favour if I dyed there. I think my poor dear Charles has expressed something of the same sentiment, and I am sure he has not less filial affection and sensibility than his brother. I therefore submit it to you and Mrs. Evance whether to let them know it now, or not—for I am not capable to think for my self.
>
> I have beged the favour of my friend Mrs. Evance to pay the children's bills punctually: but my debt of gratitude will always be due. My return to them is at present uncertain, but my heart is with them: and as soon as I can, consistent with there interest, they may be sure I shall, by Divine permission, see them.[6]

The letter to her sons must have been the hardest of the letters Eliza had to write. "How shall I write to you!" she began. "What shall I say to you! My dear, my ever dear Children! but if possible more so now than Ever. ... You have mett with the greatest loss, my children, you could meet with upon Earth! Your dear, dear father, the best and most valueable of parents is no more!" After giving them a description of their father's illness, Eliza continued by reminding them of the many virtues their father possessed: "and let it be a comfort to you, my dear babes, as long as you live that you had such a father! He has set you a great and good example. May the Lord enable you both to follow it."[7]

The boys were young when their father died—Charles was twelve years old and Thomas only seven—and to ensure that their father's image did not "wear out" in their minds, Eliza sent a miniature portrait of him to Mrs. Evance and asked that she give it a place of honor in her parlor. Eliza also did her best to keep the principles and virtues of their father alive in the minds of her sons and consequently, as adults, they had the greatest respect for him and the principles that guided his life.

Having written those letters Eliza was not capable of writing to anyone else for several weeks. Finally on September 25 she was able to write to her mother and sister in Antigua. Knowing that Mrs. Lucas had a propensity to worry, Charles and Eliza had not informed her they were leaving England and sailing to South Carolina; consequently, neither Mrs. Lucas nor Polly knew that Eliza had returned to Charleston. To her mother Eliza wrote:

> With a bleeding heart, Dear Madam, I inform you that since you heard from me the greatest of human Evils has befallen me. Oh, my dear Mother, My dear, dear Mr. Pinckney, the best of men and of husbands is no more! Oh! dreadful reverse of what I was when I last wrote to you.
>
> We left England in March (and did not acquaint you with it lest you should be uneasey from apprehensions of our being taken) and arrived here the 19th May after being at Sea ten weeks. One of my dear Mr. Pinckneys first inquirys after his arrival here was for a Vessel to Antigua in order to write to you and my brother. We heard of one but she was stoped by an Embargo till after the 12th of July, the fatal day which deprived me of all my soul held dear and left me in a distress that no language can paint.[8]

Eliza continued the letter using the same phrases she had used in other letters to extoll the virtues of her husband and express her deep sense of loss. She had learned that her brother George was on his way to England and expressed her sorrow that he had not come the year before when she and Charles would have been there to welcome him. At least her brother would be able to visit his nephews, Eliza told her mother, and comfort them.

It must have been a shock to George Lucas when he arrived in England to find that his sister, brother-in-law and niece had sailed back to South Carolina and then to learn that Charles Pinckney had died there soon after their return. It is not known when Mr. Gerrard and Mrs. Evance thought it best to break the sad news to the boys, but most likely they knew about their father's death by the time their uncle came to visit them. George was able to spend some time with his nephews and the visit enabled him to reassure his sister of their well-being when he stopped at Charleston on his return to Antigua in January of 1759.

George found his sister still living in seclusion in the country six months after the death of her husband. Gone was the active, lively and sociable Eliza he had known in the past and in her place was a pale, thin woman whose eyes were red from nights of weeping and who spent her "days in sighs," rarely stirring outside the house. Her brother gave her all the support and encouragement he could, but as soothing as his presence was, he was not able to lift her sense of despair. Consequently when he returned to his military duties in Antigua, George Lucas left his sister in low spirits and ill-health showing no interest in events taking place in the rest of the world.

Eliza had had, in her view, the perfect husband and the perfect marriage and she could not accept the fact that both were gone. While the sympathy and affection of her friends was welcome and "softened and alleviated" her sorrow, "nothing," she declared, "but the Divine Hand that gave the blow can heal the wound that is made in my afflicted heart."[9] Also weighing on her mind and dragging her spirits down was the separation from her sons. She was anxious about them and grateful for any word of their well-being.

In particular, Lady Carew and Mrs. King, a close friend and former neighbor of Eliza's in Ripley, had been very kind to the boys and Eliza confessed to Lady Carew how thankful she was to hear from so many different people that the boys were well. She had not received a letter from them as yet and had begun to fear that Mrs. Evance, Mr. Morley and Mr. Gerrard were concealing bad news about the boys from her out of pity. "But you kindly set my mind at ease with regard to them," she continued to Lady Carew. "I have since heard the poor little creatures were so much affected with their great misfortune they were not able to write."[10]

During the first part of 1759 Tom had had an attack of the measles and after he had recovered somewhat, Mrs. Evance had taken him to Bath—primarily as a treat but also to bolster his health by drinking the waters. In March after his return, his brother Charles felt they were now ready to write to their mother. How excited Eliza must have been when she saw the handwriting of her thirteen-year-old son and found at the end of his letter a little message in Tom's childish scrawl. In April Charles also wrote to his sister:

> How can I express my grief and affliction on the Receipt of Dear Mammas letter! Our most tender and indulgent Papa is no more! Our loss is truly so great that God only by preserving to us our Mammas valuable life can make it up. I know my dear Sister will do everything in her power to comfort her, let me intreat you to believe that Brother Tommy, who is just Returned from Bath, and I will de[termine] to do the same. Let us vye with one another in shewing our reverence for the memory of the best of Fathers, by loving, honouring and chearfully obeying the best of Mothers, and then we need not doubt of the blessing of God on ourselves and all our concerns.[11]

Shortly after her brother's return to Antigua, Eliza decided to move back to Charleston. She had business to conduct and it was more convenient for her to be in town close to her nephew Charles Pinckney II who was helping her with her affairs. Therefore, in February Eliza and Harriott left the seclusion of the country and took up residence in town. Lady Ann Mackenzie, the sister of Lady Mary Drayton, came to stay with them for a while as a companion to Eliza. Lady Mary and Lady Ann, the daughters of the Earl of Cromatie in Scotland, had met and become friends with Charles and Eliza during their voyage from England in spring of 1758 and both sisters had continued their friendship with Eliza after her husband's death.[12]

Once in town Eliza was dismayed to discover that the fleet which had sailed the previous August carrying her letters along with bills of exchange and the turtles and birds had been attacked by the French. Only the ship carrying a second copy of the letters managed to arrive safely in England—all the bills of exchange and the turtles and birds were lost. Eliza was anxious to pay the debt she owed George Morley and set about to procure more bills of exchange. From now on she was determined that bills of exchange would also be sent in duplicate on separate ships. Since one of her husband's last acts had been to arrange for gifts of turtles and game birds to be sent to certain friends in England, Eliza sent replacements for the ones that had been lost.

Eliza slowly plodded through the urgent business that confronted her, but she suffered from periods of lethargy that caused her to leave some of the business unfinished. Often complaining that her "eyes were tired and weak" she continued to write letters to friends in England some of whom did not yet know of her husband's death. It soon became obvious to her friends that Eliza's prolonged grieving was impairing not only her eyesight but also her health and they became alarmed. Tactfully they began to offer her advice—urging her to accept the fact that her husband was dead, as bitter a pill as it was to swallow, and moderate her grief. Ruining her health would not in any way benefit her children or herself, they warned her.

However, although she acknowledged the wisdom of their advice, she could not make herself act on it. "How stupid must I be," she declared to Lady Carew, "when I neglect any thing that may tend to the advantage of those dear pledges of the sincerest affection that ever was upon Earth [her children]; yet this creature am I. But Heaven, I trust, will still aid me and enable me to exert more resolution than I have done the last ten months especially for their sakes."[13]

It would take all the resolution that Eliza could summon to climb out of the abyss into which she had sunk; however, she was soon ready to make a start. In the summer of 1759 Eliza received a copy of Charles Pinckney's will from London and as executrix there were matters in it that needed her attention. Yet in September when George Morley asked her about it, she had to admit that she had not yet looked at any of the papers. It was vital that she now settle down and come to grips with her husband's death and begin to carry out the terms of his will. With the assistance of her nephew Charles she began to carefully go over the contents.

According to 18th-century law, the Pinckney children were considered orphans even though their mother was still living. Charles Pinckney, then, had to designate in his will two people to act as their guardians—he appointed his wife and his close friend William Bull, Jr., lieutenant-governor of South Carolina, as custodians of the "Persons and Estates of my said dear Children." It was customary in the case of orphans who inherited property to have a close male family friend or relative act as their guardian. The man chosen was usually a successful, prominent individual who could be counted on to give good, sound advice on the administration of the estates, but who would not be expected to be involved in the day-to-day management of those estates. Charles Pinckney had acted as guardian to the two Golightly girls when their father died in 1749. The day-to-day management of the Pinckney children's lives and property was Eliza's responsibility and William Bull was there to give her guidance on decisions pertaining to the enhancement of their property along with advice on the course of their education.

As was customary at the time the eldest son, in this case Charles Cotesworth, received the bulk of the father's estate: the Mansion House in Charleston, various properties, warehouses and stores in town along with Pinckney Plains (a plantation near Beech Hill), the island properties in Port Royal Sound (some 1,500 acres), and 500 acres on the Savannah River near Silver Bluff. In addition he also received all the property his father owned in England, a large number of slaves and his father's gold watch.

Thomas as the second son received the 1,100-acre plantation called Auckland on the Ashepoo River, 500 acres of land at Four Holes and a house and storehouses in Charleston. Thomas also received a number of slaves and a diamond mourning ring designed to commemorate the death of his Uncle Thomas for whom he was named. Sons in the 18th century typically inherited land and slaves while daughters received slaves, household goods and cash. Harriott received a rose diamond ring, a number of slaves and £500 to be paid to her when she reached the age of eighteen.

Widows always received one third of the husband's estate—the dower right. Eliza was to have one third of the rents on the Charleston properties as income, a house on Colleton Square and Belmont plantation along with a number of slaves, a specified number of domestic animals from Pinckney Plains plantation, household goods, furniture, a riding chair, horses and her choice of fifty books from her husband's library. All this was hers for her lifetime— after her death Charles would inherit Belmont and Thomas would have the house on Colleton Square.

Charles Pinckney had a large library and besides giving fifty books to Eliza he left his nephew £25 sterling worth of his law books—provided he help his aunt settle the estate. The rest of his library was left to Charles. The remaining two thirds of the rents collected from his Charleston properties were to pay for the education and up-bringing of his children. He specified that Charles should "be virtuously and religiously and liberally brought up and educated in the Study and practices of the Laws of England ... and that he will employ all his future abilities in the Services of God and his Country." For Thomas he directed that he "shall have the same virtuous religious and liberal Education out of my Estate with his Brother; and altho I cannot yet direct to what profession or business he shall be brought up, yet I have the same good hope and expectations of him, as of my Eldest son."[14]

As can be seen Charles Pinckney left his family very well-off. However, his Carolina estates had been sadly neglected for some time and were not producing an appropriate income. He wanted his sons to be educated in England and Eliza was resolutely determined to carry out her husband's wish. If the funds needed to maintain the boys at school were dependent on the revenues generated by the Pinckney properties in Carolina, then some order had to be imposed on their management. The time had come for Eliza to face the most daunting task of her life—managing the vast Pinckney properties, raising her daughter and continually monitoring the education and up-bringing of her sons 3,000 miles away in England.

A New Beginning

Eliza, of course, had some experience in managing plantations in South Carolina, but supervising her father's property was nothing in comparison to overseeing the large estate Charles Pinckney had bequeathed to his heirs. Besides the Carolina property there was also the villa at Ripley and property in Durham and York Counties in England. To make matters even more difficult the Carolina plantations were in disarray as there had been no one to manage them since Charles' brother had suffered a stroke in 1757. Before he became ill Charles had begun to put his plantations in order, but, unfortunately had only had time to make a start.

As Eliza looked into the accounts of the properties, she realized they were in need of equipment and supplies—a situation which she set about to rectify as quickly as possible. She had expectations that the plantations would produce enough that year for her to "clear all the money that was due upon the Estate." However, a severe drought put an end to those hopes and she soon realized this year's crops would bring barely enough to defray the expenses of the plantations.

She was optimistic about the future, though, and in her report to George Morley in March 1760 she wrote:

> I thank God there is now a good prospect of things being deferently [differently] conducted.
> I have prevailed upon a conscientious good man (who by his industry and honesty has raised
> a fine fortune for 2 orphan children my dear Mr. Pinckney was guardian too) to undertake

the direction and inspection of the overseers. He is an excellent planter, a Dutchman, originally Servant and Overseer to Mr. Golightly, who has been much solicited to undertake [work] for many Gentlemen; but as he has no family but a wife and is comfortable enough in his circumstances, refuses to do it for any but women and children that are not able to do it for themselves. So that if it please God to prosper us and grant good Seasons, I hope to clear all next year.

I find it requires great care, attention and activity to attend properly to a Carolina Estate, tho' but a moderate one, to do ones duty and make it turn to account, that I find I have as much business as I can go through of one sort or other. Perhaps 'tis better for me, and I believe it is. Had there not been a necessity for it, I might have sunk to the grave by this time in the Lethargy of stupidity which had seized me after my mind had been violently agitated by the greatest shock it ever felt. But a variety of imployment gives my thoughts a relief from melloncholy subjects, tho' 'tis but a temporary one, and gives me air and exercise, which I believe I should not have had resolution enough to take if I had not been roused to it by motives of duty and parental affection.[15]

Sometime in the late fall Eliza was ready to return to Belmont—the place where she and Charles had spent their first summer together in such idyllic happiness. She arrived to find the grounds in ruins—Belmont had gone back to woods and her beautiful pleasure garden was overgrown and choked with weeds. There was enough work to do there to occupy the most ardent gardener and Eliza set to work. First she began plans to lay out a new garden as, she reported to a friend, her former garden was "laid out in the old taste so that I have been modernizing it, which has afforded me much imployment. I am my self head gardener, and I believe work much harder than most principal ones do."[16]

Gardening was, of course, Eliza's favorite pastime and she went to work with great vigor. Overseeing the clearing of the woods and planning a new, up-to-date pleasure garden gave her thoughts a new direction, while pulling up weeds and digging in the earth to plant her seeds was soothing and brought her peace. The exercise also helped her to sleep well at night and improved her appetite. Soon her health was better despite a lingering stomach complaint.

In addition to her re-awakened interest in gardening, Eliza was slowly coming out of her self-imposed isolation and was beginning to take an interest in the lives of her friends and events taking place in the world around her. She begged her friends in England not to hesitate to send her word of their good fortunes for, she explained, "I am not so wholly ingrossed by my own meloncholy concerns to be quite insensible of the pleasure that results from hearing of the happiness of others."[17] Perhaps it was this thought plus the memories of her own happy marriage that led Eliza to act as an intermediary between two lovers: William Lyttleton, the governor of South Carolina, and his fiancé, Miss Mary Macartney in England.

Charles and Eliza had known William Lyttleton when they were in London before he was appointed governor of the colony in 1755. Upon their return to South Carolina they were able to renew their acquaintance with him and the governor became a good friend. As a result of that friendship, Eliza agreed to lend the governor her assistance in the matter of some personal correspondence he wanted sent to England, but did not want included with his official letters to the Board of Trade in London. Some of the letters were to his brother and other private individuals, but most of them were to Miss Macartney. In the fall of 1759 Eliza began to include the governor's private letters in the packet of letters that she sent regularly to George Morley asking him to send the letters on to the appropriate persons. She continued this practice until Lyttleton left South Carolina in the spring of 1760 to take up his duties as governor of Jamaica.

Eliza was also becoming more attuned to happenings in the colony. Since the beginning of the French and Indian War South Carolinians had benefited from an alliance with the Cherokee, who had resisted the arguments of the French and remained loyal to the British. The relationship was not entirely cordial, however, as the Cherokee were unhappy with the fact that British settlers were creeping westward into their territory. Tensions between the Cherokee and Carolina settlers increased until finally in 1759 the Cherokee, independent of the French and their Native American allies, declared their own private war on the British and began attacking settlements and forts on the frontier.

On November 3 Eliza included a newspaper article about the on-going problems with the Cherokee in her letter to George Morley. Governor Lyttleton, after raising an army and confronting the Indians, was able to negotiate a peace treaty with them. Unfortunately, the army had barely returned to Charleston when the Cherokee, believing that the colonists had violated the terms of the treaty, broke the peace and began laying siege to forts on the frontier. The governor was then forced to request aid from Lord Jeffrey Amherst, the British commander-in-chief in North America.

The situation was grave as Eliza explained to Mrs. Evance in March of 1760:

A great cloud seems at present to hang over this province. We are continually insulted by the Indians on our back settlements, and a violent kind of small pox rages in Charles Town that almost puts a stop to all business. Several of those I have to transact business with are fled into the Country, but by the Divine blessing I hope a month or two will change the prospect. We expect shortly troops from Gen. Amherst, which I trust will be able to manage these savage Enemies. And the small pox, as it does not spread in the Country, must be soon over for want of subjects.[18]

Eliza was concerned for her slaves in town and, deciding to inoculate them, organized a "hospital." On June 19 she wrote to Mrs. Evance: "I am just going out of town for a little air and Exercise, having, I thank God, finished my super-intendentcy over a little small pox Hospital, a very small one indeed as it did not consist of more than 15 patients. ... I lost one only—a valuable Carpenter who took it the natural way [that is died by catching smallpox not from an inoculation]."[19]

The troubles on the frontier with the Cherokee continued as more fighting broke out in August throwing the city of Charleston into a panic. A truce of six months was called while emissaries from both sides discussed peace terms. In September during the lull in the fighting, concerns closer to home demanded Eliza's attention—her twelve-year-old daughter Harriott was ill with a severe fever. Eliza was in constant attendance on her and was greatly relieved when she showed signs of recovering. Her relief was short-lived, however, for just as Harriott was recovering, the fever struck Eliza. It was a violent attack that lasted for seven straight days without intermission.

Eliza had not completely recovered her health after her long period of mourning and the fever left her weak and pulled down her spirits which had just begun to revive. It also aggravated the stomach complaint she had been inflicted with since the death of her husband. She was seriously ill. "Three times in two months I was brought to the Verge of the grave," she reported to George Morley in February 1761, "and have kept my Chamber over 4 months. I thank God I am now well and recover my strength apace."[20]

Eliza was sufficiently recovered to give Morley the latest news of the on-going hostilities with the Cherokee. The peace negotiations had broken down during the truce and war was once again on the horizon. General Lord Amherst sent Lieutenant Colonel James Grant with three British regiments to Carolina to subdue the Cherokee once and for all. Grant's forces were subsequently joined by a large number of provincial troops under the command of Colonel Middleton and Mohawk, Catawba and Chickasaw warriors—some 2,800 strong.

Colonel Grant's force of 2,800 faced a force of 1,000 Cherokee warriors on June 10, 1761, at Echoee Pass. After six hours of hard fighting, the Cherokee were out of ammunition and had to withdraw. The British burned fifteen Cherokee towns along with their attendant fields of corn, beans and squash. All Indian captives—men, women, children—were ordered executed. By July the British forces, suffering from disease, were exhausted and had to withdraw. However, they had destroyed the Cherokee's main source of food and created hundreds of homeless men, women and children who faced a winter of starvation. In August the Cherokee sued for peace.[21]

South Carolinians breathed a sigh of relief when the Cherokee War was over and were able then to turn their thoughts to more pleasant happenings in

England—the wedding and coronation of King George III. In October of the previous year King George II had died suddenly leaving the throne to his twenty-two-year-old grandson, George III. Eliza, of course, had met and spoken with the new king when he was just a teenager, and consequently took a great interest in the new monarch and his reign. She, in common with many others in the colony, was anxious to learn all the details of the monarch's marriage to Charlotte of Mecklenburg-Strelitz in September and the coronation ceremony which followed two weeks later.

"If, Madam, you have ever been witness to the impatience of the people of England about a hundred mile from London to be made acquainted with what passes there," wrote Eliza to Mrs. King, "you may guess a little at what our impatience is here, when I inform you that the curiosity increases with the distance from the Center of affairs." Mrs. King had kindly provided Eliza with a description of the new queen and the coronation ceremony and Eliza was clearly pleased to be the first to distribute that information to all her friends as she continued:

> Lady Ann Atkin happened to be with me when I received your favour [letter]. I told her as she was a woman of Quality, she should be first treated with a discription of her Majesty.... In half an hour after I was favoured with a vizet from our new Gov., Mr. Boone, lately arrived here from his former Government in the Jerseys, who I found (tho' he has an extensive good acquaintance in England) knew as little of the New Queen as we did here. I had the pleasure to read him also the discription. And the next day numbers received the same sort of pleasure.... On the whole I am a very Loyal Subject and had my share of Joy in the agreeable account of my Sovereign and his Consort.[22]

Though interest in the new king and queen took center stage for a while, Great Britain was still at war and the seas were fraught with danger. It was especially irksome to Eliza who was anxious to return to her sons. "When, my Dear Madam," she wrote to Mrs. King, "shall we have peace? Till then I have little prospect of seeing my Children and friends in England; and a Spanish warr we are told is unavoidable."[23] The rumor of impending war with Spain proved to be correct. The Spanish, who had so far avoided involving themselves in the Seven Years' War, decided in 1762 to join France and Austria in their fight against Great Britain and Prussia. The addition of the Spanish to the war caused great concern for the people of South Carolina.

However, there was a consideration other than the war that was keeping Eliza from returning to England, namely the need to put the Pinckney estates on a stable footing. Her friends in England constantly asked when she planned to return and she always replied that the date of her return was uncertain. In truth Eliza did not enjoy ocean travel and only her great desire to be with her sons could induce her to make that journey. She explained her situation:

When I can prudently leave this Country and have fixt a sume in England to soport my self and children in a retired, comfortable, and decent way—not in a ostentatious or vain one, for I have no ambitious views of any sort—nither fatigue, or suffering any thing in my own person, shall detain me longer from them, for my heart breaks at our separation. 'Tis no paradox to say nothing but the greatnesss of my affection keeps me from them, as it appears to me and my friends here that it will (with the Divine blessing) be much to their advantage for me to continue here a couple of year longer; and when the question is whether I shall please my self or do them real service I should be inexcusable to hesitate a moment.[24]

So Eliza remained in South Carolina for the present—looking after the family property and planning to return to England at some point in the future.

It was probably at this time that Eliza became acquainted with Dr. Alexander Garden and his wife Elizabeth. The doctor, born in 1730 in Scotland, had studied medicine at the University of Edinburgh where he came under the influence of Charles Alston, the King's Botanist and Keeper of the Garden at Holyrood Palace. Dr. Garden came to South Carolina in 1752 and two years later settled in Charleston, married Elizabeth Peronneau and became a partner in a busy medical practice in the city. However, his real love was botany and zoology and whenever he had a chance he traveled around the colony to study the plants and animals of the region. He wrote a description of the stillingia and fothergilla, two plants native to the Carolinas, studied cochineal insects and sent a specimen of the greater siren, an unknown species of fish, to a zoologist friend in London. He also communicated with the Swedish naturalist Carl Linnaeus—who named the gardenia after him.

Eliza possibly met him during the smallpox epidemic in Charleston in 1760. It was reported that Dr. Garden had inoculated hundreds of people during that epidemic and he might have been the person who gave Eliza the instructions for performing inoculations which she used on the patients in her "small pox hospital." They became good friends with the doctor serving as a mentor to Eliza in the matter of gardening. It was through his encouragement that she began to plant trees at Belmont—not only native trees such as the magnolia or the oak, but several foreign species as well.

Her garden occupied much of her time and she began to send seeds back to her friends and former neighbors in Ripley. To Mrs. King she sent the seeds of the sweet myrtle or bayberry plant along with instructions for making the sweet smelling, light green candles from the wax-producing berries. Lord King, Mrs. King's father-in-law, had a greenhouse on his estate and Eliza sent him the seeds of the Palmetto Royal—a native Carolina plant which Eliza explained "bears the most noble bunch of flowers I ever saw. The main stem of the bunch is a foot and a half or two long, with some hundreds of white flowers handing pendant upon it." Eliza thought it would make "a pretty ornament for my Lord's

Greenhouse."[25] Mr. King also requested that she send him seeds from South Carolina. In a letter to Mrs. King she wrote:

> I hope the seeds I now send Mr. King will arrive safe and in good order, especially the Magnolia, which I think is the most beautiful of all trees. I have seen them here in level moist Land grow to a prodigious height though they do very well also in high land. The seed of the flowering shrub I send [the] Miss Kings I found wild in the woods and have named it the Royal purple. Its colours are gold and purple, but if they chuse to alter it [the name] in honour of the Queen or any thing else I have no objection.[26]

It was not always easy to get seeds to send back to England and Eliza was sometimes frustrated when her orders for gathering different seeds were not followed. She decided that instead of sending seeds, she would start a nursery and send trees and bushes across the ocean to her friends. To give the plants a better chance of survival when they were planted in England she began to send ones that were at least two years old. "For I believe," she wrote, "a tree [or bush] will grow as much in 2 years here as in 4 or 5 in England."[27]

Eliza was beginning to be comfortable in her new life and in the winter of 1762 she was able to report to several of her friends that she was "in good health and better spirrits than I have known for the last 4 year."[28] While she appeared content with her life in Carolina, there is a slightly wistful tone in her letter to George Keate, an artist and poet who had been a neighbor when the Pinckneys lived in Richmond.

> What great doings you have had in England since I left it. You people that live in the great world in the midst of Scenes of entertainment and pleasure abroad, of improving studies and polite amusement at home, must be very good to think of your friends in this remote Corner of the Globe. I really think it a great virtue in you; and if I could conceal the selfish principle by which I am actuated, I could with a better grace attempt to persuade you that there is so much merrit in seting down at home and writing now and then to an old woman in the Wilds of America...
>
> How different is the life we live here; vizeting is the great and almost only amusement of late years. However, as to my own particular, I live agreeable enough to my own taste, as much so as I can separated from my dear boys.
>
> I love a Garden and a book; and they are all my amusement except I include one of the greatest Businesses of my life (my attention to my dear little girl) under that article. For a pleasure it certainly is to cultivate the tender mind, to teach the young Idea how to shoot, etc., especially to a mind so tractable and a temper so sweet as hers. For, I thank God, I have an excellent soil to work upon, and by the Divine Grace hope the fruit will be answerable to my indeavours in the cultivation."[29]

In the midst of all her sorrow and grieving, Eliza had not forgotten her daughter and had taken an active role in her education. Having been separated from her sons, it would have been unthinkable for Eliza to have sent her daughter away to school. She saw to Harriott's education herself and obviously derived a great deal of pleasure from doing it.

Eliza was still thinking of returning to England. She confessed a "scheme" she had to Mr. Keate. "Upon a Peace," she wrote, "(I cant think of crossing the Atlantic before) I intend to see England and after Charles has been two years at Oxford to go with my two boys to finish their studies at Geneva."[30] Since Mr. Keate had lived in Geneva for a time, Eliza wanted his advice on the matter. Whatever Mr. Keate advised Eliza to do, there was still a war going on and the time was not right for a voyage to England. Meanwhile she continued to monitor the education and lives of her sons in England and to raise and educate her daughter in South Carolina.

Raising the Children

As Harriott was just a month short of her tenth birthday when her father died, she had already received a basic education—all she needed was assistance in building on that base and her mother was the perfect person to help her. Eliza was an intelligent, well-educated woman who at this time in her life needed mental diversion—something to take her mind off her loss—and in selecting books for Harriott to read, discussing religion and philosophy with her, teaching her French, mathematics and geography she found the mental stimulation she needed. It brought her a great deal of satisfaction—as she had told Mr. Keate: it was a pleasure "to cultivate the tender mind."

Of course, Harriott's education would not have been complete without music lessons and dancing instruction from one of the many dancing masters who advertised in the *South Carolina Gazette* and she needed to learn "housewifery" skills. It was expected that Harriott would marry a planter with a large estate and as mistress of that estate she would be responsible for the domestic economy of the plantation while her husband attended to the all-important fields that produced the cash crop. Eliza made sure her daughter was well prepared for her role by including her in all the daily domestic activities of their household.

Unlike her mother who still thought longingly of London and its superior "entertainments," Harriott liked the country. When she was a young lady caught up in the swirl of activities that made up the social season in Charleston, Harriott confided to a friend: "Tho I own I love society and like to partake of some of the pleasures and amusements of the season extreamly Well, I am very serious when I say I would not live in a constant round of them upon any Account."[31]

Eliza's friends in England always remembered Harriott in their letters to her mother and inquired after her well-being. Mr. Keate sent her books and Mrs. King and her daughters sent her gifts, one of which brought her much pleasure—a fan and a tuft of ribbons called a pompon. "The fann I think a curiosity," Eliza wrote, "and the pompon the prettiest we ever saw. The little girl is quite happy, and the more so as they are the first that have reached this part of the world, so she has an opportunity of seting the fashion."[32]

In the early winter of 1762 Eliza was surprised to receive a letter from Mrs. King asking her if the rumor that was circulating in England that she was about to remarry was true. Eliza was astonished and could not understand how such a rumor could have started until she remembered that she had, in fact, received an offer of marriage. The offer, she explained to Mrs. King, "in point of fortune must have been to my advantage, but as entering into a second marriage never once entered my head, and as little into my inclination, and I am persuaded never will, the affair took not a moment's hesitation to determine, and indeed I did not think it could have got air enough to have wafted it to England."[33] The name of the unsuccessful suitor was never revealed and given the depth of her feeling for Charles Pinckney, it is not surprising that Eliza remained a widow for the rest of her life.

While Eliza was delighted to have the opportunity to watch her daughter grow and develop into a lovely young lady, she was saddened by the fact that she could not also watch her sons grow-up, that she did not know what color their hair was now or how tall they were getting. Their letters were very important to her. "I beg, my dear boys," she wrote, "you will write me a letter every month if 'tis but two lines and whether you know of ships coming or not."[34] Although she always relished news of her sons from her friends in England, the most cherished letters were the ones they wrote themselves. Tell Tom, Eliza wrote to Charles, "how much pleasure it gives his Mama to see his little scral, if 'tis but in writing his name."[35]

While letters from her sons gave Eliza great pleasure, the letters she relied on to give her the best information about their well-being came from the three people who were most closely connected with them: Mrs. Evance, Mr. Morley and Dr. Kirkpatrick, a London physician whom Charles had retained to look after the health of the boys when he and Eliza returned to South Carolina. Eliza had complete faith in their judgment when it came to the welfare of her sons: "You may be sure, My good Sir," wrote Eliza to Mr. Morley, "that I acquiesce in every thing you and my other friends do with regard to my children. You are upon the spot and must be better judges of their care than I possibly can be at this distance."[36]

In the early part of 1760 her friends suggested that Tom, who was frequently unwell, should be removed from the school at Camberwell, where the air was bad, and relocated to a school in a more healthy area. Although she was reluctant to remove her sons from the care of Mr. Gerrard to whom she would always be grateful for his many kindnesses to them, she had been anxious for some time about Thomas's health and decided to follow their advice. Since she did not want the two brothers separated, it was soon settled that both boys would be removed to a school in a western borough of London called Kensington. The school was located in a part of the village known as the Gravel Pits— considered an extremely healthy area because of its gravelly soil and clean air. In fact, King William III in the last part of the 17th century had moved there to seek relief from his asthma. Eliza explained the situation in a letter to Charles:

> In the meantime I hope my dear Charles will readily acquiesce in changing his school as the air of Camberwell does not agree with his dear little brother. I know your grateful and affectionate temper and know it will give you a good deal of pain to leave Mr. Gerrard, but your affection to your brother and the defference you will, I know, always pay to the judgment of our friends in England who advise it and can more properly judge of matters than I can at this distance. Rely intirely on their friendship and judgement in the case—which I hope will make you the more readily give up your own judgment and inclination to theirs.[37]

It is quite possible that Charles was not happy at the prospect of changing schools. He had only one more year left at Camberwell and naturally would have wanted to continue there in familiar surroundings with all his friends. Nevertheless, he went to the school in Kensington. Eliza constantly impressed upon her oldest son that it was his duty to look after his brother—a responsibility he took very seriously. Years later as an adult Thomas Pinckney was heard to remark: "I never felt myself as fatherless as I might have done, had I not had my brother to look to as an authority, and he always felt a paternal responsibility towards me, when we were alone at school."[38]

Eliza also impressed upon Charles his responsibility as the potential head of the family—"for though you are very young," Eliza told him, "you must know the welfare of a whole family depends in a great measure on the progress you make in moral Virtue, Religion and learning." Her advice to him is reminiscent of the advice she gave to her brother years ago. "What I fear most for you," she continued, "is warmth of temper. Learn, my dear Charles, To subdue the first emotion of Anger."[39] It was quite a responsibility to place upon the shoulders of a twelve-year-old boy struggling with all the anxieties of adolescence and it is no wonder that at times he showed signs of wanting to have things his own way.

Soon after the boys were removed to Kensington, Charles expressed some of his frustration by behavior Eliza's friends thought inappropriate. In a letter to an unidentified person, possibly Dr. Kirkpatrick, Eliza expressed her concern over the matter. According to Eliza Charles had always been a "dutiful, obliging and teachable child" and was made acutely unhappy if he offended either his father or mother. Not only that, but he had always been modest and excessively bashful. Eliza felt that Mr. Gerrard may have, out of pity, indulged Charles too much causing him to have difficulty adjusting to a new school, new headmaster and new rules.

The existing letter is a draft and parts of it along the sides and bottom are missing and many lines heavily crossed out. What exactly the offending behavior was is never revealed. Being aware that her boys were too far away for her to administer frequently needed advice and reproof, Eliza expressed her gratitude that her friends were willing to correct them. To the recipient of the letter Eliza continued: "and if Charles should not receive it [the correction] in the manner he ought to do, tho' I am very hopeful he will, I hope you will be so good to consider how very young and inexperienced he is and not cease to repeat it."[40]

Eliza concerned herself with as many of the details of her sons' lives as was possible—from fencing lessons for Charles to increasing his allowance from six pence a week to a shilling with a promised increase to Thomas when he was a little older. Their health was always on her mind and when she received advice from a friend in Charleston that Thomas would be the better for a glass of good red wine every day, she promptly instructed Mrs. Evance to order some sent to the new school in Kensington. She sent rice to England for the boys with instructions that they liked it boiled dry to eat with their meat instead of bread. Sweet potatoes and pomegranates and other treats were sent to them from Carolina.

In 1761 Charles was fifteen years of age and Eliza began to consult friends in South Carolina about the next step that should be taken in his education. Her Carolina friends thought it was time that Charles prepare for entrance into Oxford University and that meant attendance at one of England's public schools—a group of expensive, exclusive, private boarding schools catering to boys between the ages of thirteen and eighteen. They were called "public" schools because admission to them was not restricted to religion or place of birth and they were managed by an elected board of governors. "Private schools" in comparison were restrictive in their enrollment and run for the benefit and personal profit of the administrators. Among all the public schools in England Westminster was considered the best choice for young Charles Cotesworth Pinckney.

Charles, of course, had his own ideas as to which school he wanted to attend and there is a hint that he wanted to go to Warrington where his longtime friend and companion Tommy Evance was destined or Charter School where, he informed his mother, he could be more "under Mrs. Evance's care." "I own I prefer," Eliza replied patiently, " (and most people I know do prefer) Wistminster. ... To be patient, humble, and resigned," she reminded Charles, "is to be happy. It is also to have a noble soul, a mind out of reach of Enve, malice and every Calamity. And the earlier, my dear boy, you learn this lesson, the longer will you be wise and happy."[41] Charles went dutifully off to Westminster followed four years later by his brother Tom.

While Eliza was, quite naturally, concerned for the well-being of her two sons, she also felt a responsibility to two other young South Carolinians attending school in London—William Henry and Charles Drayton. The two boys had accompanied the Pinckneys to England in 1753 and Eliza and Charles had been their guardians during the five years they spent in England. Eliza was very fond of both brothers and continued to take an interest in them after her return to Charleston corresponding with them regularly. Since Eliza described her correspondence with the two as "very affectionate and obliging," there was obviously a close bond of friendship and affection between her and the boys. Consequently, as Eliza always wanted those she cared about to behave in the best possible manner, she felt justified in writing to Billy, the older brother, in April of 1761 to persuade him to rectify "some little mistakes" she thought he had made in his dealings with his father:

> I must inform you that your Papa showed me a letter he received from you by Mr. Wright which was not wrote in the manner you are generally used to write. There was too much warmth from you to your parent and something like abraiding. Consider, my dear child, how much duty, defference and affectionate respect is due to a parent, and I am sure one moments reflection will be enough to make you very sorry for displeasing your father in ever so small a matter. I said as much as I could in excuse for you and was much mortified I could not insist upon your being in the right.
>
> I am sure if you do me justice you must know on which side my partiallity rests and that I would much rather throw blame on your father than you. I should have wrote you on this subject long ago but a severe and long Illness prevented me till now. Pray give my love to Charles [his brother]. I also see his letter to his Mama is a very different stile from yours.[42]

In 1763 the long war in Europe finally came to an end—it had been raging for seven years on the continent and almost nine years in North America. When Charles and Eliza were getting ready to return to South Carolina in 1758 it looked as though the British would be soundly defeated by the French. However, the fortunes of war had changed and by 1763 instead of suffering a devastating defeat Great Britain emerged as a clear winner and France and Spain had been humiliated. The British had taken, among other territories, Guadeloupe and Martinique from the French and Cuba and the Philippines from the Spanish.

The Treaty of Paris which ended the war involved a complex series of land exchanges the most important of which involved territory in North America. The French decided that the sugar-rich islands of Guadeloupe and Martinique were more important to them than the cold, frozen lands of Canada and so ceded Canada in exchange for the islands. The Spanish reluctantly swapped Florida, a territory they had occupied for almost 200 years, for Cuba and the Philippines. France also ceded New Orleans and all the Louisiana Territory west of the Mississippi River to Spain. The terms of the treaty effectively doubled the size of British territory in the New World and left them in control of all of North America east of the Mississippi River.

The expulsion of the Spanish and French from the eastern half of North America was hailed with great joy by all the British colonists, but nowhere was it celebrated with more joy than in South Carolina. No longer did South Carolinians have to live in dread of a Spanish attack from the south or the encroachment of the French from the west. And most important without the French to supply them with guns and ammunition, the Indians on the frontier would no longer be a threat. The seas were safe once again for commerce and travel. It was indeed a momentous occasion.

When the Treaty of Paris was signed in February of 1763, Eliza had been separated from her sons for almost five years. Charles had turned seventeen in February and was in the process of finishing his public school education at Westminster and preparing for entrance into Oxford University. Thomas, who would be thirteen in October, was still at school in Kensington and was planning to follow in his brother's footsteps by entering Westminster in the next year or two. Harriott, now a young lady, was approaching her fifteenth birthday in August and ready to make her appearance in Charleston society.

Although the end of the war signaled the return of normalcy in ocean travel thus removing one of the impediments preventing Eliza from returning to England, she made no plans to do so. Although Eliza still thought of London as home and probably would have been quite happy to spend the rest of her days there, she realized that her children's future, and consequently hers as well, lay in South Carolina not in England. Her sons' inheritance—their plantations and properties—were, with the exception of some property in England, all located in the colony and Harriott, brought up to be a plantation mistress, would soon be entering Charleston society and would probably marry one of the eligible bachelors in her social circle. Even though it meant several more years of separation, the best thing Eliza could do for her children was to remain in South Carolina and make sure her sons' properties were well managed and see her daughter properly introduced into Charleston society.

For Eliza, who enjoyed the social scene very much, the prospect of escorting her charming and well-mannered daughter to many of the entertainments offered during Charleston's "season" was a pleasant one. Harriott, by all accounts, was a very pretty young lady—tall and willowy with a graceful, slender figure and at fifteen already taller than her diminutive mother. She had a lovely complexion with blue eyes and soft, curling fair hair and a charming voice.[43] Eliza had commissioned John Wollaston, a British artist then working in Charleston, to paint Harriott's portrait when she was eighteen, but unfortunately the painting has not survived. However, a copy of a miniature painted in 1790 when she was about forty-two years old still exists and shows that she had retained much of her youthful beauty.

The social scene in Charleston had always been light and gay, but it was even more so after the end of the war and there were numerous "entertainments" which provided opportunities for young people to meet and form attachments. Eliza and Harriott were often invited to spend the week at one or another of the country estates of their friends and in town they accepted invitations to private dinner parties, paid social calls on friends and acquaintances, enjoyed musical evenings sponsored by the St. Cecilia Society and attended dances at the Dancing Assembly—described by Joshua Quincy on his visit to Charleston in 1773 as having "bad music, good dancing and [an] elegantly disposed supper."[44]

Eliza and Harriott alternated between living at Belmont in the country and staying in the house on Colleton Square in Charleston. The two were very close and it is highly likely that Harriott had for some time been helping her mother manage their household and the Pinckney estates. At Belmont Eliza had taken up silk cultivation again with Harriott's help and it was so successful that others were inspired to do the same. Visitors often called at Belmont wanting to tour the silk works and Eliza and Harriott were often called upon to answer letters requesting information and advice on sericulture. Harriott lent one of her interested friends their copy of Samuel Pullen's work: *The Culture of Silk or an Essay on its Rational Practice and Improvement,* "which," Harriott explained, "we follow as near as we can."[45]

Harriott was popular and had her share of admirers among the eligible young men in the colony, but she seemed to have a preference for "older men." She wrote a friend, the esteem of younger men "is often founded on Whim and Caprice" and she thought the esteem of older men would be "guided by more judgment and seek a more solid Basis."[46] If there was one man amongst her acquaintances that she liked more than the others, she was careful not to mention his name too often in her letters to her friends. Gossip and rumors spread quickly in South Carolina society and Harriott was careful to avoid giving society any reason to spread stories about her.

However, a good friend and confidant identified only as Miss R. was well aware of the name of Harriott's favorite and was untiring in promoting the budding romance. The unidentified Miss R., who might have been Mary Rutledge, the daughter of John and Sarah Rutledge, was from "Santee"—that area around the North and South Santee Rivers, which, after uniting, flow into the sea between Winyah Bay and Cape Romain. The area was settled in the seventeenth century by a number of French Huguenots and the southern or lower area was often called "French Santee."

In those days there was no regular mail service and the only way to send letters to friends and family was if some obliging neighbor sent word that he or she or an enslaved servant was going to or from town and would carry any correspondence. Harriott often sent letters to Miss R. by members or servants of the Motte family who lived in Santee, but there was another person who frequently called on Eliza and Harriott offering to carry letters for them—Daniel Horry, a wealthy rice planter from Santee and a childless widower. In a letter to Miss R. Harriott wrote:

> I find Mr. Horry is the only opportunity I can rely upon to convey a line to you; have you at last got my travelling letter? I hear it went many a mile into the back country before it found its way to Santee. Mr. Horry told me at the Assembly he would call before he left town, but I really believe he is so Joked about me that it prevents his calling on us, least it should be thought that he had a serious attachment, and I am so much Joked that I believe I look so simple when he is in Company, that he thinks me half an Idiot. These are the reasons I did not ask him to take a ride and see our little silk work.[47]

Daniel Huger Horry, Jr., a third generation South Carolinian of Huguenot descent, was a "very good-looking, olive-complexioned man with a handsome mouth and chin."[48] He had been educated in South Carolina, but had traveled to London to study law at the Inner Temple and been called to the English bar. His main plantation was Hampton about forty-two miles north of Charleston in Santee, but he also had other plantations on the Santee River, a fleet of three schooners and a house in Charleston. And he most certainly did not think Harriott "half an idiot" in fact just the opposite. The two were married on February 15, 1768, at St. Phillips Church in Charleston. He was nearing thirty and she was nineteen.

Eliza must have viewed the marriage of her daughter with mixed feelings. On the one hand, she would have been pleased to see her daughter happily married and well situated, but on the other hand she was losing her closest companion. For ten years Harriott had been by her side, had comforted her as she struggled to overcome her grief and then helped her as she tried to run the household and manage the vast Pinckney estates. It would be very lonely indeed at Belmont and in the house in Charleston without her.

However, Eliza consoled herself during the months after Harriott's wedding, when she and Daniel were at Hampton, by "directing the planting and preparation" of the garden at the handsome Horry townhouse on the northeast corner of Broad and Legare, where today the cathedral of St. John the Baptist is located. She was, though, anxious for Harriott and Daniel to return to Charleston before the "sickly season" began in the country. "I must own," she wrote to Daniel in March. "I am very desireous you should come down [to town] this year by the last day of June, when I shall expect to see you both."[49]

Eliza was happy to have her daughter and son-in-law back in Charleston that summer. Harriott was now close enough so that she could see her as often as she wished and Daniel, a very thoughtful and attentive son-in-law, was there to help her with advice on estate business or to present her with fresh produce brought to town from his plantations. When the couple returned to Hampton for the fall and winter months, Eliza was a frequent and welcome visitor and mother and daughter filled in the time between visits by keeping up a constant correspondence.

As the next year, 1769, rolled in and the chilly months of January and February passed, Eliza received exciting news from England—Charles Cotesworth had finished his legal studies and was planning to return to South Carolina in the spring. As if that were not good news enough, Harriott then announced that she was expecting a child—Eliza's first grandchild—in the late summer.

The Family Re-United

Charles had finished his last year at Westminster in the late fall of 1763. He had done well at school and had been able to hold his own in competition with his fellow students. He was an outstanding Latin scholar and was known as a young man of character with high principles and a high regard for the truth. In January of 1764 he was ready to go up to Oxford and enter Christ Church— one of the University of Oxford's many colleges. Traditionally the most aristocratic of Oxford's colleges, Christ Church was the favorite destination of most graduates of Westminster. He was admitted on January 17, 1764.

However, Charles was to study the law and that meant he also needed to be admitted to one of the four Inns of Court that were responsible for legal education in England: the Inner Temple, the Middle Temple, Lincoln's Inn or Gray's Inn. The Inns of Court were not only responsible for legal studies, but they also had the exclusive right to call qualified students to the bar—thus according them permission to practice law. Residence at one of the Inns of Court for twelve terms was one of the requirements to qualify, but in the 18th century that requirement was interpreted very loosely and students could fulfill it by simply eating or paying for a certain number of meals in the great hall.

Consequently a week after he enrolled in Christ Church, Charles was back in London where he was admitted to the Society of the Middle Temple.

He ate a few dinners in the hall, determined his course of study and returned to Oxford at the end of the month. By eating a few dinners and paying for others Charles would have several terms of residence on record when he finally left Oxford to live in London and take up the exclusive study of the law.

After two years at Christ Church, Charles decided to cut short his studies at Oxford and move to London to devote his full time and attention to his legal studies. He spent long hours studying at the Middle Temple, visited London's courts to hear cases being tried and went to listen to debates in the House of Commons. Charles set himself a rigorous schedule and it soon began to take its toll. Eliza's friends in England thought he was working too hard and was on the way to ruining his health—they wrote Eliza of their concern. She wrote to Charles immediately:

> I am alarmed my dear child at the account of your being extremely thin, it is said owing to intense study, and I apprehend your constitution may be hurt; which affects me very much, conscious as I am how much, and how often, I have urged you from your childhood to a close application to your studies; but how shortsighted are poor mortals! Should I by my over solicitude for your passing thro' life with every advantage, be a means of injuring your constitution, and depriving you of that invaluable blessing, health, how shall I answer to myself, the hurting a child so truly dear to me, and deservedly so; who has lived to near twenty-three years of age without once offending me.[50]

In view of his mother's concern, Charles decided to take some time off from his studies and travel to France where he spent several months at the Royal Military Academy in Caen. There, under a routine of regular physical exercise as well as intellectual pursuits, he soon regained his health and vigor while receiving a basic course in military science. When he returned to London he was able to quickly finish his studies at the Middle Temple. He was called to the English bar on January 27, 1769, and rode one circuit for the experience.

He then made plans to return to South Carolina, but first he had some business to transact. On March 18, 1769, Charles Cotesworth Pinckney had his father's will proved in a London court and was granted his inheritance. He was now the official head of the family, though it would be some time before he would be able to assume all the duties and responsibilities that were attached to that position. A few weeks later Charles sailed from London on board the *Carolina Packet*.

What were his thoughts as he stood on the deck of the ship and watched the shores of England recede from view? This had been his home for the last sixteen years, he owned property in England and he was leaving his closest friends behind—including the younger brother whose welfare had been his concern ever since their parents returned to South Carolina eleven years ago. So many memories must have crowded his mind as the ship made her way into the Atlantic Ocean taking him to a land he had not seen since he was seven years old. He had to have felt sadness at leaving these familiar surroundings, but also excitement at the prospect of starting a new life in the land of his birth and joy at seeing his mother and sister again.

When Charles informed his mother that he was returning to Charleston, she was, of course, elated but then she became anxious—now that she was so close to seeing her oldest son again, she worried that something might happen to prevent his reaching South Carolina safely. She begged him to choose a good, safe ship for his voyage and, knowing that she would be on pins and needles the entire time he was at sea, asked him not to tell her the date of his departure so she would not be anxious.

If Charles did not let his mother know when he was leaving England, he most likely told his sister and consequently she would have been anticipating his arrival in early May. And on May 15, 1769, the *Carolina Packet* sailed into Charleston harbor bringing Charles Cotesworth Pinckney back to his native land. The last time he had seen the view that was now spread out before his eyes he had been only seven years old. How much of it did he remember? Surely he remembered the impressive steeple of St. Philip's Church and the large brick mansion house where he had been born. It must have given him a great deal of pleasure to think that this impressive house now belonged to him and he would shortly be living there.

How different his homeland was from the place he had been living for the past 16 years. He would have forgotten how bright the sun was in Carolina, how the sunlight bounced off the water in the harbor making it sparkle and the fragrant scent of jessamine and magnolia blossoms that permeated the warm, moist air. The city of Charleston lay in the distance glistening in the sun and to the young man standing on the deck of the gently rocking ship it was a welcome sight—it was home.

What a glorious homecoming it must have been. Harriott would have been on the alert for the first sighting of the *Carolina Packet* sending the news on to Eliza who, in spite of not knowing exactly when Charles was leaving England, would have been anxiously awaiting news of his arrival. What did Eliza think when she first set eyes on Charles? The last time she had seen him he had been twelve years old. How much of the twelve-year-old boy did she see in the tall, handsome young man that stood before her? Charles would surely have known his mother immediately—the change in the looks of adults not being as dramatic as the changes that occur in a child growing into adulthood. Would he have recognized Harriott? She had been a nine-year-old child when he had last seen her and now she was an attractive young lady, married to the good-looking man by her side and just entering the last trimester of her pregnancy.

The Pinckney family had a lot of catching-up to do and likely spent the next few days doing just that, which would have given Charles time to recover from the voyage and adjust to the warm, moist climate and bright sunshine of South Carolina. Eliza would have been eager to hear news of Tom—now eighteen and enrolled in Christ Church in Oxford. Charles would have told her, if she had not already learned it from Tom, that his brother was planning to study the law just as he had done. The years of monitoring the education and upbringing of her sons while being an ocean apart were drawing to a close and Eliza could not have helped feeling proud that her efforts so far had produced such good results.

Charles was anxious to relieve his mother of the many burdens she had been carrying in managing the estate, but he was not ready to assume complete control of his inheritance as yet. He had much to learn about being a Carolina planter and he would learn much of it from his mother in the weeks to come. It is likely that after he adjusted to his new environment he took a trip to inspect his property and see something of the countryside. And he would have wanted to become better acquainted with his brother-in-law Daniel Horry who could provide him with insight into the political situation in South Carolina. Charles had heard a little about the specific problems the colony was having with the mother country on his voyage home as one of his fellow travelers was Miles Brewton, a South Carolinian just returning from a short trip to England.

At some point in the summer, Charles took over the management of his own property thus relieving Eliza of most of her responsibilities—although it does appear that she continued to manage Tom's property, which would have been appropriate as he was still a minor and she was his guardian. However, she was freer than she had been in many years and was anxiously awaiting the birth of her first grandchild. On August 13, 1769, Harriott was safely delivered of a fine baby boy named Daniel after his father and grandfather.

The arrival of the baby brought great happiness to the entire family. Harriott confided to a friend that she doubted whether the baby's father "thinks there is any thing upon Earth to exceed him and my poor Mother comes little short of him in her fondness, my Brother too goes beyond what I thought a young man that had never had a Child could [go] in fondness to so young an Infant." Both the fond father and grandmother thought the baby "very pretty" while the more moderate Harriott thought him "very well, not remarkably handsom or otherways."[51]

Eliza, a very fond and doting grandmother, was a frequent visitor at Hampton—quite willing to have her grandson left in her care whenever his parents wished it. These were happy times for Eliza. She reveled in her grandson and her family and was able to spend time in her garden, attend to her silk works, visit friends and read her books while keeping up a correspondence with Tom and her friends in England. However, although she was absorbed in her own happiness, she was aware of the increasing tension between the colonies and Great Britain. It was a dark cloud that marred the otherwise clear horizon.

The results of the last war had left Great Britain standing preeminent in the world while France, her greatest rival, was left to nurse her wounded pride and dream of revenge. The French were not without hope, though, as political leaders in Europe predicted that the expulsion of the French and Spanish from North America would lead to a rift between Great Britain and her colonies and events during the first few years after the Treaty of Paris seemed to be proving them correct. When the break came, it was said, the French had to be prepared to take advantage of the situation if they wanted to avenge themselves. Everyone thought the rift would take place in the next year or two, but they were mistaken. It would take over ten years for the bonds that bound the colonies to the mother country to be severed. Meanwhile the French would watch, wait and build up their navy.[52]

Colonists, who had once been willing to cooperate with British authorities in return for military protection, were, now that protection was no longer needed, not so willing to be accommodating. And conversely, the British government, which had needed colonial help to defeat its enemies and had, therefore, been willing to take a relaxed attitude to colonial rule, now sought to tighten that rule. With victory came great expense and many problems for the British and unfortunately King George III was young and inexperienced and had allowed his intense dislike of his predecessor extend to anyone who had served in his government. Consequently he surrounded himself with men he liked and trusted, but who lacked experience and were not always qualified. This set of circumstances was a formula for disaster.

The first major controversy between the colonies and the mother-country occurred in 1765 when, in an effort to raise money to pay for the war, Parliament passed the Stamp Act. The act required that all printed materials—legal documents, licenses, newspapers, magazines and playing cards—contain an embossed revenue stamp indicating that the tax on it had been paid. A stamp tax was not a new idea, individual colonies had used a stamp tax in the past to raise money, but this was the first time a non-maritime tax had been imposed on the colonies by the British Parliament.

The legal community was the first to react maintaining that the British constitution protected its subjects from taxation without their consent—an echo of Charles Pinckney's argument in 1735. All the colonies were united in their opposition to the Stamp Act and the Massachusetts House of Representatives sent out a circular letter inviting all colonial legislatures to send delegates to a congress to be held in New York in October. Known as the Stamp Act Congress, nine colonies, including South Carolina, sent representatives to the meeting. The delegates drew up a statement in which they reiterated their position that the British Parliament had no right to tax the colonies.

Throughout the colonies stamp tax agents were threatened and harassed when they tried to perform their duties—in Charleston the South Carolina stamp tax agent had to flee for his life before an angry mob. As a result the agents either resigned or agreed to suspend their work until Parliament had time to review the petitions of the Stamp Act Congress and with no one to stamp the paper, the courts could not function, licenses could not be issued, and shipping ground to a halt. Consequently the British government backed down and in March of 1766 King George III signed the repeal of the Stamp Act, but as a matter of principle he also signed the Declaratory Act which affirmed the right of Parliament to tax the colonies.

The next year Charles Townshend, Chancellor of the Exchequer, proposed the Revenue Act which placed a duty on tea, glass, paper, and dye stuffs imported into the colonies. Parliament passed the Revenue Act and the king signed it in June of 1767. The duties, known as the Townshend Duties, met with stiff opposition from the colonists and calls for a non-importation agreement to protest them were heard in colonial legislatures.

When Charles Cotesworth returned to South Carolina, he found that a lively debate over the pros and cons of the non-importation agreement was ongoing. He, of course, did not know much about South Carolina politics, but he had a good mentor in his cousin Charles Pinckney II, one of the top lawyers in the colony and an important and influential member of the Commons House of Assembly. The proponents of non-importation won the debate and at the end of July Charleston became the last colonial port to adopt the non-importation agreement. From now on only a limited number of essential goods were allowed into the colony—the importation of everything else including slaves was prohibited.

Through the long, hot days of summer Charles Cotesworth worked on learning the ins and outs of plantation management all the while becoming more and more involved in colonial politics. A political career, if he wanted to pursue one, was eminently possible for he had all the qualifications: impeccable credentials as a lawyer and a name that was well-known and respected—people remembered and applauded his father's unselfish service to the colony and his mother, through her experiments with indigo, was one of the best known and most respected women in South Carolina. Added to that he had influential friends and relations: his cousin Charles Pinckney II was a leader in the Commons House, his guardian had been William Bull, Jr., now acting as Royal Governor of Carolina while Lord Montagu was absent in England, and one of his closest childhood friends was William Henry Drayton—another influential politician who was soon to be named to the Governor's Council.

Any county in the colony would have been happy to be represented by such a well-connected young lawyer. Consequently, in September of 1769 Charles Cotesworth was elected to represent St. John's Parish in Colleton County in the Commons House. He was following the path his father had laid out for him— "that he will employ all his future abilities in the Services of God and his Country." In January of 1770 he received his commission to practice law in South Carolina and was soon riding the circuit representing clients in other parts of the colony.

Eliza was proud of her son and could only wish that his father had lived to see his oldest son fulfill his expectations. Meanwhile, she had another son whose education she was still monitoring in England. In 1768 Tom had finished his schooling at Westminster graduating as the top Greek scholar in his class. He entered Christ Church at Oxford University in November of 1768 and then returned to London on December 16 to be admitted to the Middle Temple. He stayed in London for a month eating the required dinners in the great hall.

After being at Oxford for several months, Thomas began to wonder how beneficial four years of classical study at Christ Church would be to his career as a lawyer. To gain perspective and improve his French he took a month off from his studies and went to France. He was back at Oxford for four weeks before deciding in early August that he would not continue his studies at Christ Church. It is most likely that at this point Tom went back to France to study military science at the Royal Military Academy in Caen—just as his brother had done.

When he returned from France, Thomas threw himself into his studies at the Middle Temple and in 1771, after two years of intensive work, decided to take some time off—there was something he wanted very much to do. He would turn twenty-one on October 23 and would be entitled to claim his inheritance in South Carolina. He had not seen his homeland since he was two and a half years old and had no clear recollection of it and he had not seen his mother and sister for thirteen years. His plan was to return to South Carolina in the fall, be reunited with his mother, sister and brother and, of course, meet his brother-in-law and nephew for the first time and take possession of the property he had inherited from his father. He would then return to England and finish his education.

On September 8, 1771, Eliza was reunited with her youngest son—who after eighteen years and five months was returning to his homeland. The Pinckney family was finally together, if only temporarily, after thirteen years of separation. Eliza most likely whisked Thomas away to her house on Colleton Square to fuss over him until she was certain that he had recovered from his ocean voyage. The family must have spent hours together just talking giving Thomas the opportunity to become acquainted with his brother-in-law and his two-year old nephew.

When Thomas had recovered from his voyage and adjusted to the climate, he most likely went to visit his plantation on the Ashepoo River and his property at Four Holes. He would have also spent time with his mother learning the business of running his plantation and managing his properties in town. From now on Tom would be in charge of his South Carolina estate and when he returned to England, it would be his brother Charles who would hold his power of attorney and handle his business affairs. Eliza's responsibility for managing the estates of her two sons was now at an end—at least for a while.

There would also have been many opportunities for Tom to socialize during his visit. He would have attended the races with his brother and brother-in-law, a racing enthusiast who generally had one or two horses running in every race, played cards, gone to musical soirées, dinner parties and dancing assemblies. Good food, fine wine and attractive young ladies were all part of Charleston's social scene and Tom's brother, one of the town's most eligible bachelors, would have been happy to escort his younger brother to all the entertainments Charleston had to offer.

However, no matter how much Tom was enjoying his visit, he needed to complete his legal studies at the Middle Temple and receive his call to the bar. On March 12, 1773, after spending eighteen months in South Carolina, Thomas Pinckney stood on the deck of the ship that was to take him back to England and took a long, last look at Charleston. While he was sad to be leaving, he was also anxious to get back to England so he could finish his studies and return home for good. His visit had been a success and he had accomplished much—he had reconnected with his family, taken possession of his properties and learned much about their management and he had also gained insight into the problems between the colony and Great Britain.

Everyone in the family felt a deep sense of loss when Tom returned to England. Harriott wrote to him aboard ship just before he sailed: "I can't express what we feel at parting with you. My Brother [Charles] is at the House of Assembly well, as is Mr. Horry, but none in high Spirits. My Mother is well but very low."[53] Eliza was probably the most affected by Tom's departure and, being all too aware of the hazards of ocean travel, was nervous about his voyage—it would be four months before she could reasonably expect to hear that he had arrived safely in England. However, she was not a woman to remain idle for very long and was soon engaged in a range of activities calculated to take her mind off the dangers of an ocean voyage.

The first of these activities involved taking care of the four-year-old Daniel. Several days after Tom's departure Harriott and her husband returned to the country and, since several cases of the measles had been reported at Hampton, they decided to leave their son with his grandmother. Eliza thoroughly enjoyed having Daniel with her—a feeling reciprocated by the little boy—and would have had him stay with her more often but she did not want to overstep her role as grandmother. "Tell my dear baby," Eliza wrote later to Harriott, "I have in my heart and would always have him in my sight if I could consistently with what is right."[54]

In addition to frequent visits from her grandson, Eliza had her garden and her projects to keep her busy. She was growing cotton at Belmont and experimenting with the possibility of having it woven into cloth to make clothes for the slaves and she still had her silk works. In addition there were long visits to Hampton, outings to neighboring plantations, calls on friends and acquaintances in town, letters to write and books to read. The months passed quickly and before she realized it in December of 1774 Tom was home. Eliza's fondest wish had been fulfilled—her family was together at last.

The Road to Independence

When Tom left England in 1771 to visit South Carolina, tensions between the colonies and Great Britain had eased somewhat. The non-importation agreement implemented in 1769 had been successful—colonial trade was cut in half and British merchants were unhappy. As a result, in the spring of 1770 Parliament repealed the Townshend duties on paper, glass and dye stuffs, but kept the duty on tea as a reminder to the colonies that it had the right to tax them. The repeal had the desired effect, as the colonists, encouraged by their partial victory over Parliament, began to relax restrictions on the importation of British goods. However, in order to send a message to the British government the boycott on tea was continued.

This was the situation when Tom left England and during the eighteen months he was in South Carolina little happened to change the relationship between Great Britain and her North American colonies. However, soon after Tom's return to England in the spring of 1773, tea once again became a subject of controversy.

The prolonged colonial boycott of tea had had a devastating effect on the East India Company, the prime supplier of British tea—it had been driven to the brink of bankruptcy. In May of 1773 Parliament felt compelled to intervene to save the company. It did so by passing the Tea Act which gave the East India

Company a monopoly on all tea exported to the North American colonies and, in an attempt to diminish colonial resistance to taxed tea, Parliament also reduced the duty on imported tea to the point that East India tea was cheaper than smuggled tea the colonists had been buying from the Dutch.

While news of the passage of the Tea Act was filtering into the colonies during the summer of 1773, Eliza noticed that her oldest son was paying more and more attention to a certain young lady. Charles was twenty-seven years old, nice-looking, a successful lawyer and owned a substantial amount of property—he was, in a word, a very eligible bachelor and it was time for him to settle down, marry and begin raising a family. Of all the attractive young ladies he had met in Charleston, his fancy had fallen on one in particular—Sarah Middleton, the youngest daughter of Henry Middleton and his deceased wife Mary Williams Middleton.

He began a serious courtship that summer and, finding that his feelings were reciprocated, soon asked Henry Middleton for his daughter's hand in marriage. It was an excellent match for both parties. Henry Middleton was an extremely wealthy man owning twenty plantations and over 800 slaves in South Carolina with additional property in England and Barbados. He was also an influential member of government. Henry Middleton readily gave his consent to the marriage and Eliza could not have been happier. Her friendship with the Middleton family dated back to her earliest days in South Carolina and she could never forget the kind attention her sons had received in England from Mr. and Mrs. William Middleton—Henry Middleton's older brother and his wife. The match had her wholehearted approval. The young couple were married on September 28, 1773—Charles was twenty-seven and Sarah was seventeen.

The newlyweds settled into married life at the Mansion House in Charleston in close proximity to Eliza at Colleton Square. Eliza spent her summer months at the house in Charleston and the rest of the year at Belmont or visiting Hampton in Santee. Harriott and Charles were very attentive to their mother and letters and notes flowed back and forth between their residences and hers— sometimes their notes were accompanied by tokens of their affection and esteem. "Indeed my Children," Eliza exclaimed to Harriott, "you are all very kind, and determined I shall live well, you, (in which I include Mr. Horry) send me a quantity of eatables, and your good brother, of drinkables, Porter and Liquors, and would have forced more wine upon me than I have room for."[55] The only thing needed to make Eliza perfectly happy was to have her "dear Tom" back in Charleston and to know that the conflicts with Great Britain were being resolved. Unfortunately they were only getting worse.

Charles, who was a member of the South Carolina committee of correspondence and consequently in close communication with the other colonies, would have been aware of the latest developments resulting from the passage of the Tea Act. Knowing that his mother was always eager to hear the latest news, he probably shared information with her, but it is highly likely that he edited it so as not to cause her undue worry. So perhaps he didn't tell her that the committee of correspondence had received word that in the fall the East India Company was planning to send simultaneous shipments of tea to Charleston, Boston, New York and Philadelphia and that the northern cities were going to refuse the shipments of tea as a protest against Parliament's right to tax them.

On December 2, 1773, a ship arrived in Charleston harbor and on board were 257 chests of tea. A mass meeting of Charleston's leading citizens—planters, merchants, artisans—was called the next day to discuss their course of action. Convening in the great hall of the Exchange building, those in attendance resolved "not to import or buy any tea taxed for raising a revenue in America" and the merchants to whom the tea was being sent "resigned amid applause." A committee was then appointed under the leadership of Christopher Gadsden to collect signatures from people all over the province promising "not to import or use tea."[56]

In the 18th century women had no public voice and did not participate in government, but that did not mean that they were not well informed about current affairs or have an opinion about them—many colonial women were just as incensed by the actions of the British government as their male counterparts. Men and women throughout the colony signed the petition pledging not to import or use tea and women in particular took up the cause with great zeal. It became quite the fashion for ladies to show their support for the American cause by serving a hot beverage brewed from herbs in their parlors after dinner instead of the usual tea and many women became quite creative in mixing many kinds of herbs together to make a potable drink.

However, there still remained the problem of the tea aboard ship in the harbor. In South Carolina consignees of goods imported from Great Britain had twenty days from the time those goods arrived in port to off-load them. If they failed to remove the cargo by that time, customs officers were authorized to take the goods into custody. Since everyone knew the tea was not going to be claimed by any of the merchants in town, Gadsden and his associates planned to take the tea from the ship before the time limit had expired and store it out of the reach of the crown's customs officers. However, they misjudged the day the customs officers were going to act. Arriving a day before expected, the officials unloaded the tea and stored it in the basement of the exchange before Gadsden and his group were aware of what they had done.

In Boston the response to the arrival of the tea was not as mild. Under the leadership of Samuel Adams a group of colonists, dressed as Mohawk Indians, boarded the ships anchored in Boston harbor and threw £15,000 worth of the East India Company's tea into the water. Reaction in Charleston was one of shock. Destruction of private property was not an act that met with the approval of most South Carolinians and they echoed the sentiments of Benjamin Franklin who called the destruction of the tea "an Act of violent Injustice on our part."[57] In London Thomas Pinckney shared this feeling. In a letter to his brother he wrote: "I am extremely happy to find my Countrymen [fellow Carolinians] have acted with so much Resolution & at the same Time with Moderation in the Tea Affair, & make no doubt but a steady adherence to such Measures will ensure them Success."[58]

British response to the incident in Boston was swift. In March of 1774 Lord North, the Prime Minister, presented the Boston Port Act to the House of Commons. The act called for the port of Boston to be closed to all commercial traffic on June 1 if, by that time, the East India Company had not been reimbursed for the loss of the tea and if restitution had not been made to the royal treasury for the loss of custom revenue. When these conditions were met and when George III was convinced that the city of Boston would, in the future, observe the laws of the realm, the port would be re-opened.

While most people agreed that the East India Company should be reimbursed for the destroyed tea, closing one of the most important ports in the North American colonies and punishing the entire population of Boston for the actions of a few seemed rather excessive. The issue was debated by members of Parliament and while those who opposed the bill argued well, they were not successful—the act passed and the king signed it on March 31.

Hard on the heels of the Boston Port Act, Parliament passed the Administration of Justice Act and the Massachusetts Government Act and sent them to the king for his signature. Under the conditions of the first act soldiers or royal officials who were accused of committing a capital offence while carrying out their duties could have their trials moved out of the Massachusetts colony if the governor thought the accused would not receive a fair trial there. The second act revoked the Massachusetts colony's charter which had been granted in 1691.

The Administration of Justice Act, also known as the Murder Act in the colonies, raised fears that royal officials would be pardoned for any acts of violence against the colonists and therefore, might feel encouraged to use violence. As for the second act: if Parliament could suspend the colonial charter of one colony and change a form of government that had been in place for 80 years, it could do the same to any of the remaining colonies. News of the passage of the two acts produced shock, anger and indignation both in the colonies and among those American colonists then living in England.

At the instigation of Benjamin Franklin and others, including Ralph Izard of South Carolina, a meeting of all the colonists in London was called. At the meeting the colonists decided to band together as Americans to petition the king—on whose good will they depended—not to sign the Acts. "The Petition of the native Americans residing in London, to His Britannic Majesty in 1774" was a respectful request to the king to "suspend your royal assent to the bills." Thirty Americans signed the petition and of the 30 signers 16 were from South Carolina—Thomas Pinckney was one of them.[59]

The king, ignoring the petition, signed the Administration of Justice Act and the Massachusetts Government Act on May 20, 1774. Thomas, disheartened by the actions of king and Parliament, wanted nothing more than to return home as quickly as possible. He would be eligible to receive his call to the bar in November, but there were certain expenses attached to answering the call and then he needed money to pay for his passage home. As income from his property in South Carolina was sometimes slow in arriving, he wrote his brother in the spring requesting him to make sure the money he needed would arrive before November. "If it should prove inconvenient from the bad sale of Crops or the like to send Money at that Time," he added, "I should be glad that you would, if possible, borrow it on my Account, as I had rather undergo any Inconvenience when at home, than to be obliged to stay here a Day after I have an Opportunity of leaving England."[60] He was called to the English bar on November 25, 1774, and sailed for Charleston soon after and by the end of December was home.

Eliza was delighted to have her youngest son back in Charleston permanently. She now had her family all together and had the satisfaction of knowing that her efforts to raise her sons to be good, responsible adults had been successful. She had been fortunate because, to use Eliza's metaphor, she had had "excellent soil to work upon" and now she could sit back and enjoy the fruits of her labor. However, just as one set of responsibilities ended, another set was beginning—grandchildren were coming along who would need her care and guidance in the future. There were now two, for a little girl, Maria Henrietta, had been born to Charles and Sally in the latter part of 1774 and there would soon be more.

Shortly after his return to Charleston Tom was admitted to the South Carolina bar and was soon scheduled to plead his first case in court. Always anxious that her children do their best in any undertaking, Eliza was very nervous while she waited for news of the outcome of the law suit. To pass the time and keep herself from pacing the floor, she decided to write a long letter to Harriott. She was interrupted in the middle of her writing by Charles who stopped by briefly to tell her that Tom had won his case. Eliza was not satisfied, though, as she complained to Harriott: "I have seen nobody yet to know how he spoke but his brother, and he, you know, is very partial to him." However, visitors calling on her later in the evening assured her that Tom had performed well.[61]

While Eliza was concerned with Tom's appearance in court, South Carolinians were beginning a serious debate over a recommendation from the First Continental Congress which had met the previous September in Philadelphia. Delegates from all the colonies except Georgia had come together to plan a united course of action in response to the passage of the Intolerable Acts—the series of acts beginning with the Boston Port Act. Since the non-importation agreement of 1769 had resulted in the repeal of most of the hated Townshend duties, the delegates were willing to try economic pressure once again to bring about the repeal of the Intolerable Acts. They called for the establishment of a Continental Association that would not only prohibit the importation of British goods, but also the exportation of colonial goods to Great Britain, Ireland and the West Indies.

Since the formation of a non-exportation and non-importation association would have serious consequences for Carolina planters, South Carolina leaders convened a Provincial Congress made up of representatives from all parts of the colony to debate the issue. The Provincial Congress met in Charleston in January of 1775 and, after much discussion, voted for the Association. Non-importation of British goods was to take place immediately, while the non-exportation phase was to begin in September of 1775 if the Intolerable Acts were not repealed by that time. Since the sugar planters in the West Indies depended on the North American colonies for most of their food and other necessities, the mere possibility of an embargo on imports from the mainland colonies was enough to cause them to panic. It was hoped that their cries of protest would be loud and clear enough to influence lawmakers in London.

Rumors were rampant in Charleston in the winter of 1775 and in February Eliza reported the latest of them to Harriott at Hampton:

> I cant tell you much Public news, what I have heard is as follows, That the American affairs at home wear a more favourable Aspect, The King has promised to receive the petition, Jamaica has petitioned, the rest of the Islands are about to do it, as well as the London Merchants; the Trades people clamour extremely; Mr. Fox [British politician] is not so violent as he used to be against us. Captain Turner is also arrived and says there is a prospect of the Acts [Intolerable Acts] being repealed. Pray God Grant it may prove true.[62]

Eliza, like most of the people in the colonies at this time, was struggling with a confused sense of identity. On the one hand Eliza thought of herself as British—she still referred to London as "home" in spite of having lived in South Carolina for over thirty years—and the conflicts between the colony and Great

Britain were "American affairs." Her use of the phrase "American affairs" and not "our affairs" seems to indicate a personal detachment on her part from the colonies and their problems with the mother country. But then there is a clear indication that she did associate herself with the colonies—all the colonies not just South Carolina—in her statement: "Mr. Fox is not so violent as he used to be against us."

In the early months of the year 1775 most colonists, like Eliza, did consider themselves loyal British subjects and they would have very emphatically said so if asked. At this time the thirteen individual and very distinct colonies were just beginning to unite as one in opposition to the policies of the British government. And while the colonists still thought of themselves as loyal British subjects living in a British colony, they were beginning to bond together and think of themselves as being something else—Americans.

Hopes were high in South Carolina that Parliament would repeal the Intolerable Acts. Then on April 19 the British packet ship *Swallow* arrived in Charleston carrying a mail pouch containing letters and documents for royal officials. The pouch, intercepted by political leaders in Charleston, contained a very revealing letter outlining the intention of the British government to use force to compel the colonies into submission. The next day the Provincial Congress appointed a secret committee to take charge of the arming and defense of the colony.

On the evening of April 21 the committee made its first move. The members, William Henry Drayton, Charles Cotesworth Pinckney, Arthur Middleton, William Gibbes and Edward Weyman, along with several other men, broke into two powder magazines and removed all the gun powder. They then headed to the armory which was located in the State House and took all the arms and equipment stored there. These were serious and dangerous acts and the men involved were very much aware of the consequences should they be caught— in the 18th century men were hanged for much less. Charles would most definitely not have shared the events of this night with either his wife or his mother.

A little over two weeks later a schooner arrived in Charleston harbor from Salem, Massachusetts, bringing news of the fighting at Lexington and Concord. At a meeting of the Provincial Congress on June 1 congress voted to raise two infantry regiments and one regiment of mounted rangers. Officers to lead the infantry regiments were then voted on—Christopher Gadsden and William Moultrie were elected colonels of the 1st and 2nd regiments while Charles Cotesworth Pinckney was chosen as the ranking captain. Both Daniel Horry and Thomas Pinckney were also commissioned as captains.

The formation of a South Carolina army in which her sons and son-in-law were officers must have conjured up visions of the past for Eliza. She had worried and fretted over the safety of her father and brother in a past war and could not have been looking forward to doing the same for her sons. However, at this time a war between Great Britain and the colonies was not a certainty by any means and Eliza and many others could only hope and pray that the disputes would be peacefully settled. Even though the Continental Congress had established a Continental Army under the command of General George Washington to defend the rights of the colonies and even though that army was now besieging the city of Boston, there was still hope that the colonists could convince Great Britain to grant their requests and put an end to the hostilities.

Since reconciliation, not war and not independence, was the goal of the American colonies in the summer of 1775, the Continental Congress drafted a petition to send to the king. Known as the "Olive Branch Petition" it restated the grievances of the colonists while assuring the king of their loyalty and their desire for a reconciliation and a cessation of hostilities. The king rejected the Olive Branch Petition unread and on August 23 proclaimed the colonies to be in a state of rebellion.

Since Charleston was now considered to be in rebellion against the king, royal officials in town thought it prudent to disarm Fort Johnson, an earthwork fort standing on the east end of James Island and guarding the entrance to the harbor. They sent the British sloop-of-war *Tamar,* which was hovering off the coast, to direct the removal of the fort's guns and other military supplies.

Fort Johnson was not only the main naval defensive site for the city of Charleston, but it was also the repository of most of the round shot for the city's heavy cannon—it was essential for the Americans that the fort and its armaments remain intact. Therefore, the Council of Safety, the group charged with the direction of the defense of Charleston, ordered Colonel Moultrie of the 2nd Carolina regiment to take the fort before the British could carry out their mission.

It was the first military action undertaken by Captain Charles Cotesworth Pinckney as his company was one of the three companies scheduled to take part in the attack. It turned out to be an easy task as the British, anticipating the American reaction, had dismounted the cannons two hours before the arrival of the soldiers of the 2nd regiment. When Charles and the rest of the attacking force approached Fort Johnson, the gates were open and only the fort's caretaker and five sailors from the *Tamar* were inside. Fortunately the cannons were only dismounted not dismantled or spiked and in a matter of hours were remounted and fit for service.[63]

A flag, designed by Colonel Moultrie and reflecting the attire of the 2nd regiment, which wore blue uniforms with a silver crescent, was hoisted over

Fort Johnson to alert the *Tamar* that the American forces were in control. On board the *Tamar* was Lord William Campbell, the last royal governor of South Carolina, who must have watched in frustration as the flag—a field of blue with a silver crescent in the right-hand corner—was raised over the fort and fluttered in the breeze while shouts of "huzzah" from the soldiers inside the fort floated across the water.

At this time Eliza's sons and son-in-law were with their units preparing to defend Charleston from a possible British attack—which left the ladies of the family to make their own arrangements. Sally and the children, there were now two, went to her father's plantation on Goose Creek northwest of Charleston while Eliza, Harriott and little Daniel remained in town. The situation there was not good as the British had blockaded the harbor and there was a shortage of provisions and supplies.

Rumors were widespread during the fall of 1775. Captured British sailors warned that a bomb ketch, a ship armed with mortars that fired explosive shells, was coming to attack Fort Johnson and that Charleston would then be burned—a likely scenario as the British had already burned Charles Town in Massachusetts. Then there was the rumor of a possible naval invasion. The rumors and the presence of British war ships outside the harbor had its effect on the townspeople who were convinced that an attack was imminent. "Almost all the Women, and many hundred Men have left Town," Harriott reported to her cousin in Santee. "In a few days more I imagine we shall hardly have a female acquaintance to speak too."[64]

Preparing for the worst Eliza and Harriott had made plans to leave if and when they felt it was no longer safe to stay in Charleston. The three of them, Eliza, Harriott and Daniel, were going to Auckland, Tom's plantation on the Ashepoo River about fifty miles southwest of Charleston. Fortunately they did not have to evacuate for on January 6 the British fleet left, sailing south towards Georgia. The Council of Safety then sent Colonel Moultrie and his regiment to occupy Sullivan's Island and to begin to construct a fort on the southern shore facing the entrance to the harbor. A lookout was posted to give warning if the British fleet should return, but, although there were sightings of British warships off the coast from time to time, the enemy appeared content to leave Charleston alone. The people of Charleston breathed a sigh of relief and life returned to some semblance of normalcy.

As the royal governor and other royal officials had departed with the British fleet, there was no official government left in South Carolina—a situation that needed to be quickly addressed. In February the Provincial Congress met to write a temporary constitution under which an interim government could be established to ensure that order was preserved in the colony during the continuation of the disputes with Great Britain. Christopher Gadsden, newly arrived from Philadelphia and carrying with him a copy of Thomas Paine's pamphlet *Common Sense*, rose to speak at the meeting. He startled the entire body of representatives by announcing that he was not only in favor of forming a new independent government for South Carolina, but he was also in favor of the total independence of the United Colonies from Great Britain. Members rose in opposition to his remarks and there were angry shouts that reconciliation and not independence was the best course to follow.

The issue of independence would not be resolved for months to come and in the meantime South Carolina needed an interim government and the members decided to devote their energies to accomplishing that mission first. The new constitution basically kept the old form of government in place with a few minor changes. Instead of a governor and lieutenant governor there would be a president and vice-president—John Rutledge and Henry Laurens were then elected to hold those offices. Both these men as well as the members of the Legislative Council, as the new upper house was called, were in favor of an "accommodation of the unhappy difference between Great Britain and America" and not in favor of separation.[65] In the last week of March 1776 most of Carolina's leaders shared this opinion. However, the debate over independence was not finished—it was just beginning.

While Carolina legislators were struggling with heavy issues of forming a government and debating the advisability of independence, Eliza and Harriott took little Daniel and went to visit Tom's plantation on the Ashepoo River. They went not for the sake of safety, but to be of service to Tom. Ashepoo was Tom's main plantation and in the future he would be living there for several months of the year. The house on the property was small and needed some enhancements if it were to serve as his country residence. The two women whose opinion he valued most in the world were his mother and his sister and it was to them that he entrusted the task of making improvements to his house. It was a pleasant change for Eliza and Harriott after the anxieties they had been living with for the past few months.

They left Charleston at the end of March or beginning of April. As soon as they arrived and inspected the house, they began to make plans and, one of Eliza's first suggestions was that the house would be improved by the addition of a garden. Tom agreed and Eliza was soon involved in one of her favorite activities. However, at some point Eliza and Harriott must have been concerned for their safety—perhaps it was the rumor of a large British fleet headed south that prompted their concern—for they left Ashepoo at the end of May.

They did not return to Charleston, but went to stay with Eliza's friend Ann Elliott who had gathered a number of women and children at Sandy Hill, the Elliott plantation in St. Paul's Parish in Colleton County south of Charleston. Tom wrote to Eliza and Harriott there in the middle of June telling them that after their fellow South Carolinians had given the British a good "drubbing" he would pay a visit to Ashepoo to view the changes that had been made there.[66]

However, the British fleet, which was anchored off the entrance to the harbor when Tom wrote his letter, were certainly not anticipating a "drubbing" from the Americans—in fact just the reverse. While the bulk of the British army in America was struggling with the rebels in the north, officials in London had decided to mount a campaign to conquer the southern colonies. It would be quick and easy and success was virtually guaranteed. After all, they had been assured by the disposed royal governors of the southern colonies that the colonists in the south were basically loyal and all that was needed was for a British regiment to set foot on southern shores and the populace would rise up in support of the king.

Acting on that assumption, Sir William Howe, commander-in-chief of British forces in North America, ordered Sir Henry Clinton and a small force to sail from Boston at the end of January. Clinton was to rendezvous at Cape Fear in North Carolina with Lord Cornwallis who was sailing from Ireland with seven regiments. By May all the ships in the fleet had gathered at Cape Fear and Clinton began to make plans to launch an attack in the south.

Clinton was not sure where he wanted to strike and at first was inclined to favor the Chesapeake colonies. However, two British officers sent out on reconnaissance returned with a favorable report on the Charleston area. The Americans, they said, were in the process of building a fort on Sullivan's Island but it was not finished—only the southern wall which faced the channel and the western side were defensible. The walls on the north and east were only seven feet high. Clinton decided at that point to attack Charleston.

The British fleet arrived at the bar guarding the entrance to the harbor on June 4. Charles, who was stationed at Ft. Johnson, knew his mother would be uneasy about the situation in town and made it a point to write to her often during the coming weeks to reassure her and provide her with first-hand information. His first letter was written on June 5:

> Lest my honored mother should be alarmed by hearing exaggerated reports of the fleet off the bar, I snatch a few minutes from the duties of my station to acquaint her of the particulars of it.
>
> There are not more than fifty-two vessels altogether, many of which are very small. I do not believe there are above six or seven men-of-war and a few tenders amongst them; the rest I take to be transports—some with soldiers and some with provisions. They can not get over the bar with this wind, so that we shall have no fighting to-day. We are preparing to receive them properly when they do come over. Our men are in fine spirits and I doubt not will behave as they ought to do on the occasion.[67]

The city of Charleston had put out a call for help when it was known that a large British fleet was headed its way. As a result continental regiments from Virginia and North Carolina and experienced Indian fighters from the Carolina back country had arrived to swell the ranks of the Carolina regiments and militia gathered to defend the city—all in all a total of 6,500 men. And to lead and direct them all the Continental Congress had sent Major General Charles Lee—an intelligent, experienced and able soldier, but an eccentric with a bad temper and a habit of expressing his views with brutal candor. He was not at all impressed with the half-finished fort on Sullivan's Island, but he threw his energies into building up the defenses in the town and trying to correct some of the defects of the island fort.

On June 7 the smaller British ships and the transports carrying the soldiers had crossed the bar and sought safety by anchoring in Five Fathom Hole—a spot just inside the entrance to the harbor but out of range of the guns at Fort Sullivan. The expected attack could not take place until the large warships also crossed the bar and it seemed to the waiting Americans that the British were taking a very long time to accomplish that mission.

By June 17 when Charles wrote again to Eliza, the enemy still had not attacked, but he reported that the British had landed men on Long Island which was located north of Sullivan's Island and was separated from it by a seventy-five-foot wide inlet. If the British troops crossed the inlet onto Sullivan's Island they could attack Fort Sullivan from the rear while the war-ships battered it from the front. To confront the 2,200 British regulars now encamped on Long Island and keep them from crossing the inlet the Americans sent Lt. Colonel William Thompson, an experienced Indian fighter from the South Carolina back country, with a force of 780 militia and regulars. They threw up earthen breastworks reinforced with palmetto logs and waited for the British to make a move.

At 11:30 on the morning of June 28 the defenders at the fort on Sullivan's Island looked up to behold twenty-eight ships in full sail moving through the channel. Charles and Thomas were both on duty at Ft. Johnson and, much to their disappointment, were only spectators at the battle that took place. They watched as the enemy ships then formed two lines and a heavy cannonade began between the fort and the ships. Colonel Moultrie had thirty-one guns and a limited amount of gun powder to use against eight British men-of-war boasting a total of 260 guns. To conserve powder Moultrie ordered the cannons to be fired every ten minutes and only when a clear shot presented itself. Charles estimated that the British ships fired fifty shots for every one that came from the fort. However, the fire from the fort was deadly accurate and caused several of the British ships to run aground while others were badly damaged.

The British fired on the fort from 11:30 in the morning until 9:30 at night and yet they could not destroy it. The half-finished fort that General Lee had called "a slaughter pen" had been built of palmetto logs—a double row of the logs encircled the fort and the space between the exterior and interior walls had been filled with sand and marsh clay. Palmetto wood is soft and does not splinter. The palmetto log walls of the fort absorbed the cannon balls hurled at them and did not shatter or send lethal splinters of wood flying in all directions to lodge in the flesh of the defenders.

Clinton's plan to have his men on Long Island ford the inlet that separated that island from Sullivan's Island and attack the fort from the rear came to nothing. He had been told there was a shallow channel—only 18 inches deep at low tide—that his soldiers could easily ford to reach the island. However, after several days and nights of searching, the shallowest channel they could find was seven feet deep. When Clinton decided to have his men rowed over in shallow draught boats, they came under such intensive and accurate fire from Colonel Thompson's men entrenched behind their breastworks that they could not proceed. At nightfall, after trading shots with the Americans for most of the afternoon, Clinton withdrew his men from the inlet. And at 9:30 the British ships stopped their cannonade against the fort and drew back to the safety of Five-Fathom Hole.

To the people in town, who could see little of the battle for the clouds of smoke that drifted over the water, the silence after ten hours of bombardment was ominous—they were certain it meant that the garrison at the fort had surrendered. No fort could, in their opinion, withstand such a cannonade. Then a dispatch boat arrived bringing the news that Fort Sullivan was still standing and the British had withdrawn to Five Fathom Hole and a great cheer went up. However, no one believed it was over—surely the British would renew their attack the next day and when they did Charles and Thomas at Fort Johnson were hoping they would be part of it.

However, the dawn did not bring a new attack. The British ships remained at Five Fathom Hole. On July 7 Charles reported to Eliza at Sandy Hill:

> It is so uncertain when the Enemy will renew their attack, that it is impossible for me to form an opinion on that subject—But as the part of the Country in which you are begins to be so sickly, I think it would be the most prudent step to come to town, & if the Enemy should again attack us after you are there you will always have Notice enough to get out of Town before the Enemy can reach that place.[68]

Charles felt comfortable enough with the situation himself to take a short leave of absence from the fort to visit the Middleton plantation at Goose Creek. He wanted to see his wife, his little daughter Maria and the baby—a little girl named Harriott. Eliza, taking her son's advice, returned to town.

The British did not resume their attack. Instead sailors spent the days after the battle working to repair the damage inflicted on their ships by the Americans. When that was completed, the British then began the slow process of transferring soldiers to the waiting transports. On July 14, one by one the ships began to slip quietly away seeking safety in the broad, deep waters of the Atlantic. By August 2 the British were completely gone. The celebration in Charleston was exuberant. In the middle of the festivities an express arrived with even more joyful news—on July 2 the Continental Congress had declared the United Colonies to be free and independent states and on July 4 a Declaration of Independence, drafted by Thomas Jefferson, had been adopted.

CHAPTER FIVE

The War Years (1776–1783)

The War Begins

On August 5, 1776, the city of Charleston celebrated the signing of the Declaration of Independence with a grand parade. Men of the Carolina regiments, their officers and various civilian dignitaries led by President John Rutledge marched down Alexander Street to the Liberty Tree. There, where ten years earlier Christopher Gadsden and his associates had first met to plan their opposition to British policies, the Declaration of Independence was read out loud to the assembled crowd.

It was a joyful celebration as the majority of the townspeople, exhilarated by their recent victory over the British, viewed the prospect of independence with enthusiasm while those who had supported the king during the colony's confrontations with Great Britain prudently kept their emotions hidden and their thoughts to themselves. Although there was joy in Charleston that August day, there was also sadness. Lowcountry planters had always had strong economic and cultural ties to Great Britain and for some the separation was heartbreaking—Henry Laurens, who would later serve the American cause with distinction, confessed to a friend that he wept when he heard the Declaration of Independence read.[1]

Now that independence had been declared, South Carolinians had to decide, if they had not already done so, whether they were going to support it or not. Up to this point the choices had been relatively simple: support the colonies in their disagreements with Great Britain, side with the king and Parliament or ignore the entire matter. There was a big difference, however, between opposing British policies and declaring independence and the transition was difficult for many people to make. Charles Cotesworth and Thomas Pinckney were two South Carolinians who had no trouble making the transition as they had made their decision to support independence before the Continental

Congress had even begun a debate on the issue. It is not clear exactly when Charles made his choice, but Tom had definitely decided by May of 1776 as he wrote to Harriott and Eliza at Ashepoo on the ninth of the month: "Our Ports are now by a Resolution of the Continental Congress thrown open to all the World except the Subjects of the King of Great Britain or any Dominions belonging to the said King. A grand Step towards Independance."[2]

Charles and Thomas were not the only members of the Pinckney family to favor independence—their brother-in-law Daniel Horry and their cousin Charles Pinckney II had also declared their support for it. But what were Eliza's feelings? She had always had close personal and emotional ties to England. Did she, like Henry Laurens, view independence as a painful but necessary step or did she think the colony would live to regret its decision? Whatever her personal feelings were she did not share them with anyone. She never expressed her views on this subject one way or another in any of her letters and apparently did not try to influence her sons as they were making their decisions in the spring of 1776.

According to family tradition Eliza's granddaughter, when she asked what advice Eliza had offered her sons on the subject of independence, was told that Eliza had "given no advice and attempted no influence; for that having done her best while they were boys to make them wise and good men, she now thankfully acknowledged that they had surpassed her in wisdom as in stature."[3] Eliza was content to follow the path her sons had chosen—in fact it would have been impossible for her to have done anything else. Family unity was all important to Eliza and she would never have disrupted the family by placing herself in opposition to any course her children decided to follow. Eliza had long ago reconciled herself to the fact that the family's future lay in South Carolina not England. Therefore, because her children had done so, she embraced the American cause and was prepared to give that cause all the support she could. She had become an American, though she became one, as one historian has noted "more by chance than by choice."[4]

Eliza was fortunate that her children were united in their support for independence—it made it easier for her. Other families, however, were not as fortunate for the American Revolution was in reality a civil war which tore families apart and pitted neighbors against each other. For example, Dr. Alexander Garden, Eliza's good friend and mentor, was a staunch loyalist, but his son fought on the side of the Americans and as a result his father never spoke to him again. Eliza could take some small comfort in the fact that her brother, Captain George Lucas, had died in 1760 and her sons would not be called upon to face their uncle on the field of battle. They would, however, be called upon to face former school mates—some of whom had been good friends.

Charles and Thomas Pinckney along with Daniel Horry were all members of the elite, rice-planter class of South Carolina and they chose independence over loyalty to the king. Yet it was their class that had reaped the greatest financial benefits from being part of the British Empire and that had the closest cultural ties to the mother country. The rice planters were proud of their British heritage for they knew that British subjects enjoyed rights and privileges extended to no other people in Europe or perhaps the entire world.

On the surface it would seem this class would be the most likely to renounce independence and remain loyal to the king, yet that was not the case. Though some of the lowcountry planters did side with the British, many—like Charles, Thomas and Daniel—chose independence and many of the leaders of the American Revolution in South Carolina came from the members of this class. Why did these men turn their backs on the country they so admired and that had brought them such great prosperity and seek to establish a new country? It was a matter of respect, power and control.

In general colonists in North America felt that British authorities did not view them with the same respect with which they viewed people living in England and did not treat them the way they expected to be treated as British subjects. And nowhere was the stigma of being "a colonial" felt more keenly than in South Carolina. Charles Pinckney had certainly felt it when the king overturned his appointment as chief justice. With no thought as to whom the colonists might have preferred as chief justice or with no regard to the insult it was to Charles Pinckney, the king appointed one of his cronies in Pinckney's place for no other reason than it was politically expedient to remove the man from England. The colonists in South Carolina were made to feel inconsequential—their preferences were irrelevant and it was crown officials who chose the men to hold positions of authority in the colony and native Carolinians were seldom appointed.

Josiah Quincy, Jr., noticed the lack of control Carolinians had over the appointments of colonial officials when he visited Charleston in the early 1770s. He noted in his memoirs: "The Council, judges and other great officers are all appointed by mandamus (command) from Great Britain.... Persons disconnected with the people and obnoxious to them. I have heard several planters say, 'We none of us can expect the honours of state; they are all given away to worthless, poor sycophants.'"[5]

The lack of respect with which they were treated by the British government was a constant irritant to South Carolina planters and the passage of the Stamp Act—a direct threat to the rights they cherished as British subjects—compounded that irritation. They joined other colonists in a protest against Parliament's right to tax them for once Parliament gained the right to levy taxes on the colonists, a precedent would be set that would be impossible to reverse. Parliament could then claim the right to legislate for the colonies in other matters and representative government, the hallmark of the British political system they so admired, would be lost to them. Control would be solely in the hands of the British government and the colonists would be reduced to a subservient status—a bitter pill for wealthy rice planters to swallow.

When petitions and boycotts did not achieve the desired results, South Carolina planters along with leaders from the other colonies came to the same conclusion: if they were ever to have any control over the destiny of their respective colonies, they would have to separate from Great Britain. They would form their own government, incorporate in it everything they admired in the British political system and then adapt it to meet the specific needs of the new country. If they were going to take this step, it had to be done now for they might never have another opportunity.

Lowcountry planters were confident that they had the knowledge and experience to govern themselves, but they also knew that they would need the support of the backcountry in order to win independence. The Carolina backcountry begins fifty miles inland and stretches westward to the foothills of the Appalachian Mountains and is a land of rolling hills and lush valleys. In the 18th century indigo, wheat, hemp and tobacco were grown there for both export and domestic use. It had been settled by Scots-Irish, English, Welsh and German settlers who until now had been relatively ignored by the low-country elite. They were looked upon as second-class citizens, their needs disregarded—in fact they were treated in much the same way that British authorities treated the low-country planters.

Rice planters, anxious to maintain their majority in the Commons House, limited the number of representatives allotted to the inhabitants of the backcountry. Even in 1775 when the Provincial Congress was established and the backcountry was allowed more representation, it was still pitifully inadequate—60 percent of the white population of South Carolina lived in the backcountry and the backcountry held only 30 percent of the seats.[6] It is not surprising then, that when patriot leaders came into this area looking to win support for their protests against Parliament, they were not only greeted with little enthusiasm but also in some cases with outright hostility.

Backcountry planters were divided in their points of view. There were some who thought the confrontations with Great Britain were strictly a low-country problem and of no concern to them while others supported the protests against Great Britain. However, many of the backcountry planters, angry at the treatment doled out to them by the low-country elite, saw the patriot leaders in Charleston as more of a problem than the king and Parliament. On the other hand new settlers, especially those from Germany, were grateful to the British crown for making it possible for them to own land and they had no problem with the king or with the patriots in Charleston. They just wanted to be left alone to build a better life for themselves and their children.

In the fall of 1775, before independence was even an issue, 1,600 men calling themselves "the king's friends" staged an uprising in the backcountry. Hoping to prevent the colony from arming itself against a possible British attack, they seized gunpowder and a large amount of lead from a patriot supply train. The patriots retaliated and in a series of skirmishes were able to put down the uprising. Charleston leaders then allied themselves with prominent back-country planters and began a campaign to convince people to support the American cause.

In the early summer of 1776 just as the British were about to attack Charleston, the Cherokee began a series of devastating attacks on the southern frontier from Virginia to Georgia with settlements in Carolina receiving the brunt of the first attacks. The entire backcountry, regardless of political opinion, united against the common threat. The militia mounted a determined and efficient ninety-day campaign during which the Cherokee were thoroughly defeated and forced to abandon their lands east of the Appalachians. Among the prisoners taken in the campaign were Tories, British sympathizers, disguised as Indians. Nothing more was needed to convince settlers in the backcountry that the British had deliberately incited the Cherokee to attack on the frontier while the colonists were occupied with the British on the coast. Whether this was true or not, the presence of Tories among the Indians dealt a damaging blow to the loyalist cause and provided great propaganda for the Americans.

With the defeat of the Cherokee in October of 1776, peace came to South Carolina. Loyalists had been subdued or forced into exile and Patriots had the state of South Carolina firmly under their control. The fighting in the War for Independence was taking place in the north and the only sign of the conflict in the south was the British blockade of the harbor in Charleston. However, since skilled captains were able to evade the British and bring their ships safely into port, the blockade presented few hardships to the inhabitants of the city. Now that trade was open to any country except Great Britain and her colonies, ships from France, the Netherlands and New England rode at anchor in the harbor waiting to be loaded with goods. As the Cherokee were no longer a threat on the frontier, new settlers streamed into the backcountry and prosperity reigned across the land.

Elections were held in September for the new General Assembly—Charles Cotesworth was re-elected—and one of the first actions of the new legislative body was to pass a resolution incorporating the Carolina regiments into the

Continental Army. Charles and Thomas were now officers in the 1st South Carolina Regiment, Continental Line. Thomas remained a captain, but Charles had been rapidly promoted and was now a Lt. Colonel and second in command of the regiment under the leadership of Christopher Gadsden, the commanding officer. The 1st Carolina Regiment was stationed at Fort Sullivan now renamed Fort Moultrie.

After the excitement of the past few months, Eliza was thankful to be able to resume her usual activities. She had little Daniel with her on a regular basis now. He had turned seven in August of 1776 and it was time for his formal education to begin. As there was no question of sending the child back to England to attend school, the next best thing was for him to study with a tutor in Charleston. It is possible that at this time Daniel came to live with Eliza in town and began to work with Mr. Moreau. He was certainly one of Mr. Moreau's students by 1778.

By the age of seven Daniel would have been expected to have mastered the rudiments of education and it is quite likely that it was Eliza who had provided him with these basics. After Harriott's marriage, Eliza was alone for the first time in her life and although she kept busy with her many projects she missed the companionship of her daughter. Having her first grandchild come to stay with her and teaching him his letters and numbers filled a void in Eliza's life and Daniel's parents, recognizing her skills as a teacher and her need for companionship and activity were happy to leave their son in her care for extended visits. Daniel loved being at Belmont and always regretted having to leave for town. He had his pets in the country—his puppies and possums—he liked to watch the fields being plowed and the cows in their pens and Eliza who had not been able to watch her own sons grow-up cherished every minute she spent with him.

In April of 1777 Eliza went with Thomas to visit his plantation at Ashepoo. Thomas would have wanted to consult with his overseer on this year's crops and to check on the progress of the improvements being made to the house. Eliza, having laid out a garden there the year before, would be anxious to see how it was progressing and to make changes to it. It is possible that at this time Eliza and Tom brought family valuables—items the family wanted to preserve such as Charles Pinckney's papers and books—with them to store at Ashepoo. Although the war was far away in the north, no one in South Carolina was foolish enough to think that the British would not return to the south. Since the capture of Charleston would be their prime objective, the family thought that Ashepoo would be the best place to keep the family valuables safe.

In June the people of Charleston were excited by the arrival of distinguished visitors from Europe—the Marquis de Lafayette, the German-born Baron de

Kalb and eleven French officers. The Marquis and his party had come ashore at Benjamin Huger's plantation on Winyah Bay near Georgetown as they had not wanted to risk running the British blockade of the Charleston harbor. Major Huger then escorted them to Charleston where they were entertained at a dinner given by the officers at Fort Moultrie followed by another dinner hosted by Christopher Gadsden. Charles and Thomas who both spoke fluent French and had attended the military academy in Caen were present at both dinners and no doubt enjoyed talking with the French officers.

At the end of June Lafayette and his entourage were escorted north to General Washington's headquarters where they were planning to offer their services in America's war with Great Britain. A few weeks after they departed, Charles Cotesworth decided to follow their example. All the fighting was taking place in the north and Charles wanted to improve his military knowledge by observing the war firsthand. He received leave from his commanding officer and with letters of introduction to Washington from Henry Middleton, his father-in-law, and Thomas Lynch, Jr., a signer of the Declaration of Independence, Charles traveled north. He was received by General Washington at his headquarters on August 19 and welcomed into the General's military family. There he had the opportunity to become better acquainted with Lafayette and also to become friends with Alexander Hamilton, an aide to Washington, and young John Laurens, son of Henry Laurens, who at that time was an unofficial aide to the General.

There was a joyful celebration in Charleston that fall when news of the American victory at Saratoga reached town. On October 17 British General John Burgoyne had been forced to surrender his entire army to General Horatio Gates. Charles had stayed with Washington's army until October 15 when he left for Yorktown, Pennsylvania where the Continental Congress was in session. He wanted to visit Henry Laurens, one of the delegates from South Carolina, and observe the meetings of the Congress. It was while he was there that he learned of the great American victory at Saratoga. He left Yorktown soon after and returned home arriving at Fort Moultrie by December 4, 1777.

While he was with Washington's army Charles had witnessed the Battles of Brandywine and Germantown and had observed first-hand the noise and confusion of battle. He had gained much valuable military knowledge and he had come away with a tremendous respect for George Washington—a leader he felt he would be willing follow the rest of his life. When he returned home he discovered that during his absence Christopher Gadsden had resigned his command of the regiment. Charles Cotesworth Pinckney found himself the commanding officer of the 1st South Carolina Regiment of the Continental Army.

The General Assembly had recently met to write a new constitution to replace the temporary one passed two years before and one of the changes made to the new, independent government of South Carolina involved the upper house of the legislature—it was now called the senate instead of the legislative council. And when new elections were held in the fall, members of the Pinckney family were to be found in both houses of the General Assembly. Daniel Horry and Charles Pinckney II were both members of the new upper house and in the lower house were Charles Cotesworth, who had been re-elected to his former seat, Thomas Pinckney who was holding his first elected office and Charles Pinckney III, son of Charles Pinckney II, just turned twenty-one and also holding his first elected office.

Under the new constitution all male inhabitants over the age of sixteen were required to swear an oath of allegiance to the state of South Carolina promising to defend it from the armies of King George III. Loyalists who were unwilling to take the oath had sixty days in which to leave the state and many of them did just that making their way back to England or removing to Canada or one of the island colonies. Some of the king's supporters, however, went to the British at St. Augustine. Once there they formed into militia units under the command of Governor Tonyn and began to conduct raids into Georgia and South Carolina.

In Georgia the situation was becoming alarming. In the early spring groups of loyalists from the Carolina backcountry began to move through Georgia making their way south to join British forces in Florida. The groups traveled light and raided near-by farms for provisions and supplies causing havoc in the countryside. The large number of loyalists and the constant menace of raiding parties from Florida were seriously threatening the stability of the state. To combat these threats Governor Houston had only a weak, undisciplined militia and the help of a small force of continental soldiers under the command of General Howe in Savannah

Governor Houston and General Howe were both agreed that it was imperative to eliminate Florida as a British base from which to attack Georgia and South Carolina. They decided to mount a campaign to capture Fort Tonyn just over the border on the St. Mary's River and then continue on to St. Augustine. General Howe wrote to General Moultrie in Charleston requesting assistance in the forthcoming expedition into Florida and on April 19 the 1st South Carolina Regiment commanded by Colonel Charles Cotesworth Pinckney marched out of town.

Eliza, remembering all the miseries of the St. Augustine expedition led by General Oglethorpe in 1740, confessed to Harriott: "I take all the pains I can to support an equal mind, but I find it impossible not to be anxious about this

Augustine expedition, having so much at stake as I have."[7] While concern for the welfare of Charles and Thomas occupied her thoughts, she had other matters that needed her attention—the property belonging to her sons. Someone had to look after it during their absence and who better to perform this service than the person who had managed it so well while the boys were growing up? Eliza's immediate concern at this time was the condition of the slaves at the Beech Hill plantation belonging to Charles. An epidemic of some sort was spreading through the countryside and had affected a number of the slaves on his plantation. She was extremely anxious about their well-being as she wrote to Harriott:

> I have been busey fryday and Saturday, collecting, packing, and dispatching, some necessaries for your poor brothers, The boat with them is gone; and I have had a messenger every day upon the road between Beach Hill and Charles Town for several days; I am afraid they have the same distemper there that they hade at Mr. Lynche's; We lost George and Phebe in a few day's, and before I heard they were sick; Abram and little Toby lay at the point of Death on Saturday, some more down; I expect to hear from thence this morning, I ordered and they had a Doctor to Toby and Abram.... Pray God put a stop to this raging disease!
>
> If I had had a horse to carry me I should have gone to Beach hill my self (tho' I dont imagine I could have done much good)

Eliza soon had her own slaves to worry about as she continued:

> Sibby has been extremely ill with a Rheumatic fever which did not go off for 5 days though she was blistered. I had her in the house and she has been well nursed tho' is still very weak. little Dick has been extremely ill; I was afraid we should have lost him also. I believe taking him in the house and good nursing was a means of saving him also, so you may pretty well judge what a time I have had in your Absence.[8]

Eliza eagerly followed the progress of the expedition to the south reading and re-reading the letters she received from Charles before passing them on to her daughter-in-law and daughter. Edward Rutledge, knowing how much Eliza appreciated any news of the progress of the army, called on her in early June to share a letter he had just received from Charles. General Howe's army had reached the Altamaha River on the 9th of May where they had set up camp to await the arrival of the supply boats. Charles's letter was dated May 27 and he reported that, in spite of the fact that their provisions and other supplies had not yet arrived, General Howe had decided to cross the river and that they were now on the other side and "upon the March." "Your brother," Eliza confided in a letter to Harriott, "thinks that an Army grows sickly by long encampments, and that it is for the health of the people to keep them in motion."[9]

After crossing the river Howe's forces encamped at Reid's Bluff to await the arrival of the militia from Georgia led by Governor Houston and Colonel Williamson's South Carolina militia. The supply boats had still not arrived and the army was short of many essentials—kettles for cooking, canteens, medicines and tents. The lack of canteens meant that many of the soldiers had nothing to drink during the long march to Reid's Bluff and those who did not have tents were forced to make bowers from the branches of trees and palmetto fronds which provided shelter from the sun, but were not waterproof. The country was low, swampy and full of mosquitoes and the lack of adequate shelter, food and water took its toll on the soldiers. Charles Cotesworth succumbed to a bout of sickness but soon recovered while Eliza sent Tom two containers of bitters which was thought to prevent chills and fever.

Tom was an excellent correspondent writing frequently to both his mother and sister. He tried to keep his letters positive and made it a point to describe the hardships of the campaign in a light-hearted manner. However, even in the midst of the difficulties of the expedition Tom rarely forgot to mention in letters to his sister the subject that was foremost in his mind: his "charmer." Towards the end of May just before the army crossed the Altamaha River Tom wrote to Harriott:

> I am still hopeful that before the sickly Season comes on we shall be in the neighbourhood of Augustine which lying on the Sea must be a more healthful Situation than the interior parts of the Country. As our Absence from Carolina will probably be much longer than we at first expected I am afraid my Charmer will be run away with by some of the gay Sparks left behind, as her Attractions both with respect to the Accomplishments of her Mind and the Graces of her Person must daily increase. I imagine she has passed some Time with you before now and expect a long Account from you very soon.[10]

Tom's "charmer" was Elizabeth (Betsey) Motte, the oldest daughter of Jacob and Rebecca Brewton Motte of Fairfield plantation in Santee. The Mottes were neighbors and friends of the Horry family. Tom had frequently referred to Betsey, "his charmer," in letters to his sister before the expedition began and in April had even requested: "If Chance should throw my Charmer in your way I charge you to make strong Love for me."[11]

By June 21 the army was within a two-day march of crossing into East Florida when General Howe learned from captured British dispatches that General Prevost was not marching north towards Georgia as rumor had implied and furthermore, that he had ordered the garrison at Ft. Tonyn to evacuate. Hoping to catch the soldiers at the fort before they retreated, Howe crossed into Florida on the 28th and prepared to attack the fort. At that point Governor Houston arrived with his Georgia militia and immediately entered into an argument with Howe over who should command the assault on the fort. Houston seemed to think he should be in charge, but Howe, who had been appointed the Commander of the Southern Department by the Continental Congress, would not relinquish his post. Governor Houston then departed with his militia to undertake his own independent action against the British.

By the time the Continental forces arrived at Ft. Tonyn it was deserted and in ruins. General Howe and his officers then took stock of their situation. The army was not up to full strength as half the men had been lost to sickness and disease and the lack of grain and pasture for the horses—the British had previously driven a large herd of cattle through the area—had caused the deaths of so many of them that there were now not enough horses to pull all the supply and artillery wagons. In their present circumstances it would be impossible for the army to continue south to pursue the British. They had accomplished one of their major goals—their presence had forced the British to evacuate and destroy Ft. Tonyn. They decided they could in good conscience return home. By the end of July Colonel Charles Pinckney and his brother Major Thomas Pinckney (he had been promoted during the expedition) returned to Charleston thinner than when they had departed but in good health.

Eliza was greatly relieved when the St. Augustine expedition was over and her sons returned home. She was prone to worry, especially where her family was concerned, and in addition to having been anxious for her sons she was also anxious about her daughter who was expecting her second child in the fall. She was not content until Harriott came to town at the beginning of June to avoid the "sickly season" in the country. Consequently, both Eliza and Harriott were in Charleston to welcome home the soldiers of the 1st South Carolina Regiment at the end of July.

After she satisfied herself that neither of her sons had sustained any lasting harm from the expedition, Eliza settled down to await the birth of her fourth grandchild. The baby, a little girl named Harriott, was born on October 4, 1778, in Charleston. Tom was disappointed not to be present at her birth. He was riding the circuit defending clients in Orangeburg when his little niece was born. "If you could by any Means contrive to remain in Town with my little Harriott 'till I return from Circuit," he wrote to his sister, "I think we might make an agreeable Journey to Santee all together ... at all Events do not forget in Case of a Christening to procure a Proxy for me."[12]

Meanwhile events were taking place in other parts of the world that would affect Eliza, her family and everyone who lived in South Carolina. In May 1778 while Charles and Thomas were taking part in the St. Augustine expedition, the Continental Congress had ratified a treaty of alliance with France. The French, who were already supplying Britain's rebellious colonies with weapons and money, had been following the progress of the war very closely waiting for a sign that the Americans were capable of facing the British on the field of battle. The impressive American victory at Saratoga was the sign they had been waiting for—France declared war on Great Britain and signed a treaty of alliance and trade with the United States.

The French declaration of war was disturbing news to the British—the French were a traditional enemy located just across the English Channel and posed a serious threat. While there was no fear that the Americans would invade the homeland, attack the valuable sugar islands in the West Indies or threaten British possessions in India, Africa and the Mediterranean, there was a very good chance that the French would do so. The War for America had suddenly metamorphosed into a global conflict with more at stake than the possibility of losing thirteen North American colonies.

In an attempt to end the war in America and free up the army and fleet to defend British territory in other parts of the world, the British sent commissioners to the Continental Congress to offer terms of reconciliation—the colonies would be given dominion status but still be dependent colonies. Ironically, if that offer had been made three years earlier it would have had a good chance of being accepted—but now it was too late. The Americans wanted the British to withdraw their troops and ships from the area and recognize the independence of the United States—an unacceptable alternative for the British.

The British were in a quandary—they had a tough decision to make. What was more important to them: the thirteen American colonies or their possessions in the rest of the world? There was a strong feeling in London that Canada and Florida should be defended for, as recent acquisitions, they were essential to British prestige and the southern colonies with their rich crops of rice, indigo and tobacco were also worth keeping. The northern colonies, however, were a different matter—they were expendable. The war in the north was bogged down and at an impasse—it was time to move the military action to the south. The Southern Campaign was about to begin.

The Southern Campaign

British officials in London predicated their strategy for the southern campaign on the assumption that legions of loyalists would flock to the king's banner as soon as British troops landed on their shores—indeed, loyalist support was fundamental to the success of the "southern strategy." The plan was to "roll-up the south" by first conquering Georgia, re-establishing it as a royal colony and turning it over to loyalist forces to govern and control. The same procedure would then be followed in the Carolinas and Virginia. American loyalists along with token British forces would then hold the south for Great Britain freeing up soldiers to fight in other parts of the world.

With the plan in place, the British set about to implement it. On November 27 a force of 3,500 British soldiers set sail from New York for the coastal city of Savannah. At the same time Major General Augustine Prevost and his troops began marching north from St. Augustine. Upon receiving word of Prevost's advance towards Georgia, General Howe, who had only a small force of continental soldiers under his command, quickly sent off an express to General Moultrie in Charleston requesting that he send the South Carolina regiments to his aid as quickly as possible.

Although Moultrie was able to send some units south to Howe immediately, the bulk of the army did not march for several weeks. General Benjamin Lincoln, who was replacing Howe as Commander of the Southern Department, had only arrived in Charleston on December 6 and needed time to settle in to his new command. He also wanted to wait for the arrival of continental soldiers from North Carolina before moving out. Therefore, it was not until December 27 that the American force numbering 1,200 men was ready to march.

Eliza was still in Charleston with Daniel at the end of December when the Carolina regiments left for Georgia. She had intended to go to Hampton before that time and her continued absence was causing her daughter a great deal of uneasiness. Harriott, imagining that her mother was detained in town because she, Daniel or one of Harriott's brothers were ill, sent a hasty note to her wanting to know the reason for "her dear Mama's" delay. Harriott was alone at Hampton with her baby and the enslaved servants—her husband was with the army, her Horry relations had left after spending Christmas with her and even the weaver and overseer were absent. She was anxious and had fallen prey to fears fueled by rumors that spread like wild fire through the countryside.

"I have heard various reports," she wrote her mother, "the last of which was that all the first regiment were gone to Georgia! I had heard before, that there were an hundred sail of Vessels within the Bar, then that there were but forty, and that those had never been within forty leagues of it, and that the fleet had gone to Georgia, where also Generals Lincoln and Moultrie were gone."[13] Fortunately, Eliza and little Daniel arrived at Hampton by the beginning of January and Eliza was able to give Harriott more accurate information.

However, the news from the south was disappointing. General Lincoln, who had marched to Savannah to join forces with Howe and check Prevost progress into Georgia, arrived to find the British in control of the city and what was left of Howe's army on the South Carolina side of the Savannah River. The British fleet from New York had reached the mouth of the Savannah River the same day that Lincoln and his army had left Charleston and the British had lost no time in landing troops and launching an attack on Howe's forces in town.

It was an unequal battle. Howe's continentals were quickly overwhelmed and driven through the streets of Savannah and although he managed to bring a portion of his army across the Savannah River into South Carolina, Howe's losses were heavy: 550 men plus most of his artillery and supplies. When Lincoln arrived all he could do was join forces with what was left of Howe's command and establish an encampment in Purrysburg, a little town in Jasper County on the South Carolina side of the river. Charles Cotesworth and Thomas, who came south expecting to give the British "a good drubbing," could only look with frustration across the river to the city of Savannah now firmly in the hands of the enemy.

There was little at this point for the army to do but watch and wait; consequently, Charles and Thomas had ample time to keep their mother and sister well informed of the situation in camp and the frustration they felt at not being able to engage the enemy. Since there was little action taking place, Eliza thought her sons, both members of the legislature, should attend the sessions of the General Assembly which was meeting that January in Charleston and had written urging them to return to town.

In some amusement Tom wrote to his sister in early January: "My Mother must have strange notions of the Duty of a Soldier when she imagines that we could leave Camp to attend the House of Assembly, when nothing but the River Savannah parts us from the Enemy."[14] However, Eliza's wishes were to be partially gratified for in February General Lincoln did send two of his top officers, William Moultrie and Charles Cotesworth, back to Charleston to attend the legislative assembly—the general hoping that the two men would be able to persuade the legislators to strengthen the terms of enlistment for the militia.

Eliza always liked to be well-informed and was fortunate in having a wide circle of friends and acquaintances to supply her with the latest news. One of her most valuable sources of information at this time was her nephew Charles Pinckney II who, as president of the senate, was always up-to-date on the latest happenings. When the South Carolina regiments marched off to Georgia, Eliza had made her nephew promise that he would send her all the news he thought worthy of her notice. The result was a very long letter in February in which he described the situation in Charleston:

> There is almost a total stagnation of every kind of business; and we daily expect a Proclamation from the Governor and Council for stopping the Courts of Justice and prohibiting all commercial proceedings whatsoever until the removal of the enemy from Georgia.... Our town, once the seat of pleasure and amusement, is now dull and insipid; a sameness prevails through everything.[15]

Knowing that the ladies at Hampton would be very interested in hearing the latest news with regard to Daniel Horry, Charles was happy to inform them that Daniel, a consummate horseman, had been elected colonel of a regiment of light cavalry that had been recently established.

The news from Georgia was not as good, however. Within ten days of taking Savannah the British had all of coastal Georgia under their control. They then marched north up the Savannah River and occupied Augusta and by the end of the month were in command of the outlying areas of the state. When American forces under General Ashe tried to drive the British from Augusta, they suffered a devastating defeat—the Americans losing a quarter of their army in the attempt plus a large quantity of arms and ammunition. However, Charles assured his aunt "that our officers pledge themselves, that they will, with the assistance of only a small part of our militia, free Georgia from the present invasion."[16]

Charles was a little too optimistic. General Lincoln did not have a force strong enough to oust the British from Georgia, all he could do was to prevent them from connecting with the Indians on the frontier and try to interrupt their flow of provisions from the backcountry. Leaving Moultrie and a small unit of continental soldiers plus 1,000 militia at Black Swamp, twenty-five miles up-river from Purrysburg, Lincoln marched north to cross the Savannah River and place his forces in a favorable position to disrupt British activities in the area. However, Georgia, for all practical purposes, was a royal colony once again and it would remain so until 1782.

The British, having secured Georgia, were anxious to move on to South Carolina. On April 30 General Moultrie was greatly alarmed to discover that General Prevost with 2,000 men had crossed the Savannah River into South Carolina undoubtedly with the capture of Charleston as his goal. Moultrie could not stop the British from advancing with the force he had at his disposal and so sent an urgent message to Lincoln to send him 1,000 continental soldiers. With this addition to his force, he was confident he could prevent the British from reaching Charleston. Unfortunately, Lincoln and his officers thought Prevost's march was a diversion to lure the patriots away from Georgia and Moultrie's request was denied.

The hard-pressed Moultrie began to retreat towards Charleston ordering his men to burn bridges and ferries along the way to slow the British advance. He sent frantic messages to Charles Pinckney II in Charleston to shore up the town's defenses and throw up breast works across Charleston Neck to block the land approach to town. His force made up of mostly militia began to slowly dwindle as the men whose homes lay in Prevost's path slipped quietly away to see to their families and property. For as Prevost and his men pushed north, they burned and plundered every plantation in their path carrying off able-bodied slaves to be sold later in the West Indies.

News of the British advance up the Carolina coast spread quickly through the lowcountry and people began to seek refuge wherever possible. Judging that Hampton was far enough away from Charleston to be safe, Harriott gathered friends and members of the family together at the Horry plantation. Besides Harriott, her two children and Eliza, Charles's wife Sally, who was expecting a baby in September, her two daughters, her two sisters, her sister-in-law and her step-mother were also there along with several other women whose husbands were away in service to their country.

Prevost continued his drive all the way to Charleston Neck and was within one mile of town by the middle of May when he received news that General Lincoln, who had finally realized the threat to Charleston was real and not a diversion, was making all possible speed to Charleston. Not wanting to be caught between Moultrie's defenders in town and Lincoln's approaching army Prevost decided to withdraw south of Charleston near Stono's Ferry.

The people of the lowcountry had just been introduced to the realities of war with all its brutality and wanton destruction—something they had not experienced before. Some who had been lukewarm about the patriot cause or had even supported the loyalists were turned into ardent patriots after witnessing the devastation of Prevost's march to Charleston. But there were others who continued to support the British even joining their ranks, betraying their patriot neighbors and friends and helping to destroy their property. It was an ominous portent of what was to come.

Eliza was at Hampton when she received news of the damage done by the British to her plantation at Belmont. While the troops did not destroy the brick house, they looted the inside demolishing everything they could not carry away—the china, crystal, paintings, books and furniture. The animals not immediately used for food were slaughtered and all the horses and provisions were seized. Belmont, the place that held so many memories for Eliza, where she and Charles had begun their married life together was in ruins. Neither Eliza nor any other member of the Pinckney family would ever live there again.

As devastating as this news was for Eliza, there was even worse to come. Tom's house at Ashepoo, where all the papers and books belonging to Charles Pinckney along with other family valuables were stored, had been completely destroyed. Tom wrote his mother this description of Ashepoo in May:

> A North Carolina soldier was 5 Days sick at my House at Ashepoo & was there when the enemy came there; he reports that they took with them 19 Negroes among whom were Betty, Prince, Chance & all the hardy Boys but left the women with Child or young children and about 5 fellows who are now perfectly free & live upon the best produce of the plantation. They took with them all the Horses they could find, burnt the dwelling House & books, destroyed all the Furniture, China, etc., killed the Sheep & Poultry and drank the Liquors. The Overseer concealed himself in the swamp & afterward returned; I hope he will be able to keep the remaining property in some Order.[17]

Eliza was more upset over Thomas's loss than her own. She wrote to him:

I have just received yours with the account of my loses and your almost ruined fortunes by the Enemy, a severe blow! but I feel not for my self, but for you; 'tis for your loses, my greatly beloved child, I grieve; the loss of fortune would affect me little but that it will deprive my dear children of my Assistance, when they may stand most in need of it. One happiness however I have ever enjoyed, that of being free from Avarice, which will lighten the present evil with regard to my self, and a very little, at my time of life will be sufficient; I can want but little, nor that little long.

Your brother's truly generous offer to devide what remains to him among us, is worthy of him. I am greatly affected with, but not surprised at his liberality. I know his disinterestedness [unselfishness] his sensibility and affection.

You say I must be sensible you cant agree to this offer, indeed, my dear Tom, I am very sensible of it, nor can I take a penny from his young helpless family. Independence is all I wish, and a little will make us that, Dont grieve for me my child, as I do assure you I do not for my self, while I have such children as I have, dare I think my lot hard. God forbid![18]

With the arrival of Lincoln's army in May military action in Charleston came to a standstill. And on June 18 when Eliza received a report on the situation from her nephew, things were still "at a Stand." The British, he told her, had entrenched themselves on John's Island and at Stono's Ferry on the mainland and appeared to be waiting for reinforcements. Since the British commanded inland navigation between Carolina and Georgia and had the sea open to them, the Americans could not possibly prevent reinforcements from arriving. They could only hope, he wrote, that the reinforcements would not come.

That hope was fulfilled for no additional British troops arrived, instead, taking one regiment with him, Prevost returned to Savannah. When he realized that the British force at Stono's Ferry had been reduced, General Lincoln decided to attack. Tom Pinckney must have felt a little thrill of excitement as he rode south in the wee hours of the morning of June 20 with the 1st South Carolina Regiment. He was second in command of the 2nd Battalion of Light Infantry and this would be his first military engagement. Facing the continentals was the 71st Regiment, a crack British unit known as the "Highlanders" and one of its officers was Captain Charles Barrington McKenzie, an old friend of Tom's from his school days at Westminster.

Tom's first venture into battle was a personal success as he was commended for bravery and daring during the first stage of the action, but, unfortunately for the Americans, although they fought with great courage, their losses were heavy and they were forced to retreat leaving the field to the British. However, by June 24 Colonel Maitland, the British commander, seeing that the patriots were about to cut off his communications on the Stono River decided it was time to leave.

The British moved south by way of the sea islands that guard the southern coast of South Carolina all the while shadowed by Colonel Horry and his cavalry.

At the beginning of July Horry was able to report to General Lincoln that the British were occupying Port Royal Island near the town of Beaufort. Charles Pinckney and the 1st Regiment were sent south to keep an eye on the British who, it was thought, might be planning to launch a new campaign against Charleston from that area.

However, by the middle of July, Lincoln and Moultrie both agreed that it appeared the British were content just to hold Port Royal with its large, natural harbor for the time being. And since the General Assembly was meeting in Charleston and there were important military issues to be voted on, General Lincoln requested that all officers who were members of the legislature and who could be spared from their military duties return to Charleston. Eliza would have been pleased that both her sons were able to attend to their legislative duties at that time.

While Tom was in Charleston he decided to take care of some personal business. He had long admired Betsey Motte and though his military duties had kept him from spending much time with her, he had told her of his feelings and ascertained that they were reciprocated. It was not an auspicious time to marry, but Tom had no idea when he would be able to get leave to come to Charleston again. Mr. and Mrs. Motte gave their enthusiastic approval and the young couple were married on July 22, 1779. Betsey was one month short of her seventeenth birthday and Tom was twenty-eight.

Eliza was delighted. The Mottes, like the Middletons, had been good friends for many years. It had been Betsey's grandparents who had invited Eliza to bring her husband to their home at Mt. Pleasant to recover from the "country fever." It was where he had died. Eliza, who had married well while marrying for love, was pleased that her children had been able to follow her example.

The Carolina countryside was quiet during the remainder of the summer—the inhabitants and soldiers, both British and American, being content to relax and conserve their energy during the long, hot days of August. The British were miles away from Charleston on Port Royal Island or back in Georgia for the moment, but everyone knew that as soon as the excessive heat of summer was over they would return to try to take the capital. The best way to avoid another British attack on Charleston would be to drive the British from Savannah. But how was this to be accomplished?

The state of South Carolina had tried to entice more men to join the Continental Army by offering a huge bonus to new recruits, but the bonuses had not brought in the desired number of men. They had been somewhat more successful in their efforts to raise money to finance the war. That summer the state initiated a campaign to sell war bonds and to make the bonds more attractive were offering 10 percent interest.[19] Many people took advantage of the offer and bought the bonds—Eliza Lucas Pinckney was one of them. In the fall of 1779 she made a significant personal contribution to the War for Independence by investing £4,000 in South Carolina bonds.[20]

However, these efforts were not enough. Even if the ranks of the six South Carolina regiments were filled, the number of fighting men would only total 5,000—hardly enough to expel the British from Georgia. State officials then devised another plan: to enlist the aid of the French fleet now operating in the West Indies. In the summer of 1779 Governor Rutledge, General Lincoln and Monsieur Plombard, the French consul in Charleston, sent a proposal to Comte d'Estaing, the Commander of the French Fleet in the West Indies. It was proposed that Comte d'Estaing and his fleet take a short respite from cruising in the Caribbean during the dangerous hurricane season and join with American forces in a cooperative effort to re-take Savannah.

The Comte, flush from victories against the British in the West Indies, was agreeable to the proposal and in early September he sent his adjutant general, Vicompte de Fontages, to Charleston aboard the frigate *Amazone* to confer with General Lincoln. When the two men had completed the plans for the joint attack on Savannah, the Vicompte relayed an urgent request from Comte d'Estaing. The Comte asked that some American officers who spoke fluent French be assigned to him to act as liaison officers—Major Thomas Pinckney and two others were selected. They boarded the *Amazone* commanded by Compte de la Pérouse and two days later joined d'Estaing on board his flagship the *Languedoc*, lying off the southern coast of South Carolina.

As the *Languedoc* sailed down the coast past Port Royal Island, Tom informed Comte d'Estaing that Colonel Maitland "with a considerable part of the British force was stationed at that place" and made the Comte "aware of the advantages which would result from preventing his junction with the main body at Savannah."[21] Unfortunately d'Estaing took little notice of Tom's advice.

The fleet continued south to the coast of Georgia and just before reaching Tybee Island the *Amazone* captured a small British sloop commanded by Captain Thomas McKenzie. During the conversation between La Pérouse and McKenzie it was mentioned that Thomas Pinckney was one of the American liaison officers with the French fleet. All military and naval officers at that time were considered to be gentlemen and when taken prisoner by the enemy were treated with the formal courtesy one gentleman always extended to another. Therefore, when McKenzie was captured by the French, La Pérouse asked him what services the French could offer him to make him comfortable. He replied: "Let me have the pleasure of receiving the comforts I stand in need of from Thomas Pinckney; let him know what my wishes are and he will not fail to have them fully gratified."[22]

Thomas McKenzie and his brother Captain Charles McKenzie of the 71st Regiment had been friends with Tom when they were all in school together at Westminster and Captain McKenzie was sure Tom would not forget an old schoolmate even though they were fighting on opposite sides. He was quite correct—Tom took great care to see that his friend was provided with everything he needed to be comfortable. Centuries before Aesop wrote that "no act of kindness, no matter how small, is ever wasted" and Tom would find that his kindness to Captain McKenzie would later be repaid a hundred times over.

The French fleet arrived off the Georgia coast on September 11 and began to disembark soldiers 15 miles south of Savannah. By the 16th of the month 3,000 troops were encamped in front of the British held city. Comte d'Estaing, not waiting for General Lincoln to arrive, arrogantly demanded the surrender of the British in the name of the king of France. He made no mention of the Americans although it had been agreed beforehand that this was to be a joint venture. General Prevost asked for twenty-four hours to consider what terms he would ask if he decided to accept the French demand.

The British request was granted by the French—d'Estaing being certain Prevost would surrender—but it was a huge mistake. Prevost did not want twenty-four hours to consider terms, he wanted a delay to give Colonel Maitland and his men time to march the forty miles from Port Royal to Savannah. By the time the twenty-four hours were over Maitland had arrived and Prevost then sent a message of defiance to the French instead of the expected surrender.

General Lincoln arrived the next day, September 17, with 1,500 men and was visibly dismayed to learn that the French had demanded a surrender before his arrival and that the surrender had been issued in the name of the French king only. The matter was eventually smoothed over and the joint effort continued, but the good feeling that had existed between the two sides was noticeably diminished. The French and Americans then set up camp on September 23 about one mile from the enemy lines. Tom, irritated that d'Estaing had not heeded his advice concerning the British force at Port Royal, was happy to be allowed to return to his own regiment at this time.

Ten days had now elapsed since the demand for surrender had been made and the British had used the time to build up their defenses which were formidable. The only way to take the town now would be by siege—a slow but effective method of taking a heavily fortified position. Savannah was completely surrounded. The French fleet was blockading the harbor preventing access to the town by water while the allied troops were guarding the land approaches.

Siege warfare required much patience. In order to safely move men and artillery close enough to the enemy's fortifications to assault their defenses, the attacking army had to dig a series of trenches. The trenches were known as parallels as they were essentially dug parallel to the defenders' lines and contained batteries in which cannon were mounted to bombard the enemy. The first parallel was generally started anywhere from 600 to 1,000 yards from the defenders' lines. When it was completed and the guns mounted and the shelling of the enemy had commenced, soldiers started digging approach tunnels, known as saps, pushing out from the front of the parallel towards the enemy's fortifications. Saps were dug in a zigzag pattern to give the men working in them as much protection from enemy fire as possible—an approach trench dug directly at the defenders' position would allow a clear shot down the trench. When the sap had reached a point approximately 300 to 500 yards from the defenders' lines, a second parallel was begun. After it was completed, men and artillery were then brought up and the bombardment of the enemy was continued at a closer range.

Typically only three parallels were needed. If the enemy did not surrender after the besieger's guns had battered the town or fortress from the third parallel, then the besieger had to make a direct assault on the defenders. In general, most besieged sites surrendered before that happened. Sometimes, though, the attacking army might decide to "raise the siege" and attack early—especially if food or ammunition were in short supply or if a relieving force was known to be nearby.

The French and Americans began to dig their first parallel trenches at the end of September and by October 4 were ready to position their guns and begin a heavy bombardment of the town. The allied forces then began to push the sap forward from the first parallel. Work on the sap continued until October 8 when the officers of the French fleet became impatient and urged d'Estaing to lift the siege. The French had only expected to spend a short amount of time on this expedition and they had already been in Georgia over a month. The hurricane season was coming to an end and d'Estaing's officers were anxious to return to the West Indies. D'Estaing decided to lift the siege and informed General Lincoln "that he must withdraw his force but to prove his desire to serve the cause he offered to cooperate in an assault on the British lines."[23]

General Lincoln had no choice but to agree. The joint assault was a disaster as the French attacked before the flanking American troops were in position. Tom later wrote an account of the battle:

> Thus was this fine body of troops sacrificed by the imprudence of the French general who, being of superior grade, commanded the whole. If the French troops had left their encampment in time for the different corps to have reached their position & the whole attacked together the prospect of success would have been infinitely better, though even then it would have been very doubtful on account of the strength of the enemies' line which was well supplied by artillery.[24]

Tom was of the opinion that if the combined French and American forces had attacked shortly after Lincoln's arrival on the 17th, before the British had time to build up their defenses, they would have been successful.

Charles Cotesworth wrote to Eliza on the night of the battle to assure her that he, Thomas and Daniel, who had been in the thick of the fight with his cavalry regiment, and most of their friends were well. His young cousin, Charles Pinckney III had fought with the Charleston Militia who, Charles reported to his mother "behaved extremely well" a piece of information he knew his mother would pass along to the young man's father.

Eliza was relieved to hear that everyone was well, but she was becoming frustrated with Tom. She was still looking after her sons' property and she felt she was not getting the attention from Tom that she needed. Charles wrote to her on October 15, six days after the attack on Savannah:

> I was exceedingly uneasy to find from a Letter of yours to my Brother that you imagined he had been guilty of designed inattention in not writing to you, as I am certain he has of late wrote very often, & if you have not received his Letters it must be owing to their miscarriage; with regard to his mentioning that he would see the overseer before he wrote, it is evident that he really meant that he would see the overseer before he wrote to you on the subject which you had mentioned to him in your Letter, and as the overseer was then doing Militia Duty in Camp no great delay could be occasioned by it. As to his writing oftener to his Wife than to you, surely that my Dear Mother is excusable. He has already given you every proof of filial affection; he has still to convince his [newly] Married Wife that absence does not diminish his regard for her; that he could not write as often to you as to her has [proceeded] from a want of time, & if you reflect on the very hard & constant duty we have been upon I am sure upon reconsideration you will think him blameless.[25]

Eliza loved all her children very much and would have willing made any sacrifice to help any one of them, but Tom, because he was her youngest child, was her darling and for the past five years she had played a prominent role in his life— a role that had necessarily changed somewhat now that he was married. And while she was pleased that he was happily married, Eliza was having trouble adjusting to her new position in his life. Undoubtedly, Charles's soothing and reasonable words did much to restore her peace of mind.

Charles had his own personal concerns, however, to lay before his mother which diverted her thoughts from her perceived inattention from Tom. In September Sally had given birth to a baby boy—the son that she and Charles had wanted so badly—and though the baby had been sickly after his birth, he appeared to be doing better. However, Charles in his letter confided to his mother: "I begin to have my fear again on account of my Dear little Cotesworth."[26] Unfortunately, the little baby would not survive—a source of great sorrow to his parents and his grandmother.

Both Charles and Thomas were disappointed with the failure to take

Savannah from the British. Charles wrote to his mother: "What a pity it is that Count D'Estaing could not be prevailed upon to stay longer, the Enemy I believe are in want both of provisions & ammunition & it is impossible for them to hold out long even if we were only to blockade them."[27] Without the French fleet, though, a blockade was not possible and wistfully thinking of what might have been General Lincoln and the South Carolina regiments slowly made their way back to Charleston to await the next series of events.

The Siege of Charleston—A Gallant Defense

When General Sir Henry Clinton, the British commander-in-chief in North America, learned that Comte d'Estaing and the French fleet had left Savannah for the West Indies, he immediately began to prepare for the second stage of the British plan to "roll up the south." On October 25 he ordered 3,000 soldiers to sail from Newport, Rhode Island to Savannah. Then three months later on December 26 he followed—sailing from his headquarters in New York at the head of a sizable force: 8,700 British troops and a fleet of fifty ships under the command of Vice-Admiral Arbuthnot. His goal was the capture of Charleston and the conquest of South Carolina.

The weather was not kind to the British fleet as it made its way south in January of 1780. Storms, high seas and wind took its toll—many of the cavalry horses and the horses used to pull the supply wagons died during the voyage and one ordinance ship sank with most of General Clinton's artillery aboard. Therefore, it was a weary and depleted army that landed in Savannah at the end of the month. However, the British quickly regrouped. They sent out search parties to round-up enough horses to replace most of those lost on the voyage and took the needed artillery from the defensive works of Savannah. Soon they were able to load men, horses and equipment onto transports and sail northward. They landed at John's Island just thirty miles south of Charleston on February 11.

It was a formidable force the British put ashore on John's Island—twelve regiments, four flank battalions, a large detachment of artillery and a cavalry unit numbering 300 men. Once the slow process of landing men, horses, artillery and supplies had been accomplished, Clinton began to move his army over to James Island—bringing them one step closer to Charleston. Admiral Arbuthnot ordered several of his men-of-war to block the entrance to the harbor and stationed some of his other ships in the rivers and creeks near the military encampments.

To oppose this large force General Lincoln had relatively few men. The six South Carolina regiments had recently been consolidated by the Continental Congress due to the declining number of soldiers in their ranks. The remaining regiments only totaled 800 men. In addition to the South Carolina regiments, General Lincoln had 400 Continental soldiers from Virginia and some local militia units as well as militia from North Carolina.

However, reinforcements were expected. Governor Rutledge had issued an urgent call for militia units from all over the state to report for duty and he was anticipating the arrival of a large number of men to add to the ranks of the defenders. South Carolina had also appealed to the Continental Congress and reinforcements from the Continental army and militia from Virginia and North Carolina were expected to arrive at any time.

General Lincoln deployed the men he had available as best he could. Charles Cotesworth and his 1st South Carolina Regiment were ordered to Fort Moultrie, which everyone felt was vital to the defense of Charleston. Lincoln then sent General Moultrie with a detachment of 200 light infantry under the command of Colonel Francis Marion to Bacon's Bridge on the Ashley River twenty-four miles from Charleston. Also at Bacon's Bridge was Colonel Daniel Horry and his cavalry regiment which, although not at full strength, numbered some 380 men. Horry was to "hang on the enemy's flanks" and provide intelligence of their movements while General Moultrie was to coordinate the activities of Horry's cavalry, Marion's infantry, the local militia and militia units from around the countryside that were expected to report there for duty.

Lincoln also sent a small command of approximately 200 men to protect the crossing at Ashley Ferry while other Continental infantry and artillery companies were sent to man the defenses on Charleston Neck where the General expected the most severe fighting to take place. Local militia along with the North Carolina militia were to occupy the batteries facing the harbor.

Having taken care of the land defenses, General Lincoln sought to protect the Charleston harbor with the aid of the small navy he had at his disposal—twelve ships under the command of Commodore Whipple. Lincoln ordered the commodore to place his ships just inside the bar to prevent the British from entering the harbor. However, Whipple had another plan. He wanted to position his ships in the middle of the harbor opposite to Ft. Moultrie. Then as the British ships tried to sail past the fort they would be caught between fire from the American ships and the artillery at the fort.

Commodore Whipple's plan was adopted and at the end of February the American fleet abandoned its position just inside the bar and dropped anchor in the middle of the harbor. Charles and Thomas at Fort Moultrie were delighted and confident that the combined naval and military forces would be able to score as significant a victory over the British fleet as the Americans at the fort had done in the summer of '76.

Having done all he could with his available resources, General Lincoln looked for other ways to increase his potential while he waited for the reinforcements he had been promised. One idea that came to mind was to seek foreign assistance. In June of 1779 Spain had joined her ally France and declared war on Great Britain; however, unlike the French, the Spanish had not recognized the independence of the thirteen colonies. Nevertheless, the Spanish were at war with Great Britain and General Lincoln decided to ask for their help. In February he sent Lieutenant Colonel Jean Baptiste, Chevalier de Ternant to Havana, Cuba, to prevail upon the Spanish governor there to send naval assistance to the Americans at Charleston.

Meanwhile General Clinton was moving his army slowly and methodically. He had failed in his first attempt to take Charleston in '76 because he had made mistakes. He was taking no chances on this occasion as he was not about to fail a second time. There were reinforcements from Savannah on the way to join him and with these additions to his force Clinton was confident that he could defeat the Americans.

In early March the British army began to move closer to Charleston crossing over from James Island to the mainland and establishing encampments on the banks of the Ashley River. From his headquarters Clinton could now look out over the river to view his objective: the city of Charleston glimmering in the soft sunshine of early spring. The British then began to build batteries on the banks of the Ashley River at Wappoo Cut—the entrance to Wappoo Creek where years before Eliza had experimented with indigo on her father's plantation.

With the British encamped just across the river from Charleston, many of the townspeople, especially the women and children, began to leave. Eliza, who usually spent the winter months in Charleston with Daniel who was studying with a tutor there, was among those who thought it prudent to leave town. It is not clear exactly when the two of them left, but they were at Hampton by the first week in March at the latest. They were not the only ones seeking refuge at Hampton. Charles's wife Sally, who was expecting a baby that summer, was also there with their two daughters, Maria and Harriott. The Horry plantation once again became a gathering place for women and children providing temporary shelter that spring for a range of family members and friends.

Eliza, Harriott and Sally were quite naturally anxious about the situation in Charleston and the safety of their husbands, brothers and sons, but life on the plantation continued in spite of the war and the ladies had enough to do to keep them fully occupied and give their thoughts another direction. Eliza was still supervising the plantations of her sons and for the past two years Harriott had been managing Hampton plantation as well as the other Horry plantations on the Santee River. In addition to these added responsibilities, a whole range of domestic chores required their daily attention.

Sally was busy preparing for the birth of her child hoping the baby would be a boy to replace the son she and Charles had recently lost—the "little Cotesworth" that Charles had been so concerned about the previous fall. And then there were Harriott and Sally's children to consider. The Pinckney family valued education and were not about to allow the war to interfere with that important part of the lives of the children.

Eliza, who took great delight in educating the young, most likely took on the task of instructing her granddaughters—Maria and Harriott Pinckney, aged six and four, and little Harriott Horry, aged two. It was spring and time to plant seeds in the kitchen garden. There Eliza would have supervised her granddaughters as they pressed the seeds into the ground and showed them how to care for the tender young plants that sprang up from the earth. An advocate of Locke's theory of children "playing their way into learning" she probably invented entertaining ways to teach them their letters and the basics of reading, writing and arithmetic.

Unfortunately, the one child Eliza could not help was Daniel whose studies were beyond her capabilities. He was, therefore, left to struggle with his lessons alone. Fortunately, his Uncle Thomas, stationed at Fort Moultrie, came to his assistance. Tom corresponded regularly with his mother and sister and was in the habit of including lessons he had prepared for Daniel in his letters to them. Daniel then sent his uncle the completed exercises to read and correct. Tom also sent Harriott recommendations of books for his nephew to read— books he knew his brother-in-law had in his library at Hampton.

The ladies at Hampton were always eager for news about the situation in town and relied on letters from Tom and Daniel Horry to keep them well-informed of the latest happenings. At the end of March they heard from Tom that the British fleet was beginning to take some action. The American ships had removed from the area inside the bar at the end of February and the British had then begun the slow process of lightening their men-of-war in preparation for entering the harbor. By March 20 all the artillery had been removed from seven warships enabling them to easily cross the bar and anchor at Five Fathom Hole. The next day another three joined them. All the guns were then painstakingly remounted aboard the ships.

At this point Commodore Whipple thought better of his plan to anchor his fleet in mid channel across from Fort Moultrie and rake the British ships as they sailed past Sullivan's Island. Instead he ordered his fleet to town where the ships' guns were removed and mounted in the batteries facing the harbor. Twelve hundred sailors were then ordered off the ships to man the batteries. The Americans sank several of their ships at the mouth of the Cooper River using them as supports for cables and chains that were strung from one side of the river's mouth to the other—from the waterfront on East Bay Street to Shutes Folly Island. These obstacles, it was hoped, would be enough to prevent the British from moving up the river.

General Moultrie along with both Charles and Thomas Pinckney were bitterly disappointed by the actions of Commodore Whipple. General Moultrie commented: "The reasons for altering the plan fixed upon to dispose of our fleet, was, that Commodore Whipple did not choose to risk an engagement with the British fleet." If he had stayed in his second position in the channel, Moultrie continued, "it would have been impossible for them [the British] to pass without losing some of their ships; I scarcely think they would have attempted it."[28]

There was more disappointing news for the defenders at Charleston. On March 24 the enlistment period for the brigade of North Carolina militia was up and they were preparing to leave. The government offered large bounties to any man who chose to stay, but only 200 elected to do so and so far no militia from the countryside had reported for duty at the camp at Bacon's Bridge. The country militia were happy to patrol in their home counties, but could not be prevailed upon to come to Charleston for fear of smallpox. Even though the authorities assured them that there were no cases of the disease in town, they still refused to report for duty. General Lincoln then re-called Moultrie's men to Charleston leaving Colonel Horry's cavalry outside the town to harass the British and gather intelligence.

In spite of these setbacks the morale of the soldiers and the townspeople was good. They were convinced their defenses were strong enough to withstand a British attack and that large numbers of reinforcements were on their way to assist them and they were, therefore, optimistic about the future. Thomas's letter to Hampton at the end of March reflected that confidence. He wrote:

> The Batteries in Town which are very numerous and joined all round by lines of Communication are almost entirely man'd by Seamen which leaves the whole of the Infantry with a strong reserved Park of Artillery to act as occasion may require. The whole Garrison there are in high Spirits and Matters are getting fast into the best order.
> We have intelligence that 4,000 Virginians and North Carolinians are making forced Marches to our Assistance; the first Division of Virginia Continentals must have crossed the Santee before you will receive this.
> The Enemy's Fleet remain quiet in five fathom Hole.... It seems to be not improbable that

the Spanish Fleet may come off our Coast soon after Reinforcements come in; if this should
be the Case I think Sir Henry Clintons Situation, which is now by no means eligible, will be
truly deplorable indeed; we have by the blessing of Providence a very favorable Prospect
before us.[29]

Thomas Pinckney's optimistic prediction of the "favorable Prospect before
us" was not to be realized. At the end of March Ternant returned to Charleston
with disappointing news: Spanish authorities in Cuba had rejected General
Lincoln's plea for assistance. The Spanish were not interested in helping defeat
the British in South Carolina—their interest lay closer to home where they
hoped to retake Minorca and Gibraltar from their longtime enemy. The dis-
appointments continued: the first Division of Virginia Continentals, said to
number 900, that Tom thought were already crossing the Santee on their way
to Charleston, never arrived; General Charles Scott of the Continental army,
who was expected to arrive with troops, rode into town alone and only 300
militia from the countryside could be persuaded to answer the governor's
urgent summons—the rest were still afraid of the smallpox.

In the meantime, General Clinton was gradually moving his men across
the Ashley River to Charleston Neck and by March 31 the British were facing
the batteries described by Thomas in his letter to his mother and sister. The
British army was larger now than it had been when it first landed on John's
Island in February as reinforcements from Savannah had arrived. The new
arrivals included the British Legion—a regiment of cavalry and foot soldiers
made-up of loyalists from the state of New York. The commander of the British
Legion was a young Lieutenant Colonel by the name of Banastre Tarleton.

The foot soldiers of the British Legion were mounted, traveling on horse-
back but fighting on foot. The Legion had stayed behind in Savannah when
the bulk of the British army left in early February due to lack of horses. They
had spent the ensuing time searching far and wide for suitable mounts to replace
the ones they had lost on the voyage. Now at the end of March, poorly mounted
on swamp ponies and farm horses which were the only ones they could find,
they had finally made their way north to join General Clinton. In the spring of
1780 no one in South Carolina had ever heard of Banastre Tarleton and the
British Legion, but it would not be long before they would not only be well-
known but also hated and feared throughout the south.

The next day, April 1, at a spot some 800 yards from the defenders' fortifications the British began to dig their first parallel. The men digging the
trenches were bombarded day and night by the American forces in town, but
that did not stop their progress. On April 4 the British retaliated and began to
shell Charleston from their batteries at Wappoo Cut and from ships anchored
in the Ashley River. On April 6 four houses in town were hit with cannon balls

and it was fortunate for Eliza that she was at Hampton for her house was one of the four that was hit.

The next day the British ships which had been anchored at Five Fathom Hole began to make their way through the channel past Fort Moultrie. Since the British did not intend to attack the fort, the ships sailed past in single file without firing, moving smoothly on the spring tide. However, as each vessel passed the fort the ship turned and fired once before making for safe anchorage near James Island. Although the men at Fort Moultrie fired at the passing ships, they were only able to damage one and disable another. Three days later three shallops passed the fort without incident. Unfortunately for Charles and Thomas, Fort Moultrie was not destined to play a role in the defense of Charleston during this engagement. Eventually the 1st South Carolina regiment would be recalled to town leaving only a small garrison at the fort.

On April 7 there was cause for great joy in Charleston. Some of the long awaited reinforcements finally arrived: Virginia Continentals under the command of Brigadier General Thomas Woodford. They were war-hardened veterans who had just marched a great distance in a short amount of time and they were heartily cheered as they trudged wearily through the streets—but there were only 700 of them instead of the 1,500 that had been expected.

The first British parallel and redoubts were completed by April 10 and Charleston was now surrounded on three sides: Charleston Neck, the Ashley River and the harbor. The only side left open was the Cooper River. At this point it was customary in siege warfare for the attacking general to send a demand for surrender to the besieged commander—it was a formality as no one expected the besieged to surrender at this point. Tom reported to his sister that "The British Commanders sent to General Lincoln two days ago with the modest request that he would deliver up the Town, the answer was 'No.'"[30]

However the situation in Charleston was becoming more serious as the British began to haul boats across Charleston Neck to the Cooper River in preparation for landing troops on the other side. Once there they could challenge the Americans for control of the river crossings eventually sealing off the city of Charleston and trapping the defenders inside. However, at this time it was the Patriots who controlled the countryside across the Cooper River and the Americans in town seemed to feel there was little need for worry.

Thomas wrote optimistically to his mother on April 10 that the defensive works around the town were as strong as possible and "thronged with men and matters in general in the best posture for a vigorous defence." He continued:

> I heard it reported that the Governor is shortly to take the field and draw down as many of
> our country militia into a camp to be formed somewhere on this side of the country as he
> can collect, as our militia in general cannot be prevailed on to come into town, and it is hoped

this measure will be productive of very good consequences. The enemy continue their approaches but slowly; none of their works are nearer than 600 yards from our lines. Their men-of-war continue opposite to Fort Johnson.... The North Carolina and Virginia troops which cannot now be at a very great distance, together with such of our country militia as the Governor may collect, will, it is thought, be sufficient to oblige the enemy to raise the siege, or at all events will much incommode them and in the end render their repulse the more certain.[31]

On April 10 General Lincoln had suggested that Governor Rutledge and three of his council members leave town. It was thought that the executive authority of the state should be preserved. If Charleston should fall, it was important that the government be able to continue functioning in another part of the state. On April 11 Governor Rutledge accompanied by Charles Pinckney II, Daniel Huger and John Lewis Gervais left Charleston for Georgetown. The governor established two camps: one at Lenud's Ferry, a crossing point on the Santee River, and another between the Santee and Cooper Rivers where troops could be assembled to harass the British and where provisions and communications could flow into Charleston. That day the British began firing on the town from all their batteries.

There was some discussion at this point whether it would be advisable to evacuate the Continental army from town—allowing them to remain free to continue the fight another day. At a meeting with his general officers Lincoln admitted that the engineers had informed him that the town's fortifications were not capable of holding for more than a few days and sadly he also told them that he had little hope of receiving any additional troops and that provisions were low. Considering the overpowering strength of the enemy, Lincoln felt they should consider the possibility of evacuating Charleston. General Lincoln, however, was not ready to make the decision to evacuate and asked his officers to consider the matter and they would discuss it again at a later meeting.

By the second week in April the British had landed a sizable force across the Cooper River—two regiments commanded by Lt. Colonel Webster plus Tarleton's British Legion and the American Volunteers, a group of Loyalists from the northern colonies under the command of Major Patrick Ferguson—a total of 1,400 men. Their immediate goal was the supply depot at Monck's Corner—a crossroad near the west branch of the Cooper River thirty-two miles north of Charleston—where supplies and provisions were collected before being sent into town. The depot was being guarded by Brigadier General Isaac Huger and the American cavalry which included both Daniel Horry's cavalry and cavalry from Virginia under the command of Colonel William Washington.

Banastre Tarleton, commanding both the British Legion and the American Volunteers, was given the assignment of attacking the Patriots at Monck's Corner. Hoping to surprise Huger's force, Tarleton decided on a night attack. Leaving the main British army at Goose Creek at ten o'clock on the evening of April 13 Tarleton and his corps rode quickly through the night and attacked Huger's forces at 3:00 in the morning catching them unprepared. The British killed fourteen Americans, wounded nineteen and captured sixty-four—Colonel Horry, General Huger, Colonel Washington and other officers escaped only by abandoning their horses and fleeing on foot into the swamp. Tarleton also captured fifty supply wagons loaded with arms, ammunition and clothing along with most of the horses belonging to the American cavalry—a tremendous bonus for the poorly mounted British Legion.

Monck's Corner was Banastre Tarleton's first major victory in South Carolina and established the pattern for the style of attack he would favor in future battles—a sudden approach catching his opponents off-guard followed by a swift assault with swords and bayonets. The men of the British Legion rode hard covering great distances in a short amount of time and were utterly fearless and ruthless during battle. They were also reluctant to cease fighting once the attack was over. At Monck's Corner a French officer fighting with the Americans asked for quarter and instead of being allowed to surrender was fatally hacked and slashed by Tarleton's men—a pattern that would, unfortunately, be repeated in future engagements.

With the British capture of Monck's Corner and the subsequent victory by the British Legion three weeks later at Lenud's Ferry the opportunity to evacuate the Continental army was fast slipping away. Then, when it became known that General Lincoln was contemplating an evacuation, another problem arose: Christopher Gadsden, the acting-governor, and the citizens of Charleston expressed their total opposition to it. In fact, the townspeople were so much opposed to the idea of evacuation that they threatened to destroy the boats needed to carry the soldiers across the Cooper River and then to open the gates to the enemy if General Lincoln attempted to abandon the town.

Another alternative at this point was surrender, which was also not acceptable to either the soldiers or the townspeople. The weak condition of the town's fortifications, the lack of provisions and the improbability of reinforcements arriving had not been adequately communicated to either the army or the townspeople. Therefore, they refused to believe that they could not stop the British on this occasion as they had done twice before.

However, the British were approaching Wando Neck on the Cooper River and threatening to close the last American link to the countryside. A few days later fourteen ships were seen approaching the bar—the ships were bringing

more reinforcements for General Clinton from the north. The British bombardment of Charleston was causing considerable damage and the number of
people killed and wounded was increasing daily. The exploding shells fired by
the British mortars caused the most damage and several of the wooden houses
in town were destroyed. The besieged were living on rice, sugar and coffee—
meat was almost impossible to be had.

At the end of April it was felt that a verbal message needed to be gotten
to Governor Rutledge, who was in Georgetown trying to rally a counter force
to relieve the city, urging him to send whatever troops he had as quickly as possible. Reportedly there were Continental soldiers and militia units marching
south from North Carolina and Virginia to join him. Major Thomas Pinckney
was entrusted to carry this verbal message to Governor Rutledge—he knew
the Santee countryside well and also had a reputation for being quick-witted
and calm in the face of danger. He had a difficult ride, though, having to cross
two rivers and traverse a countryside heavily patrolled by the enemy. He arrived
safely, but before the Virginia Continental soldiers under Colonel Buford, who
had just arrived in the area, reached the Santee River, they received word that
Charleston had surrendered.

After Thomas left on his mission the situation in town had grown steadily
worse. By May 7 the British had completed their third parallel and Lord Cornwallis, crossing the Cooper River, had taken Mount Pleasant and Haddrell's
Point just on the other side. The small garrison that had been left at Fort Moultrie was now isolated and forced to surrender. The loss of Fort Moultrie was a
great psychological blow to the soldiers and citizens of Charleston.

On May 8, knowing the situation was hopeless for the Americans, General
Clinton called for a cease fire and once again asked General Lincoln to surrender the town telling him that the responsibility for "whatever vindictive severity
exasperated soldiers may inflict on the unhappy people" of Charleston was on
his shoulders if he did not surrender and the British were forced to storm the
town.[32] Lincoln sent Clinton his terms for surrender which contained more
favorable conditions for the citizens of the town and the militia than the British
had offered. However, they were rejected by the British general who demanded
unconditional surrender. Clinton then announced that hostilities would begin
again at 8 o'clock that evening.

General Moultrie described the scene that night:

> At length, we fired the first gun, and immediately followed a tremendous cannonade (about
> 180 or 200 pieces of heavy cannon fired off at the same time), and the mortars from both sides
> threw out an immense number of shells; it was a glorious sight, to see them like meteors cross-
> ing each other, and bursting in the air; it appeared as if the stars were tumbling down. The
> fire was incessant almost the whole night; cannon-balls whizzing and shells hissing continually

amongst us; ammunition chests and temporary magazines blowing up; great guns bursting, and wounded men groaning along the lines: it was a dreadful night! It was our last effort, but it availed us nothing.[33]

The following day the townspeople and most of the militia had had enough and informed General Lincoln that they were willing to accept the British terms of surrender. Still Lincoln hesitated. It was not until May 11 when the British troops were within twenty-five yards of the defenders lines and waiting for the signal to storm the town that General Lincoln finally surrendered.

The next morning at 11:00 Colonel Charles Cotesworth Pinckney led the men of the 1st South Carolina Regiment of the Continental Line out of Charleston to the place just outside the city's fortifications where they were to lay down their arms. Although Colonel Pinckney and the other officers were allowed to keep their swords, they were not allowed to wear them during the surrender ceremony, the drummers were not allowed to beat a British march— instead the Americans walked to the beat of the "Turk's" march—and their flags were cased not flying proudly in the spring breeze. The British had not allowed the Americans all the honors of war.

After laying down their arms, Charles Pinckney led his men back to their barracks where they were to remain prisoners of war until exchanged. The remainder of the Continental soldiers followed after them. The British were surprised that the defenders were so few in number and according to General Moultrie they asked him, "Where our second division was? they were told these were all the continentals we had, except the sick and wounded; they were astonished, and said we had made a gallant defence."[34]

While Continental troops and sailors were to remain prisoners of war until exchanged, the militia were allowed to return to their homes as prisoners on parole—prisoners who had given their word not to take up arms again. As long as they observed their parole, they were promised they would not be molested by British troops. All civil officers and citizens in the town were also considered to be prisoners on parole and subject to the same terms as the militia.

Naval and military officers were allowed to keep their horses, swords, pistols and baggage, which was not to be searched, and were permitted to keep their servants. Enlisted men and junior officers were placed on board prison ships floating at anchor in the harbor while senior officers were confined to houses in and around Charleston. Charles Cotesworth was fortunate—he was allowed to go to his house on East Bay Street after the surrender.

Those that favored the Patriot cause were left stunned and disconcerted by the fall of Charleston. Upon hearing the news militia units in the backcountry quickly disbanded, the men returning to their homes determined to keep a low profile while the military forces that had been operating in the Santee area scattered seeking a safe haven from the British forces that would inevitably be moving north from Charleston. The Continental army in the south was practically non-existent. Brigadier General Isaac Huger was the highest ranking Continental officer left who was not a prisoner of war and Colonel Buford's corps of 350 soldiers were all that remained of the army.

General Huger was gravely ill as a result of the four days he had spent in the swamp after the attack at Monck's Corner and was at home recovering when Charleston fell. He immediately ordered Buford and his troops to withdraw to Hillsborough, the Patriot capital of North Carolina. Governor Rutledge and two of his council members, also headed for Hillsborough, traveled along with them as did General Caswell and his North Carolina militia who, like Buford and his corps, had arrived too late to assist in the defense of Charleston.

The South Carolina cavalry, now under the command of Lt. Colonel Anthony White, Huger's second-in-command, had been in disarray for some weeks. They were still reeling from their humiliating defeats at the hands of Banastre Tarleton at Monck's Corner and three weeks later at Lenud's Ferry. They had made their way back to Georgetown to refit—many of them had lost saddles, pistols and swords along with their horses during their run-ins with the British Legion.

After the fall of Charleston Colonel White took what was left of his corps and retreated to Halifax in North Carolina. Some of Colonel William Washington's Virginia cavalry chose to join Buford's Virginia Continentals on their way to Hillsborough. Washington then took the remainder on to Halifax where he and Colonel White began to rebuild and refit their regiments—they had not given up, they would both return to South Carolina and fight another day. Daniel Horry's cavalry disbanded, the men returning to their homes to wait for better times.

When Governor Rutledge left Charleston on April 11, he had been accompanied by three of his council members: Daniel Huger, John Lewis Gervais and Charles Pinckney, II. However, when he left Georgetown for Hillsborough with Buford's corps only Huger and Gervais were with him—Charles Pinckney II had returned home. The British had been operating in the area north of the Cooper River since the middle of April and many of the plantations in the area had been raided and plundered. Pinckney's Snee plantation located eight miles north of Charleston was one of the places that had suffered at the hands of the British. It was reported that his family had been plundered of all their silverware, linen and provisions. Worried that his wife had been left destitute, he decided to return to Charleston, give himself up and become a prisoner on parole.

After his regiment disbanded Daniel Horry returned to Hampton. The number of ladies seeking refuge there had increased as Thomas's wife Betsey and her younger sister Mary had joined the group. The ladies were all anxious for the latest news, but what Horry had to relate to them was not what they were hoping to hear. Like Patriots all over the state, they were stunned by the fall of Charleston and worry over the fate of family members in town threw a pall over their thoughts and activities. This was especially true for Eliza who was deeply troubled by the fact that her oldest son was now a prisoner of war.

Tom was in Georgetown with Governor Rutledge when Charleston surrendered and thus escaped becoming a prisoner like his brother and comrades in the Continental army. He was all on his own now, for not only was he an officer without a command but there was also no army in the vicinity for him to report to—the closest Continental army being far away to the north. Tom had a few options open to him. He could travel to Hillsborough with Governor Rutledge and await events there or he could go north and offer his services to General Washington until an army was formed to liberate South Carolina or he could wait until that army arrived in the area and then report for duty. However, before making any decision he wanted to see his wife who was expecting their first child that summer and the rest of his family. He headed for Hampton.

The British Occupation of South Carolina

Although General Clinton was satisfied with the capture of Charleston, he knew the campaign was not over as there was still much work to be done. The surrounding countryside needed to be brought under British control, the people had to be pacified and Loyalist militia had to be formed to govern and hold the state for the crown. It was a large undertaking and Clinton wanted to strike quickly while the Patriots were still reeling from the loss of Charleston.

A few days after the surrender Clinton ordered Lord Cornwallis to cross the Santee River to strike at Buford's corps and thus eliminate what was left of the Continental army in South Carolina. By May 18 Cornwallis and his army had reached the south bank of the river and while preparations were being made to transport 2,500 men and five pieces of artillery across the river, Banastre Tarleton and the British Legion were sent on a mission. Crossing the river first Tarleton and his men rode to Georgetown where they were ordered "to chase away or take prisoners all violent enemies to the British Government and to receive the allegience of the well affected." Tarleton returned to Cornwallis by the 22nd and reported that the mission had been accomplished "without opposition."[35]

The British did not capture and occupy Georgetown until July and until then there were no British troops in the vicinity. There were, however, Loyalist militia units who were determined to continue the mission begun by Tarleton—the rounding up of "all violent enemies to the British Government." Acting on information given by local Tories, they began to conduct surprise raids on the nearby Santee plantations hoping to capture any lingering Patriots. Toward the end of May they paid a visit to Hampton.

It was late at night and everyone had gone to bed. Harriott Pinckney, Charles and Sally's daughter then aged four was sleeping on a cot at the foot of Eliza's bed when they were both awakened by a loud noise and screams. Suddenly the bedroom door flew open and fifteen-year-old Mary Motte, Tom's sister-in-law, came running into the room crying: "Oh, Mrs. Pinckney, save me, save me! The British are coming after me." Eliza immediately got up and pushed Mary down onto the bed and pulled the covers over her. "Lie there," she is reported to have said, "and no man will dare to trouble you."

Eliza then took Harriott by the hand and the two of them stood by the foot of the bed waiting. It was not long before the door was suddenly thrown open and armed men began to rush into the room. However, upon encountering an icy stare from the diminutive, but dignified elderly lady (Eliza was fifty-seven at the time) standing with a small child at the foot of the bed, they fell over themselves trying to back out of the room. They were Tories under the command of Major Fraser and they were, of course, looking for Major Pinckney and Colonel Horry.

Tom managed to escape, but Daniel Horry was not so fortunate and was soon seized by Major Fraser's men and made to give his parole promising that he would not take up arms against the British again. Silently the inhabitants of Hampton then watched as the Tories—fellow South Carolinians—plundered the house and carried away their personal possessions. They were fortunate, though, as neither the house nor any of the outbuildings were burned.[36]

Meanwhile, the British army under Lord Cornwallis had reached Nelson's Ferry on the Santee River where Cornwallis had received some vital information about Buford's forces. According to local Tories, Buford had passed Nelson's Ferry ten days before and, even more interesting, they told him that Governor Rutledge and two of his council members were traveling with him.

Lord Cornwallis now saw an opportunity to eliminate the remainder of the Continental army and capture the rebel governor of the state at one stroke. However, he was faced with a problem: Buford had a ten-day lead and Cornwallis knew he could not possibly overtake him with his infantry. His only chance lay in sending the hard-riding British Legion after the Americans. Always ready for a challenge, Tarleton left Nelson's Ferry on the 27th of May with 270 men—forty British regulars of the 17th Dragoons (cavalry), 130 Legion cavalry and 100 mounted Legion infantry.

Blissfully unaware that Tarleton and the British Legion were in earnest pursuit, Buford was making his way to Camden where he would take the Great Wagon Road north to Hillsborough some forty miles south of the Virginia border. It was a long journey, but he was making good time and there seemed to be no reason for undue haste. At Camden Buford's corps and General Caswell's men parted company—the general and his troops heading home to North Carolina.

Eleven miles north of Camden was a place called Rugeley's Mill, the home of Colonel Henry Rugeley, a well-known local Tory. Colonel Rugeley, not the only Loyalist in the state who would hedge his bets during the war, offered the governor and his party food and overnight lodging. Buford and his men continued on headed for an area a few miles south of the North Carolina border called Waxhaws where they intended to rest.

Riding hard in horrendous heat Tarleton and his men reached Camden on the evening of the 28th and rested briefly. By two o'clock in the morning they were ready to leave and by dawn were at Rugeley's Mill. By a stroke of luck Henry Rugeley had received word that the British were coming and had managed to hustle his visitors out of his house just before midnight. At Rugeley's Mill Tarleton learned that Buford was only twenty miles ahead and he continued his relentless pursuit coming up with Buford's force by three o'clock in the afternoon.

Not waiting for stragglers to catch-up Tarleton attacked immediately with his cavalry. In 18th-century warfare a cavalry charge upon an opponent's infantry followed by a bayonet charge was always a very brutal affair and Waxhaws was especially brutal. Overwhelmed Patriots trying to surrender were hacked down and some of the wounded were cruelly stabbed as they lay on the ground. After 15 minutes the battle was over and 113 Americans lay dead on the field and 203 had been captured—150 of whom were so badly wounded they could not be moved with the rest of the prisoners. They were taken to the Presbyterian Meeting House and looked after by the local inhabitants and the British surgeons that Tarleton requested from Camden. British losses were slight: sixteen killed and twelve wounded.

Patriot propaganda made the most of the fact that Americans had been slain while they were trying to surrender and the reputation of Banastre Tarleton and the British Legion, which had its beginnings at Monck's Corner, mushroomed out of proportion after Waxhaws. Tarleton earned for himself the nickname "Bloody Ban" and "Ban the Butcher" and in subsequent battles the words "Tarleton's Quarter" or "Buford's Quarter" (signifying that no mercy would be given) became a rallying cry for Patriots.[37]

After successfully eliminating what was left of the Continental army in the south, Tarleton and his men joined Lord Cornwallis who had seized control of Camden, a busy settlement 124 miles northwest of Charleston. The town was strategically located on the Great Wagon Road which led north all the way to Pennsylvania. From there the British could control the area to the east and stop any Continental army from invading the state from the north.

The British soon marched into the backcountry and occupied Ninety-six, a trading post 175 miles west of Charleston and then the hamlet of Cheraw on the Pee Dee River just south of the North Carolina border. They went on to establish two important outposts north of Camden at Hanging Rock and nearby Rocky Mount. The British soon held key positions in the state that stretched in a great semi-circle from Georgetown in the low country through the backcountry all the way to Augusta just across the Savannah River in Georgia. The Patriots in the backcountry, stunned by the loss of Charleston and the bloody encounter at Waxhaws, had offered no resistance—even the most ardent Patriots had accepted parole.

General Clinton, satisfied that his plans for the conquest of South Carolina were being successfully implemented, began to make arrangements to leave. He had never intended to remain long in the south after the capture of Charleston and he was now planning to take part of the army and return to New York leaving General Lord Cornwallis in command. Before he left, however, he issued a series of proclamations calculated to re-instate the majority of the people of South Carolina to the status of loyal, British subjects.

The proclamations of May 22 and June 1 promised amnesty and pardon to all who would once again swear allegiance to the king. The proclamation of June 1, however, included an added inducement: all inhabitants who took the oath of allegiance would be "re-instated in the possession of all those rights and immunities which they heretofore enjoyed under a free British government, exempt from taxation, except by their own legislature."[38] Since the original cause of the dispute between Great Britain and her colonies had been the right of the colonists to be taxed only by their own representatives and not by the British Parliament, this offer had great appeal.

However, the next proclamation issued on June 3 undermined the good intentions of the previous proclamations by repealing the terms of surrender which had allowed prisoners on parole to remain neutral for the duration of the war. After June 20, according to the new proclamation, prisoners on parole were to be restored to all the rights, privileges and duties of British subjects, would be required to take an oath of loyalty to the king and would be expected to take an active part in the British war effort. For example, all young, unmarried men would be required to join Loyalist militia companies. Those who did not swear the oath of loyalty would be considered rebels and traitors and be treated accordingly and, as a matter of course, their property would be confiscated.

As General Clinton blithely sailed away to New York on June 5, he was confident he was leaving a state firmly under British control and a population primarily restored to allegiance to the king. He could not have been more mistaken. As news of the proclamation of June 3 spread through the countryside it provoked outrage among those who were on parole. They had been promised they could remain neutral and now they were being told they had to take up arms against their comrades still in the field of battle or be considered traitors and lose their property.

As the long, hot days of summer settled over the state of South Carolina, those with Patriot sympathies struggled with an ever increasing sense of despair and frustration. For Eliza worry over the whereabouts and safety of Tom added to the feelings of despondency that loomed over the household. Slowly the group that had gathered at Hampton dispersed. Sally, leaving her two little girls with Eliza, went into Charleston to visit her husband at their home on East Bay Street where he was being held. Betsey and her sister traveled to Mount Joseph, the Motte plantation on the Congaree River, to join their mother and other members of the family.

On June 5 Eliza was relieved to receive a short note from Tom telling her that he was staying at the plantation of Captain Thomas Giles, a former officer in Daniel Horry's disbanded cavalry regiment. He was well, he told her, and had seen his brother in Charleston two days earlier and was happy to report that he, too, was in good health. He was hoping to be able to visit them soon at Hampton.

During the days after his escape from Hampton Tom had come to a definite decision: he would travel north and offer his services to General Washington until he could join the army he felt must soon be formed to liberate South Carolina. Before he left the area, however, he wanted to see his brother. Therefore, he applied for and received permission to come into Charleston under a Flag of Truce. He was allowed to talk to his brother at the home of Mr. James Simpson, a leading Charleston Loyalist. During his visit he told his brother of his plans to join the army in the north and a few days later Charles sent Tom a letter of introduction to General Washington and instructions to take some gold he had placed in the care of his sister-in-law, Henrietta Rutledge, to defray the expenses of his journey. "I shall not think you act affectionately if you do not make use of it," wrote Charles.[39]

After his visit with his brother, Tom made his way to Camden and was there by June 11. Daniel Horry was also in Camden that day—he had come to town to take the oath of allegiance to the king. After much thought he had finally decided to take British protection rather than lose all his property and leave his family destitute. Daniel Horry was not the only Patriot to take such a step—the proclamation of June 3 had caused many Patriot supporters to think long and hard about taking the oath of loyalty in order to protect their property. Henry Middleton, Charles Cotesworth's father-in-law, and Eliza's nephew, Charles Pinckney, II, were among those who chose that course of action. However, it was a bitter blow to Tom to discover that his brother-in-law, who had supported the Patriot cause so ardently from the very beginning, had now changed his position. He wrote the following letter to his mother and sister:

> Driven by the Fate of War from my Family, Friends, and Country I have a mind ill at ease to write, but I can not pass by the opportunity of Mr. Horry's return of bidding Adieu for (I hope) a short Time to my dearest Mother & Sisters before I quit this Country. I was hopeful when I went in with a Flag of Truce I might have been permitted to return by the way of Santee, but in that as in other Matters I have been disappointed: I had however the Satisfaction of half an hours conversation with my Brother at Mr. Simpson's in his Presence. This Gentleman behaved with the greatest Politeness & indeed in a friendly way to me, offering to render me any services in his Powers. If you should have any occasion for his Assistance I dare say he will afford it to you.... Mr. Horry will inform you of my future Intentions. I need not say that if I thought I could remain at home consistently with my principles I should not think of proceeding, but let my fate be what it may, I hope I shall not act in such a way as to call up a blush on the Cheek of those who wish me well. The trial is at present rather severe but I firmly trust that we shall not be entirely given up to Misfortune. Certain I am that Matters are not so bad with us as the despondency of our own People and the high hopes of our adversaries would induce you to think.
>
> Tho' I am sorry for the Step Col. Horry has taken in one Sense, yet it can not but give me the greatest Pleasure to consider that you will have a Person with you to support & protect you. Adieu, my Dearest Friends, may Heaven protect and make you Bear this cloud with Resignation & be assured of my letting you hear from me by every opportunity & that I am with the greatest sincerity your most dutiful & Affectionate Son & Brother.[40]

Before he began his northern journey, Tom had been able to spend some time with his wife at Mount Joseph. It must have been with a heavy heart that he continued his journey. Betsey was very near her due date and considering the uncertainties attending childbirth in the 18th century, not to mention the uncertainty attached to a soldier's life, it had to have occurred to him that they might never see each other again.

Eliza felt the departure of her son very acutely. "My heart bleeds at my separation from my dear and greatly beloved son," she wrote to Betsey on June 18. However, as great as her grief was, Eliza realized that Betsey's grief was even greater and she urged her daughter-in-law to keep up her spirits and "imitate your husbands fortitude, it is as much a female, as a male virtue" and, she continued, "the greatest favor you can do him, will be to take care of your self, and bear with an equal mind your present trials."[41]

Everyone in South Carolina would have "trials" to bear that summer. An outbreak of a virulent form of fever spread through the countryside. Betsey reported to Eliza that several of the children in the family and many of the slaves at Mount Joseph had been struck with it and the rest of the family was expecting to have it soon. While they had managed at Hampton to escape the fever, they knew they would not escape the next threat that appeared—a small pox epidemic that swept the entire area sending people scurrying in all directions to be inoculated. Harriott, who had gone to Charleston on business, called on Eliza's good friend, Dr. Garden, and received written instructions from him on how to perform the inoculation.

Eliza immediately sent a copy of the instructions to Mount Joseph expressing the hope that Betsey would be able to "keep out of the way of the small pox" until after the birth of her baby. "Nothing would tempt me to wish you to be inoculated in your present situation, unless You were almost certain you could not escape it in the natural way," she wrote. Meanwhile Eliza and Harriott could find no one to inoculate Daniel and little Harriott and were forced to perform the procedure themselves. Charles had sent for Sally and the girls to come to Charleston where he immediately made arrangements for the girls to be inoculated.[42]

The threat of fever and small pox was not the only "trial" the civilian population in the countryside had to deal with that summer—they also had the British army and its constant demands. Swooping down on a farm or plantation, the British commandeered horses, provisions, carts, wagons, boats, slaves and whatever else they needed. The slave population in the country was becoming depleted as many slaves, hoping for freedom, had runaway to join the British while others had died from the small pox that had come with the conquering army. The loss of slaves meant there were fewer workers to grow food and do other necessary jobs.

In the backcountry Tory militia were zealous in their efforts to round-up traitors—men who had not taken the oath of loyalty. Their visits were often attended with violence as homes were burned, livestock slaughtered and the inhabitants—young and old, male and female—were abused and, in some cases, killed. Tory violence coupled with the proclamation of June 3 galvanized Patriot supporters in the backcountry. Paroled militiamen, who would have been content to sit-out the remainder of the war as neutrals, began to rally to the Patriot cause under the leadership of Colonel Thomas Sumter, former commander of the 6th South Carolina Regiment.

On May 28 the British Legion, while in hot pursuit of Buford's corps, had passed close to the home of Colonel Sumter. Tarleton, who knew Sumter had been a regimental commander in the South Carolina army, sent a detachment to bring him in. Warned by a neighbor that the British were coming, Sumter and his body servant left immediately and headed for American headquarters in Salisbury, North Carolina. There Sumter let it be known that he was proposing to raise a volunteer army and return to South Carolina to fight the British. He was soon joined by disgruntled militia from all over the backcountry. Loosely organized under Sumter's leadership, they were known as Sumter's Brigade.

On July 12 at Williamson's plantation men of Sumter's Brigade won a decisive victory over Captain Christian Huck of the British Legion who was commanding thirty-five Legion cavalry, twenty mounted infantry of the New York Volunteers and sixty Tory militia. British losses were high and only twelve Legion dragoons and twelve Tory militia managed to escape, the rest were either killed or taken prisoner. The Americans had one man killed and one wounded. The victory was as much a psychological one as a military one, for partisan soldiers had overwhelmingly defeated regular Loyalist forces including members of the dreaded British Legion.

Patriots began to take heart and the cloud of despondency that had been hanging over them dissipated somewhat. The men from Daniel Horry's cavalry regiment, who had been waiting for better times, began to form militia units in the Santee area. These units were then loosely united under the leadership of Lieutenant Colonel Francis Marion. Marion, the former commander of the 2nd South Carolina Regiment, had been in Charleston with his regiment during the siege, but by a curious quirk of fate, had not been in town for the surrender. Having broken his ankle, he was away recovering when the city fell to the British. Consequently, he was free to assume leadership of the partisan fighters in the lowcountry who would be known as Marion's Brigade.

While Patriot spirits were beginning to revive, Eliza was waiting for some word of Tom. On July 17 she heard from Betsey: "I sincerely sympathise with you in The separation from our Dear and greatly beloved friend which has lately left us, God only knows when to meet again.... I have not heard from him since he left Camden but hope ere now he is safe with General Washington as it was his Intention to join him as soon as possible."[43]

Tom, however, was not with General Washington. He had gotten as far as Hillsborough, North Carolina, where he learned that the Continental Congress had appointed General Horatio Gates—the victor at Saratoga—as the new Commander of the Southern Department and that Gates was on his way to Hillsborough to take command. Waiting in Hillsborough for his arrival were Major General Baron de Kalb and his Continentals. They were encamped south of town and Tom decided to join de Kalb's men and wait for the opportunity to present himself to General Gates when he arrived. Toward the end of July he sent Eliza a short note under a Flag of Truce telling her that he was well "and as eligibly situated as I could expect."[44]

General Gates arrived in Hillsborough on July 25 and assumed command of the army. Tom immediately offered his services to him. Gates, who had been given permission by Congress to name his own staff officers, thought it would be politic to have an officer from South Carolina on his staff and appointed Tom as one of his aides. His desire to include South Carolinians in his army did not extend to Francis Marion and his poorly dressed partisan fighters who, hearing of Gates's appointment, had come to Hillsborough to offer their services. Gates promptly sent Marion and his men back to South Carolina with orders to gather intelligence.

General Gates was anxious to proceed and on July 27, just two days after taking command, he ordered his troops to break camp and prepare to move out. Choosing the most direct route to his goal—the British-held town of Camden—Gates led his men through the central part of North Carolina and on August 4 Thomas Pinckney's greatest wish was fulfilled—he was back in South Carolina. By August 13 the Americans were encamped at Rugeley's Mill just 11 miles from Camden.

General Gates had been told that the British garrison in town was weak consisting of only 700 men. While American forces numbered a little over 3,000, two-thirds of the men were inexperienced militia and Gates was not anxious to engage the British in battle. He planned, instead, to build defensive works a few miles north of Camden and by cutting British supply lines force Lord Rawdon, the British commander, to abandon the town. The most appropriate site for constructing the defensive works was located north of Saunders Creek about five and a half miles from Camden. General Gates decided to move his men there at night so they could establish their camp and begin to build the works the next morning. At ten o'clock on the night of August 15, then, the entire army led by a van guard of cavalry began their journey to Saunders Creek heading south on the road to Camden.

Unfortunately, General Gates had received outdated information about the strength of the British forces in Camden. On August 9 Lord Rawdon had sent an urgent dispatch to Lord Cornwallis in Charleston telling him that General Gates was reported to be moving toward Camden with a force numbering about 5,000. Cornwallis lost no time in leaving Charleston with 1,500 men and was able to reach Camden by the 13th of August prepared to meet the American threat.

Lord Rawdon had told Cornwallis that the Americans were encamped at Rugeley's Mill and Cornwallis, ever ready to take the initiative and thinking that the American force was twice the size of his own, planned an early morning, surprise attack on the encampment. Therefore, on the night of August 15, with the cavalry of the British Legion leading the way, the British marched out of town heading north on the road from Camden. At two o'clock in the morning moving in darkness broken only by the light of the stars, the cavalry forming the van guards of each army literally ran into each other on the Camden road. Chaos ensued for the next fifteen minutes then each side managed to draw back to collect their wounded and regroup.

From captured British prisoners, the Americans learned, to their dismay, that a few hundred yards ahead of them stood an army of 2,200 battle-hardened British regulars under the command of General Lord Cornwallis—known as the "fighting general." And from captured Americans Cornwallis learned, to his relief, that the army under Gates numbered only 3,000 men two thirds of whom were unseasoned militia. Both Generals began to make plans for combat.

At first light the battle of Camden commenced. After an exchange of artillery fire, the British began to advance on the left side of the American line which was made up of inexperienced Virginia militia commanded by General Stevens. As the Americans looked across the field in the early morning light, they saw the British advancing in solid formation with muskets held waist high and eighteen inches of gleaming steel in the form of bayonets protruding from the ends of their guns. General Stevens, seeing that the British were mounting a bayonet charge, told his men that they would have to use their bayonets after firing a round or two at the British. That command caused consternation among the militia who had just received their bayonets the night before and had no experience in using them.

As the British marched resolutely forward with their deep-throated cries of "huzzah" ringing across the battlefield, the militia panicked, many fired once and then dropped their muskets and ran while others did not wait to fire, but threw down their loaded weapons and fled. The panic was contagious and spread to General Caswell's North Carolina militia, posted to the left of the Virginians, who also threw down their weapons and ran.

Tom was some 200 yards behind the front line with General Gates when the first wave of fleeing militia came streaming past them. He immediately rode forward to try to rally the next group of bolting men while Generals Gates, Stevens, Caswell and others tried to stop the first group and make them reform. However, no one was able to stop the onslaught of fleeing men and General Gates and the others finally decided to retreat from the field. It was while he was covering their retreat that Tom was wounded—his left leg shattered by a musket ball. In great pain he managed to ride four miles to the rear of the American lines where the non-combatants were encamped with the supply wagons and the baggage train. Someone lifted him into a wagon and there he lay while off in the distance the battle continued.

While the left flank was collapsing Maryland and Delaware Continentals under Baron de Kalb were gallantly checking the British advance on the right. For forty-five minutes 600 Continental soldiers held off a superior force of British regulars. However, de Kalb finally fell, having been wounded eleven times, and though he still lived (he would die three days later in Camden) his men seeing that their leader was down and that they were being surrounded either fled or surrendered. Only those men who ran into the swamps located on either side of the battlefield—where cavalry could not follow—managed to escape. It was reported that the British Legion chased fleeing Americans for twenty-two miles, capturing or killing many of them hours after the battle was over. General Gates, riding a very fast horse, retreated all the way to Hillsborough covering the 180 miles in three days.

The exact number of Americans lost at the battle of Camden is not known. Cornwallis put the number of Americans killed between 800 and 900 while Tarleton reported that seventy officers and 2,000 soldiers were killed, wounded or taken prisoner. He reported that eight cannon, the wagons, carriages, munitions, stores and baggage belonging to the Americans had also been captured.[45] British losses were sixty-six killed and 256 wounded.

Thomas Pinckney knew nothing of what happened after he was placed in the wagon. The pain of his shattered leg was overwhelming and he fainted. He was found lying there unconscious after the battle by Captain Charles Barrington McKenzie of the 71st Regiment—an old school friend from Westminster and the brother of Thomas McKenzie, the navy captain captured by the French off the coast of Georgia in 1779. It was Tom, then an aide to Comte d'Estaing, who had been responsible for the comfortable circumstances of the captain's captivity. Seeing a chance to repay his old school mate for his kindness to his brother, Charles had Tom taken into Camden with the British wounded.

It was late at night before the wagon bearing Tom reached the home of Mrs. Ann Clay who had been ordered by the British to take the wounded into her home. Tom asked that Mrs. Clay not be disturbed so late at night and had the men place him on a table on the piazza. When Captain McKenzie returned the next morning to visit his friend, he realized that Tom would in all likelihood lose his leg and possibly his life unless he received prompt medical attention. He persuaded Banastre Tarleton to send his regimental surgeon to examine him.

Eliza was pleased when she learned that Tom was with General Gates and that he was making his way back to South Carolina with the army. She had returned to Charleston by that time and was staying with Daniel and Harriott at their house on Broad Street. Actually Daniel Horry had invited Eliza to make her home with them as the British occupation of Charleston had left her in serious financial difficulty. Under the terms of her husband's will she was entitled to one-third of the rental revenues collected from the Charleston properties owned by her sons. Since these properties had been seized by the British, the greater part of her income had ceased leaving her with little or nothing to live on and Daniel Horry's invitation had been most welcome.

If Eliza had hoped to be near Charles at the Mansion House when she came to town, she was disappointed for at some point in the summer the British had transferred him along with General Moultrie to Snee plantation. However, British officials had allowed Sally, who was in the last weeks of her pregnancy, to remain in the house with her two daughters. Consequently, Eliza's fifth grandchild—a little boy named Charles Cotesworth—was born there some time in August. Tom had also become a father that summer for from Mount Joseph had come the joyful news that Betsey had given birth to a baby boy named Thomas and that mother and child were doing well.

When Eliza heard the news of the disastrous defeat suffered by the army under General Gates at Camden she was stunned. All the pleasure she had felt on learning that Tom was back in South Carolina changed to alarm. Not knowing the fate of those she loved was never easy for Eliza and the uncertainty surrounding the fate of her youngest son filled her, she wrote, with "a thousand fears and apprehensions."[46]

It was not until August 20, four days after the battle, that Tom was able to write to his brother and tell him of his situation. Both bones of his lower left leg were broken and splintered. It was a compound fracture which meant that part of the bone was protruding through the skin and there was a very good possibility that he might lose his leg. Tom was counting on his brother to break the news to Eliza and to dissuade her from immediately setting out to nurse him—which he knew she would want to do. Camden was crowded with the sick and wounded and the nearby swamps made the town even more undesirable. He did not want his mother to risk her health and wellbeing by coming there.

Eliza could tolerate with the greatest fortitude all adversities to herself, but the misfortunes of her children were very difficult for her to bear. It was bad enough that Charles was a prisoner of war, but Tom's condition caused her more anguish than she could find words to express. "Gracious God support me in this hour of distress," she wrote to Tom after learning of his wound, "You can more easily conceive my feelings upon this occasion, than I express them." She then continued: "'tis saying little at my age to tell you how readily I would part with life, could that save your Limb; but how little can I do for you!... I find you will by no means consent that I should come to you, least I should got sick."[47]

Though she assured Tom that she was not at all worried about the dismal conditions in Camden, he still urged her not to come. Mrs. Clay, the ladies with her and the British doctors were all taking very good care of him, he declared. Therefore, "to prevent giving him pain," she explained to Betsey, "I did not go to him my self: that his mind should be kept quiet and easey must be of great consiquence to him in [his] present situation."[48] Instead she contented herself by writing a letter to Mrs. Clay expressing her deepest gratitude to her and sending Tom ten guineas—gold coins worth twenty-one shillings each—and a box of "necessaries."

In 18th-century warfare, captured enemy officers were allowed certain privileges not extended to enlisted men and were able to correspond with their relatives and friends who were allowed not only to send them letters but also boxes containing food, clothing, wine, medicine and other personal items. Eliza and other members of the Pinckney family took full advantage of this privilege and corresponded regularly with Charles and Thomas while they were prisoners-of-war and sent them articles to make their captivity more pleasant and to keep them in good health.

However, getting these items to Charles and Thomas required some maneuvering and the assistance of British officials. Sometimes an enslaved servant provided with a special pass delivered the letters and boxes and sometimes letters were carried by an obliging British officer who happened to be going to Camden or Snee. Most of the time, however, the items were placed on a supply wagon carrying provisions for the British army. Eliza entrusted letters and boxes for Charles to Major Dellient who saw that they were safely delivered to him at Snee while Major Money, an aide to Lord Cornwallis, and Captain McMahon, the barrack-master in Charleston, were extremely helpful in getting letters and boxes to Tom aboard one of the supply wagons headed for Camden.

Another privilege officers enjoyed were better accommodations—especially senior officers who were generally confined in a home rather than a crowded prison. They were allowed to have visitors and could even have their wives and children come to live with them if they wished. Mrs. Moultrie, for example, joined her husband at Snee and stayed with him during the months he was held there.

Charles, however, did not consider Snee, surrounded by swamps, a healthy location for his wife and children during the summer months and did not even want them to visit him there. "Nor," he informed Eliza, "would I have her [Sally] write to me, as Letters between Husband & Wife are too apt to be turned into ridicule by Persons of no delicacy of feeling; and any Letters she might write would in all probability be perused before they came into my hands; you or Harriott will be so good as to inform me of any thing she would wish to acquaint me with."[49]

Consequently, Eliza became the intermediary between Charles and Sally. It was Eliza who saw that the items that Charles requested: port wine, sugar, tea, and, to help him pass the time, a French dictionary and his flute were packed in boxes and taken across the river to Snee. She wrote to him regularly keeping him informed of the well-being of his family and giving him the latest report on Tom's condition and news about relatives and friends in town. When he became ill with "country fever" and was suffering from the chills, fever and aches typical of malaria, she sent him supplies of "the bark"—quinine made from the bark of the cinchona tree—the only thing known to alleviate or ward off the symptoms of malaria at that time.

Since Eliza could not be with Tom and see for herself how he was progressing, she worried that he was shielding her by not telling her the whole truth about his condition. She had had much the same anxiety about the well-being of Charles and Thomas just after the death of her husband when she imagined that Mrs. Evance, Mr. Morley and Mr. Gerrard were concealing bad news about the boys from her out of pity. Therefore, she was extremely pleased when Captain McKenzie called on her in Charleston to give her the latest report on Tom's condition. Captain McMahon also called to tell her he had heard that Tom "was in a fair way of doing well." "This account," she wrote to Tom, "has greatly relieved the extreme distress into which your misfortune had thrown me."[50] Her friend Dr. Garden also relieved her anxiety by writing to Dr. Hayes, the British surgeon in charge of Tom's recovery. Thomas, Dr. Hayes reported, "is in a very good way, and as well as he could expect, though the cure will be Tedious."[51]

By early September Eliza and the rest of the family were greatly relieved when Tom's doctors announced that he stood in no danger of losing his leg. However, there was still a chance of infection. In an age that knew nothing of the existence of germs, surgeons did not sterilize or even wash their medical instruments before using them and also rarely washed their hands before examining a patient. Consequently, infection was a viable possibility.

To further complicate Tom's recovery, malarial mosquitoes bred in the swamps surrounding Camden and the danger of becoming infected with "country fever" was pronounced. He, too, requested his mother to send him supplies of "the bark" and because he did not want to be a financial burden on her, he applied to his sister for another item "so essential to my Health," he wrote, "indeed I believe to my very Existence that I must rather venture to put you to some Inconvenience than to be without it. What I mean is good Port Wine, which, I believe, with the Bark must be my main Support this Fall."[52]

Eliza was cheered by the accounts Tom sent her of the favorable treatment he was receiving from his British captors. The medical staff was very attentive, he told her, and the officers he came in contact with were respectful and kind—Banastre Tarleton, hardly known for his compassion, sent Tom wine and other "delicacies" and even offered to restore several of Mrs. Motte's horses which his men had impressed from her stables.[53]

One officer in particular, however, was singled out by Tom as being particularly friendly and attentive. He was Captain Coffin, an American Loyalist with the New York Volunteers, and Tom asked his mother to pay him special attention when he came to visit. Eliza, always disposed to like anyone who treated her children well, greeted the young officer warmly when he appeared at the Horry house carrying letters or messages from Tom. He was well liked by the whole family and was often invited to stay and dine with them. Another frequent visitor at the house in Broad Street and an overwhelming favorite with Eliza was Captain McKenzie—to whom she would be eternally grateful for saving Tom's life. He, too, was often a dinner guest at the Horry house.

In all her correspondence there is never a hint that Eliza thought the British had an ulterior motive for their kindness and attention to her family. Always seeing the best in people, Eliza viewed the British officers she came in contact with as polite, respectful men who had kindly come to her assistance during a particularly stressful time in her life and she was extremely grateful to them. However, her sons were under no illusions about their captors. The British would have been very happy to have Charles and Thomas Pinckney change sides and become loyal British subjects once again. The favorable treatment meted out to both brothers was in part an attempt to persuade them to do just that. However, both Charles and Thomas remained staunchly loyal to the Patriot cause.

Tom had long wished to be removed from Camden and be paroled to Mount Joseph where he could be with his wife and son. However, before he could even think of asking permission to do so, he had to be sure his leg was strong enough to withstand the journey. By the end of September the doctors gave him the good news—he was pronounced fit to travel. Major Money then obtained the needed permission from General Cornwallis and Tom was to be paroled to Mount Joseph until his leg "was sufficiently healed" for him to travel to Orangeburg where the rest of the field officers on parole were being held. In early October Tom made the journey to Mount Joseph.

The closing months of 1780 were especially trying for Eliza and her family. Charles continued to have bouts of malaria at Snee and in early October the

British evicted his wife and children from the Mansion House. The baby, little Charles Cotesworth, was not thriving and Charles and Sally feared that he would not survive. Tom no sooner settled in at Mount Joseph when the small-pox hit the household and his wife and child were taken with it—Betsey so ill that for a time it was thought that she would not live. Fortunately, she recovered but the recovery was slow. Although Tom remained in good health, his wound did not improve and Eliza was anxious that he be allowed to travel to Hampton or Charleston so his leg could receive proper medical attention. Mount Joseph located on a bluff overlooking the Congaree River and continually swept by cold winds was not, Eliza felt, conducive to Tom's recovery.

The Pinckney family may have been going through a stressful time during the waning months of the year 1780, but the Patriot cause had taken a decided turn for the better. Partisans fighters under Francis Marion in the Santee area and Thomas Sumter in the backcountry had scored significant victories over the British—the most important coming on October 7 when 1,100 partisan fighters from the mountainous regions of western Virginia and North and South Carolina attacked and overwhelmingly defeated Major Ferguson and his 1,000 Loyalist militia at King's Mountain.

Consequently, as the year 1780 came to a close, patriot hopes were high. The Continental Congress had appointed a new Commander of the Southern Department and this time they had asked General Washington for his recommendation—General Gates having previously been selected by congress without the commander-in-chief's endorsement. Washington was now able to appoint the man he had always wanted to appoint—General Nathanael Greene. Greene arrived in early December—the tide was beginning to turn.

The Liberation of South Carolina

The Christmas of 1780 was a sad and lonely one for Eliza. Her family was scattered—Charles was at Snee with his oldest daughter Maria while Sally, Harriott and the baby were in Charleston; Thomas was at Mount Joseph with his wife and son and Harriott and Daniel were at Hampton with their two children. The Horrys had gone to Hampton in the early part of December with their daughter leaving Daniel in town with his grandmother. The war had seriously disrupted his education as many schoolmasters and tutors had left Charleston before the British laid siege to it. However, in September a tutor had been found and Daniel was once again engaged in his studies. He had taken some time off from his lessons, though, and gone to Hampton for the Christmas holidays to enjoy some hunting with his father.

Eliza had not accompanied Daniel to Hampton, but had remained in town to keep Charles apprised of the condition of his son now in Charleston with his mother. The baby, constantly plagued by fever and pain, was frail and found it hard to suckle and twice had appeared on the verge of death before recovering. There was still hope that he would survive, but the prospects were not good. At the end of December Charles, weak and low from his own bouts of fever, confided to Eliza: "I almost dread to hear of my poor little boy."[54]

The subsequent death of the baby, while not unexpected, cast a spirit of sorrow over the family and must have reminded Eliza of her own feelings after the death of her baby thirty-three years before: "Young as it was, the pain was sharp we found at parting with it," she had written to a friend in England. It was a melancholy end to the year. Harriott writing to her mother from Hampton on Christmas Day expressed her wish for "a more fortunate new year than the last."[55]

Fortunately, January started off with some good news. Eliza was relieved to learn that Tom had been given permission to come to Charleston to receive medical attention for his leg. The bones in Tom's leg had re-joined, but, as the outer edges of the bones had been splintered by the musket ball, tiny fragments of bone remained in the wound—their sharp points causing Tom a great deal of pain. Individual pieces of bone eventually worked their way to the surface— much as feathers work their way through the covering of a down pillow—and they had to be painstakingly removed. Eliza had a pair of small forceps specially made for Tom which she hoped would make the extractions easier. Tom warned the family: "I have Reason to fear there are a great many yet to come away, tho' a very considerable number has already been extracted."[56]

At first Thomas had been reluctant to ask permission to come to Charleston for he did not want to be a financial burden on his mother. As captured enemy officers both Charles and Thomas were entitled to be fed and lodged by the British, but, as they were not receiving any income from their confiscated properties, they had to rely on the generosity of their families for the "extras" they needed for their comfort and well-being. Thomas was especially averse to becoming a burden to either his mother or the Motte family both suffering financially from the British occupation. He relied, instead, on his sister, whose husband's estates had not been confiscated, to supply him with the more expensive items he needed—such as port wine. Charles' father-in-law, Henry Middleton, had also taken British protection and it is highly likely that he provided the items Charles requested—Eliza passing on his requests to Sally who then relied on her father to supply them.

According to the proclamation issued by Lord Cornwallis on July 22 only planters who had sworn allegiance to the king could ship rice and other articles of produce to Great Britain or Ireland—providing, of course, that these items were not needed for the use of the military or the inhabitants of South Carolina. Similarly, only merchants who had taken the oath of loyalty were allowed to conduct business. A special license was needed to sell land, houses or slaves, but selling property was difficult as hard currency was scarce and the paper money issued by the Continental Congress was basically worthless.

On September 6 the British issued a proclamation concerning the sequestration of the estates of rebels. For humanitarian purposes, the proclamation stated, one quarter of the net income from the estate was to be paid to the wife and children of the former owner. Charles was then able to have some sheep and hogs sent from his Beech Hill plantation for the use of his family. He also advised Eliza to take an authorized copy of his father's will to the British authorities to prove that Belmont was hers so that it would not be sequestered with the rest of his property and since some of her Belmont slaves had gone to Beech Hill after the British plundered her house, the will would be useful in identifying her slaves and separating them from his.

Tom did not have all the resources available to his brother as his plantation at Ashpoo could not have been very productive after the British plundered and burned it in 1779. If he came to Charleston with his wife and son, he would be financially dependent on his mother and he knew she was not in affluent circumstances and he also knew she would sacrifice her own well-being to provide for him and his family. However, Eliza had not been idle and triumphantly wrote to him at the beginning of December: "I have a prospect to subsist you and yours (for some months at least)."[57]

As a widow who had committed no crime and not been charged with any offense Eliza felt that what remained of her estate must, "when the present confusion subsides, be my own."[58] She was correct. She had an authenticated copy of Charles Pinckney's will presented to the Board of Police, who after examining it, ruled that she had a legal right to a third of the rent from a house on Bay Street belonging to her son Charles—a decision that was upheld by the British Commander in Charleston. Then Mr. Cruden, the Commissioner of Sequestration, informed her that she was also entitled to a third of the rent from another house in town owned by Charles. Captain McMahon had already returned her house on Elroy Street to her and she had very easily found a tenant for it. "These will procure necessaries," she told Tom, "and till the rents become due, I make no doubt, I can get Credit, with this prospect of paying. Belmont, is not yet Let [rented], but I still have hopes of geting something for it. Mr. Horry gave me an Invitation of making his house my home, so that I keep no house, and consiquently, can want but little for my self."[59]

Then Daniel and Harriott, who were at Hampton, offered the use of their townhouse to Tom and his family. No more persuasion was needed and Tom applied for and received permission to come to Charleston. On January 15 he and his family arrived at the Horry house to be welcomed by a very happy and excited Eliza and Daniel. Eliza, a very adoring grandmother, was then able to hold her newest grandchild in her arms for the first time and make a great fuss over him.

Soon after Thomas and his family settled in at the house on Broad Street, exciting news about a Patriot victory in the backcountry reached Charleston. In early December General Nathanael Greene had arrived in Charlotte, North Carolina to take command of the Southern Department. He had re-organized the army and divided it in half giving command of one half to General Daniel Morgan. On the 21st of December Morgan headed west with his troops towards the British outpost of Ninety-six. His orders were to act "either offensively or defensively as your own prudence and discretion may direct" and his goal was "to give protection to that part of the country and spirit up the people" and to annoy the enemy.[60]

Lord Cornwallis, fearing an American attack on the outpost at Ninety-six, responded by sending his favorites, Banastre Tarleton and the British Legion, to stop them. On January 17, 1781, the two armies clashed at a place called the Cowpens. There General Morgan and his men won a decisive victory over the hated British Legion and its commander. When, after an hour of fighting, the battle was over, 86 percent of the participating British forces were either dead, wounded or had been captured. In one hour Lord Cornwallis had been deprived of his light troops—swift moving, versatile troops who were an essential component of any army. It was a devastating blow.

The victory undoubtedly brought smiles to the faces of the American prisoners-of-war being held in Charleston and to Patriots all over the country. Charles and General Moultrie, eagerly following events at Snee, would have been delighted with the news but also frustrated because they were not free to take part in military action. There was no hope either that they would soon be exchanged for the official channels needed to implement the trade of prisoners had not as yet been established in the Southern Department. It would not be until May 3 that the British and Americans agreed to create an official board to process exchanges. Charles and General Moultrie would have to wait many months before they were free to fight again.

After the victory at the Cowpens, General Greene joined forces with Daniel Morgan and took the army into North Carolina. Lord Cornwallis followed for not only did he want to destroy Greene's army but he also wanted to conquer North Carolina. Annoyed by the actions of Patriot militia who were making life difficult for the British, Cornwallis thought the best way to keep

South Carolina under British control was to eliminate North Carolina as a safe haven for partisan forces. Consequently, for the next six weeks or more, General Lord Cornwallis and his army chased General Greene and his army over the state of North Carolina—coming close to catching up, but never being quite able to do so.

Notwithstanding the fact that Greene's strategy appeared to be one of playing cat and mouse with the British, he was not averse to facing Cornwallis in battle, but it would be at a time and a place of his choosing. On March 15 he decided the time was right and the place he chose for the confrontation was a small hamlet in the backcountry of North Carolina called Guilford Courthouse. The ensuing battle was the largest and most fiercely contested battle of the American Revolution in the south and although it resulted in a tactical victory for the British, the cost was high. Cornwallis lost 28 percent of his men that day. As Charles James Fox, a British politician, quipped in the House of Commons: "Another such victory would ruin the British army." Cornwallis then took his battered and weary troops to the Carolina coast to rest and be resupplied. When the army had recovered and was ready to move out, Lord Cornwallis turned his back on South Carolina and headed north to face his destiny in the tiny port city of Yorktown in Virginia.

Meanwhile, Daniel and Harriott had a family matter that was weighing heavily on their minds—the education of their son. Young Daniel would turn twelve in August and it was time for him to be enrolled in a proper school. Before the British began to implement their "Southern Strategy," the Horry's had thought fleetingly of sending their son to a school in Europe, but the danger of an ocean voyage during war time was deemed too great. However, now that the British controlled South Carolina, it was possible to send him to England to complete his education. On July 6, 1781, Daniel and his son set sail from Charleston for London and on August 24 young Daniel Horry was entered into Westminster School to follow in the footsteps of his uncles.[61]

It was heart wrenching for Eliza to be separated from her oldest grandchild. She was, of course, excessively fond of all her grandchildren, but the two oldest, Daniel and Maria, were her favorites. She was especially attached to Daniel for she had spent a great deal of time with him ever since his birth and the two of them were very close. That she missed him very much is apparent from the rather mournful note she made two years later at the bottom of her copy of a letter to him: "This day to [two] year, we parted with our dear Child. Heaven grant this painful parting may answer all the good purposes we hoped from it."[62]

Now that South Carolina was British again, Eliza had resumed corresponding with her friends in England and she now wrote to ask them to extend their friendship to her grandson who had never traveled outside South Carolina before and never been separated from his family. The whole experience of attending school in a strange country was quite overwhelming for him and it is no surprise that he expressed "dissatisfaction" at being so far away from home.

When Eliza heard that he was unhappy in England, she wrote to him: "I know by my own feelings how much firmness is necessary to support properly the absence of those we love; at this moment my heart overflows with tenderness and a longing impatience to take you in my arms and tell you how truely, how fondly I love you."[63] If she had only her own feelings to consider, Eliza continued, she would wish him back in South Carolina. However, the prospect of acquiring a good education, she pointed out to him, must outweigh all the sufferings of separation. Her friends responded kindly and soon Daniel was feeling more at home. Eliza continued to correspond with him, encouraging him to study hard and to strive to be "a blessing and an ornament to your family." Her letters to her grandson echoed the advice and encouragement she had given her sons almost a quarter of a century earlier.

As difficult as that separation had been, there was an even more difficult one ahead for Eliza. The commission for the exchange of prisoners-of-war had finally been established and Philadelphia was designated as the site for captured American officers to wait for their exchanges to be arranged. Consequently, in the early summer of 1781 Colonel Balfour, the British Commander at Charleston, ordered all paroled officers and their families to leave for Philadelphia. The deadline for their departure was August 1.

In the middle of July, just days after the departure of Daniel and his son to England, both of Eliza's sons and their families along with nearly eighty others set sail for Philadelphia. Eliza had endured separation from family members in the past, but that did not make the present separation any easier for her to bear. It was heartbreaking for her to see her sons and their families exiled from their native country. She worried about Tom's wounded leg and Charles's bouts of recurrent fever. They would have little money to support themselves and their families in Philadelphia and the fact that she was not able to help them financially added to her grief at their departure.

Anxiously awaiting news of their safe arrival, Eliza was relieved when she heard from Charles. On July 25 he wrote: "I have the pleasure to acquaint you that we are all well; and arrived here after an agreeable passage of Eight days. The Female part of our Passengers were alarmed but once during our whole Voyage, and that was on our approaching rather too near to the Breakers of Cape Look-out." Knowing his mother would be worried about the condition of Tom's leg, he added: "My Brother walks a Mile and a half with his stick without being fatigued."[64] The next day she received a letter from Tom assuring her that he and his family were well and that he had walked a mile that day without tiring his leg.

The two Pinckney families shared a house in Germantown some ten miles outside Philadelphia with Charles's brother-in-law Edward Rutledge and his family. Stenton, as the handsome brick house was called, had been lent to them by Dr. George Logan and had previously served as George Washington's headquarters in August of 1777 and later as the headquarters of British General Sir William Howe. The ten occupants of the house were a little crowded, but they settled in and were able to manage a certain degree of comfort. Tom exercised his leg by walking whenever possible, but all three of the men were restless having little to do but follow the war effort and yearn for their exchanges.

Eliza spent the stressful summer and early fall of the year 1781 in Charleston with her daughter and granddaughter. The departure of her grandson for England followed closely by the exile of her sons and their families to Philadelphia had left Eliza despondent and anxious. However, she rallied and resorted to her time-honored tradition of overcoming stress by keeping busy. Only once in her life had grief and sorrow held her in such an iron grip that she was incapable of action and that had been the period following the death of her beloved Charles in 1758.

She endured the present separation from those she loved by indulging in her favorite activities: gardening, reading and writing letters. She had the garden at the Horry house to work in, books to read and a grandson and friends in England to correspond with along with her sons in Philadelphia. She also had a delightful three year old granddaughter, who by all accounts was a little chatterbox, to bring a smile to her lips. Although anxious for news of her sons and their families—Betsey was expecting a baby in October—she kept her mind occupied and followed the progress of the war hoping for a speedy end to it.

Meanwhile General Greene was doing his very best to accomplish that feat. After Cornwallis moved north into Virginia, Greene brought his army back to South Carolina where he put in place a carefully constructed campaign to rid the state of its British conquerors. His plan was to keep his army in the field engaging the enemy in battles and sieges while partisan militia destroyed British lines of supply and discouraged Loyalist support. The plan was successful. General Greene's forces did their part while partisan fighters were effective in frustrating the British—none more so than General Francis Marion and his brigade who operated in the Santee area.

Francis Marion was well-known to both Daniel and Harriott. Many members of the brigade had been in Daniel Horry's cavalry regiment before the fall of Charleston and were neighbors and friends. In spite of the fact that Daniel had sworn allegiance to the king and taken British protection, his accounts during this time period indicate that he provided rice, pork, beef, fodder, the use of boats, etc., to the partisan fighters in Santee. When Daniel was absent in England, Harriott continued the practice and there are vouchers showing that she provided both equipment and food to Marion's brigade.[65]

Partisan forces had been so successful in disrupting British supply routes from Charleston that spring that on May 9 the British were forced to evacuate Camden and later that same month they abandoned Georgetown and their forts along the Santee. Meanwhile on May 22 General Greene and the army were busy laying siege to the British outpost at Ninety-six in the western part of the state. Even though the siege was not successful, Lord Rawdon marched to the rescue of the fort and Greene was forced to retreat, the British position there was untenable—the outpost could not be permanently held. At the end of June British troops abandoned the fort and, after destroying what they could of it, began the long, weary trek to Charleston.

On September 8 the British and Americans clashed at the battle of Eutaw Springs—a violently contested battle that lasted three to four hours with heavy casualties on both sides. Unfortunately, the Americans, on the threshold of victory, stopped to celebrate their success by looting the supply wagons of the enemy and helping themselves to the great quantities of liquor found there and were ultimately defeated. However, after Eutaw Springs the British army was badly damaged and in no condition to continue its field operations. The British withdrew to the safety of Charleston. General Greene then established his headquarters at Bacon's Bridge on the Ashely River 24 miles from Charleston where he could keep an eye on British activity and thwart their attempts to send skirmishing parties out into the countryside to gather provisions.

There was exhilarating news for Patriots in the fall of 1781. In September General Washington, leading a combined force of American and French troops, had managed to trap the British under Lord Cornwallis in Yorktown, Virginia. The British position was untenable and on October 19, after a siege of almost three weeks, Cornwallis was forced to surrender. While South Carolinians rejoiced at the news of this significant victory, they could not afford to let down their guard—the British were still an active force in their state.

Meanwhile there was good news in Philadelphia for captured American officers. Some of the junior officers were being exchanged—their exchanges being easier to arrange than those of higher ranking officers. Captain Edward (Ned) Rutledge was one of the fortunate ones and leaving his family in the care of his brother-in-law, Charles Cotesworth, Ned left Philadelphia in November to make his way back home.

Since General Greene had established his headquarters at Bacon's Bridge 20 miles from the town of Jacksonborough, Governor Rutledge felt that Jacksonborough was a secure enough place for the legislature to meet. Consequently, he called for elections to be held in November to choose delegates for the first meeting of the General Assembly to be held in South Carolina in two years. Ned, Charles and Thomas had all been elected as representatives, but only Ned was able to attend the meetings which began on January 18, 1782. At that time the legislature chose John Matthews as the fourth governor of the independent state of South Carolina.

After Ned's departure from Philadelphia both the Pinckney men were even more anxious than ever to be on their way home. Betsey had given birth in October to a baby girl and by January she and the baby were strong enough to travel. Having heard that the British were abandoning their outlying posts and retreating towards Charleston, Tom decided it was safe for him to return home even though he had not been exchanged. He and his wife and two children set out by carriage at the end of January for Santee arriving there in the middle of March.

Tom left his wife and children at Fairfield, the Motte plantation in Santee, and then traveled on to Jacksonborough where the General Assembly was meeting. Harriott had gone into Charleston in the middle of March to join her husband who had just returned from England and it is quite likely that Eliza remained at Hampton with little Harriott. If so, then Thomas would have paid her a visit before going on to Jacksonborough and Eliza would have been sure to have called at Fairfield after he left to see her new granddaughter—Elizabeth Brewton Pinckney.

Back in Philadelphia Charles was heartened by news that he and General Moultrie were to be part of the exchange for British General John Burgoyne. Not waiting for the official papers granting the exchange to arrive, Charles started for home traveling by carriage with his wife, daughters and the family of Ned Rutledge. On March 3, 1782, General Moultrie sent Charles the papers that made him a free man. On reaching South Carolina Charles took his family to the plantation of Tom Middleton, Sally's brother, which was near Jacksonborough—far enough away from Charleston that a British raiding party could not capture him. He then reported to General Greene at Bacon's Bridge.

As the year 1782 progressed it soon became apparent that the war in America was winding down. There were indications that the British were not as concerned about the war with their former colonists as they were about the war taking place in other parts of the world against the French, Spanish and Dutch. On July 11, 1782, the British evacuated Savannah and in August rumors of negotiations being held in Paris began to flitter through the countryside. One of the issues being discussed in Paris was the recognition of the independence of the thirteen former British colonies.

Now that the British had withdrawn from Georgia, discussions on the evacuation of Charleston began. The Americans were afraid the Loyalists who were leaving with the British troops would burn the city or damage it in some way as they left and the British were reluctant to have the Americans enter the city before all their troops had left fearing reprisals against them. The two sides finally reached a satisfactory agreement: American forces would enter the town just as the British rear guard was leaving; the Americans would not harm the guard in any way and the British would not damage the city.

On December 14, 1782, as the sun rose over the Atlantic Ocean British troops began to withdraw from the outer edges of the city of Charleston marching through the city gates across town to Gadsden's wharf where they were to board the waiting transports. Two hundred yards behind them came the American light infantry, cavalry and artillery led by Brigadier General Anthony Wayne. At three o'clock in the afternoon Governor Matthews and General Nathanael Greene entered the city preceded by a cavalry guard of honor. They were followed by Major General William Moultrie and Brigadier General Mordecai Gist. Riding behind them were a group of Continental Army officers, including both Colonel and Major Pinckney, with the council and other distinguished citizens. The war was not officially over and the army could not be disbanded as yet, but South Carolina was at last free of the British.

CHAPTER SIX

The Final Years (1783–1793)

The Aftermath of War

Once the Patriots had gained control of the state, they were anxious to seek revenge against those who had supported the British cause from the beginning and those who had later taken British protection. In January of 1782 before the British had even evacuated Charleston, the General Assembly began the process of retaliation by passing an act to confiscate the property of Loyalists and to either confiscate or amerce the estates of those who had taken British protection. While there were some who opposed the legislation, they were in the minority and the bill passed easily. Then the legislators began the long process of compiling a list of men whose property was to be either confiscated or amerced.

Ned Rutledge, responsible for writing the first draft of the act, wrote to his brother-in-law Arthur Middleton in Philadelphia on February 8: "I wish to God you or the Pinckneys, or all were here. I do assure you my dear Friend the passions of some People run very high. Tho' I am for Confiscating some Estates yet I fear some men will give way to private Resentment—it is an odious painful Business."[1] Ned Rutledge was quite correct. Personal feelings would play a prominent role in the selection of names to be placed on the list and many men would fall victim to the vindictiveness of their peers. Eliza's nephew Charles Pinckney II was one of them.

During his long career in government Charles had made political enemies. He had been a strong Patriot supporter at the beginning of the war and had donated 20,000 guineas towards the war effort, but later he had taken British protection and his adversaries now joined to denounce him in the General Assembly. There were two serious charges leveled against him. The first was that Charles had been one of the approximately 160 Charlestonians who had signed a letter congratulating Lord Cornwallis on his victory at Camden and condemning the Patriot cause. The second was that he had voluntarily returned to Charleston and taken British protection after the surrender instead of staying with Governor Rutledge and the other two members of the council. Although Charles had his supporters in the legislature, regrettably, his detractors were more persuasive and his estate was amerced or taxed 12 percent of its net worth.

Unfortunately amercement was not the only penalty threatening Charles Pinckney II. Former Patriots now living under British protection in Charleston had until the General Assembly met in August to leave town and report to American headquarters at Bacon's Bridge. Those who did not "come out" faced confiscation of property and banishment from the state. Charles, ashamed of his actions and humiliated by the criticism he had received from members of the legislature, recoiled from coming out of town and facing his former associates.

When Charles Cotesworth reported to American Headquarters after his exchange, he soon learned that his cousin was making no effort to leave Charleston and he became seriously alarmed. Charles did not want to see his cousin, a man he had always admired, stripped of all his property and banished from the land of his birth. He wrote to his cousin in July and, assuring him that his respect and regard for him had not changed, begged him to leave town before the prescribed time. The letter was effective and on August 13, 1782, Charles Pinckney II left Charleston and British protection to face his peers at American headquarters on the Ashley River.

Unfortunately, the stress he had been under for the past months had left him exhausted and demoralized and his removal to the low-swampy countryside outside of Charleston and away from ocean breezes was not beneficial to his health. He was soon stricken with "country fever" and on September 22, within five weeks of having left Charleston, Charles Pinckney II died. He was buried in the graveyard at St. Andrew's Church; however, his body was later re-interred in the family plot at St. Philip's in Charleston.

Eliza could not help but feel great sorrow at his passing. She remembered him as the little boy who had been part of his uncle's household when she used to visit the Pinckney's in the days before her marriage. Then after her marriage, little Charles had become her charge. She also had fond memories of him as the young lawyer who had helped her with all the legal matters attending to the death of her husband and showed her such kindness and support. She would never forget either the role her nephew had played in aiding the career of her oldest son when he returned to Charleston. She heartily agreed with her son's sentiments when he wrote: "Give vent to your Tears, for he was a man of worth."[2]

Charles Pinckney II was not Eliza's only relative to find himself in trouble with the legislature. Daniel Horry returned from England sometime in February and was dismayed to discover that his name was on the list and that his property might be confiscated. Ned Rutledge reporting to Arthur Middleton in March wrote: "Poor Horry is come in [arrived in Charleston from London] & truly to be pitied he is.... He has made several applications for Leave to come out of Town, but as might have been expected, he has been as repeatedly refused. I have sent him my Opinion as to his line of Conduct—It is really a cruel Case."[3] On March 10 Harriott received permission from the British to travel to Charleston to be with her husband. A few weeks later she wrote an appeal to an unidentified person, perhaps the governor or a member of the General Assembly:

> Forgive good Sir the trouble now given you by the anxious solicitude of a Mother for her innocent and helpless children; A report prevails that Mr. Horry's Estate is to be sequesterd which, if true, is such an addition to the sorrow I have experienced from the many Injuries and mortifications which myself, my Mother and brothers with their Families have suffered in various ways from our attachment to our Country that I am oppressed with the thought of becoming a Victim to Misfortune both from friends and Foes; If Mr. Horry is so guilty as to deserve this forfeiture, I hope it will be remembered that it is impossible to seperate him from the many innocent ones connected with and who must suffer with him; and the American troubles, with the severity of British measures, have put it wholey out of the power of my own nearest relations and natural connections to assist us; even my Mother tho' a Widow has fared little better in her fortune than Men who have had their Estates sequesterd for bearing Arms against the British Government.

She rejoiced over her country's victory, Harriott continued, even though that victory meant the ruin of her own family—a ruin that was certain "unless Gentlemen of Influence in the assembly will exert themselves to Moderate [the] angry passions of those whose sufferings have irritated them to severity." She then begged the recipient of the letter to use his influence to interfere "in this matter and that if it can't be prevented" she asked that it might be postponed.[4]

Daniel Horry had many friends in the General Assembly and his estates were not sequestered. However, he was not allowed to escape without penalty. His estate was amerced 12 percent of its net worth. The amercement was postponed, however, as Daniel appealed the decision. In 1783 he presented an account of the expenses he had accrued by supporting the partisan forces in Santee from 1780 to 1783 and in 1785 he petitioned the General Assembly to have his name removed from the list of people whose property was to be amerced.[5]

Eliza was saddened by the vindictive behavior displayed by many in the state. She had lost her entire fortune during the British occupation and had seen her sons made prisoners-of-war and then, wounded and in ill health, exiled to Philadelphia. However, she wrote to her grandson, all she wanted was "to forget as soon as I can their cruelties, I wish to forgive ... and hope our joy and gratitude for our great deliverance, may equal our former anguish."[6]

She was also proud of the attitude her sons had taken. She continued: "And when I contemplate with what philosophick firmness and calmness they both of them supported pain, sickness, and evils of various sorts, and withstood the utmost efforts of the enemies malice, and see with what greatness of mind they now generously conduct themselves to all; my heart overflows with gratitude to their great preserver, for continuing to me such children!"[7] Eliza, her sons and others in the state believed that leniency and forgiveness, not vengeance, were needed to bind the people of the state together so that South Carolina could recover both economically and emotionally from the ravages of war.

It is not an exaggeration to say that Eliza was destitute after the war. She owed her old friend Dr. Garden, now living in England, a small debt of under £60 which she was not able to pay. In May 1782 she wrote to him: "It may seem strange that a single woman accused of no crime, who had a fortune to live Genteelly in any part of the world, that fortune too in different kinds of property, and in four or five different parts of the country, should in so short a time be so entirely deprived of it as not to be able to pay a debt under sixty pounds sterling, but such is my singular case."[8]

Since Dr. Garden had been a staunch Loyalist, Eliza wanted him to know who was responsible for the fact that she could not pay his bill and therefore gave him a detailed account of her financial difficulties. First British officials had taken possession of her house on Elroy Street in order to house Hessian soldiers and then they had claimed her plantation at Belmont for the use of the cavalry. Consequently she was left with no place to live. If her son-in-law had not invited her to live with his family, she told Dr. Garden, she would have had no place to lay her head either in town or in the country.

She would also have had no money to rent a lodging for the glowing prospects of income that Eliza had written so excitedly about to Tom at the end of 1780 never fully materialized. Eliza had been able to rent both her house in town and the plantation at Belmont, but the British seizures of both meant the eviction of the tenants and the loss of rental income and although the British were supposed to pay her for the use of both properties, as of May 1782 they had not done so.

Eliza was entitled to one third of the rent of the two houses in Charleston belonging to her son Charles. Each house in the past had rented for £300 a year providing Eliza with an annual income of £200. However, the British would only allow £150 a year rent for each house cutting Eliza's income in half. She had received a total of £200 for the rental of the houses, she wrote Dr. Garden, but it had been paid out in small amounts at irregular intervals over the two years the British had occupied Charleston.

She had not yet come to the end of the recital of her problems, however. She had received permission to graze thirty to forty head of cattle on her son's plantation at Beech Hill. The cattle were subsequently seized for the use of the British army who paid her nothing for them. At Belmont Eliza was further irritated by the actions of the British officer in charge of the plantation. She confided to Dr. Garden: "To my regret and to the great prejudice of the place, the wood has also been all cut down for the use of the garrison, for which I have not got a penny."[9] There was, however, a chance that the British would now pay her something for the wood and Eliza promised Dr. Garden that as soon as she received payment from them she would settle his bill.

The loss of the trees at Belmont was more distressing to Eliza than the loss of income for many of the trees had been planted there by her husband. She was, as she had once written a friend, an enthusiast "in my Veneration for fine trees" and had once had her patience tried over "the Cutting down one remarkable tree which was directed by an old man by mistake, and I could not help being very angry with the old fellow tho' he had never offended me before in his life. Indeed it was planted by my dear Mr. Pinckneys own hand, which made it doubly mortifying to me."[10]

Once the British had evacuated the city of Charleston on December 14, 1782, the former residents were free to inspect their property and assess the damage done to it by two and a half years of military occupation. Eliza's garden at her house on Elroy Street would have certainly shown signs of neglect as well as the house as it had served as a barracks for almost two years. It is likely that at this time Eliza began to live in her own house once again and she would have immediately started to work to re-design and re-plant the garden and refurbish the house.

The first order of business for South Carolinians in the months after the British evacuation, while they waited for a definitive peace to be signed, was to restore their property and livelihoods. South Carolina had been the scene of more Revolutionary War battles and skirmishes than any state in the union and the countryside bore the scars of the fighting that had taken place there. Many plantations had been completely ruined and others almost ruined as fields had been burned, houses destroyed, livestock taken, carts, wagons and boats confiscated or burned. An even greater problem was the lack of workers as many slaves had been confiscated by the British—as many as 25,000 slaves, it was reported, had been taken to be sold in the West Indies. South Carolinians had much work to do to restore their plantations and farms and to rebuild the state's economy.

Charles Cotesworth and Thomas immediately had the overseers and enslaved workers on their plantations begin cultivating rice in earnest and picked up the threads of their law practices once again. Charles and his law partner Ned Rutledge had had a well-established law practice before the war and were able, after a few lean months, to acquire enough cases to keep them both busy. Tom, on the other hand, had not had time before the war to make a name for himself as a lawyer and had to slowly begin to build a practice. He was handicapped somewhat by the fact that he was still troubled by the splinters of bone that worked their way through his wounded leg.

In February of 1783 Eliza received bad news. The house on her plantation at Belmont had been accidently set on fire by enslaved workers cutting wood on the property. Eliza had not lived at Belmont since before the British looted it in 1779, but she may have had plans to repair the house, refurnish it and restore the gardens making it her country residence once again. The house and grounds certainly held many happy memories for her and served as a link to the past and people that she had loved.

She must have discussed the possibility of rebuilding the house with Charles as he would inherit Belmont after her death. Most likely they both came to the same conclusion: that it was better not to restore the house—neither of them having the money at that time to undertake the project. Also at her time of life, Eliza may have felt she did not need the responsibility of managing her own plantation and country home. Consequently, although the property remained in the family and was used to provide wood, pastures for grazing cattle and fields for the cultivation of crops, the house was never rebuilt. Harriott and Daniel then invited Eliza to make Hampton her country residence.

On August 10, 1783, the General Assembly changed the name of the state's capital from Charles Town to Charleston and on September 3, 1783, the Treaty of Paris, officially ending the war with Great Britain, was signed in London. The most important element of the treaty, as far as the former colonists were concerned, was the recognition of the independence of the United States of America. Under the terms of the treaty the British kept Canada but ceded the area east of the Mississippi River and south of the Great lakes to the United States and returned Florida to the Spanish.

A New Country

By the time the Peace Treaty was signed in Paris the number of Eliza's grandchildren had grown. Tom and Betsey had had another daughter. They named her Harriott Lucas Pinckney but generally called her "Lucas" or "Lucy"— perhaps to distinguish her from the two other granddaughters named Harriott. Charles and Sally had also had another child—a little girl named Eliza Lucas

Pinckney. Sally, however, was not well. She had been suffering from consumption or tuberculosis for some time and had been stricken with a lingering fever while she and Charles were staying at her brother's plantation near Jacksonborough after their return from Philadelphia. In the fall of 1782 her doctor had suggested a change of location and she went to stay at her father's plantation at Goose Creek until the British evacuated Charleston and she was able to return to town.

As Charles struggled to resume his law practice and restore his plantations, Sally struggled with her health. In the spring of 1784, she seemed a little better and Charles set out on the circuit not believing her to be in any danger. Unfortunately, she took a turn for the worse while he was gone and on May 8, 1784, she died. Charles was a widower at the age of thirty-eight with three daughters—the youngest one hardly more than a baby. He promptly placed the girls in the care of the person he considered the most capable of raising and educating them—his mother. Eliza welcomed the task—to have her grandchildren around her was always a pleasure and Maria, the oldest of the girls, was one of her favorites. The three girls would fill the void in her life left by her other favorite—Daniel—when he went away to school.

Rice production was once again very profitable for Carolina planters and many, including Charles Cotesworth, also started growing indigo again. However, indigo was not as lucrative as it had been before the war. The bounty from England, of course, was no longer being paid and the British were not as inclined to favor indigo from Carolina over indigo from the West Indies and the Far East as they had been before. Indigo production would gradually decline in South Carolina over the next decade and by the end of the century whatever indigo was being produced would be for domestic use only. Cotton, which grew well on land that had once produced indigo, would become the new cash crop in Carolina.

In 1784, much to Eliza's delight, Tom and Betsey inherited Fairfield, the Motte plantation in Santee, upon the death of Betsey's father. Since Tom's house at his plantation on the Ashpoo River had been burned by the British, he and Betsey decided to make Fairfield their country residence. Eliza now had Tom and his family in close proximity to her at Hampton. At Fairfield Tom, who was interested in scientific farming, began to experiment with ways to improve the yield of his fields and the quality of his livestock—projects that captured his mother's interest and had her wholehearted support.

Eliza divided her time between the house in Charleston and Hampton plantation always in the company of her four granddaughters—Maria, the two Harriotts and little Eliza. In early November of 1785 she was in town with the girls when she received a letter from Harriott, who had just returned to Hampton.

Upon her arrival, Harriott informed her mother, she had found Tom at the house attending her husband who was seriously ill with a "bilious fever." Tom, who had ridden over from Fairfield after learning that Daniel was ill, had already sent for the doctor from Georgetown to examine him.

Two days later Harriott was able to report to her mother that Mr. Horry was free from fever, but was "as yellow as the darkest Orange" and had had "the hiccough's almost continually these two days." Daniel Horry rallied the next day and seemed better, but suffered a relapse that night. "He speaks very thick and is much confused, is scarce ever free from the hiccoughs and his tongue is much crusted," Harriott informed her mother. On November 8 Harriott was so concerned about her husband that she sent for a doctor from Charleston. Daniel complained of a "great oppression at his stomach" and though he talked a great deal his speech was very confused. Unfortunately, there was little the doctor could do for him and on November 12, 1785, Daniel Horry died.[11]

Harriott was thirty-seven years old when her husband died—one year older than her mother had been when she was widowed and like her mother she would never remarry. The Horry estate was large, but Harriott had managed it while her husband was away during the war and again when he went to England with their son. She had experience and was soon to acquire an able assistant— she asked her mother to come and live with her. Together mother and daughter managed the vast Horry estates, worked to improve cultivation on the plantations and raised Harriott's and Charles's daughters.

Harriott had an additional responsibility, though, one that was in keeping with the traditional role of the 18th-century woman as a helpmate to her nearest male relations. As an important man in South Carolina political circles, Charles Cotesworth was expected to entertain, but as a widower he had no one to act as hostess when he invited guests to his home. His sister came to his rescue. At one point he warned her that she would be busy when she came to town as he had several dinners to give and was just getting a new cook. He knew he did not need to worry. Harriott, like her mother, was known as a "notable housewife" (a high accolade for the 18th-century woman) and had a book full of delicious "receipts" (recipes) and could be counted on to make sure the new cook properly prepared the various dishes which would be served to his guests.

Charles, however, soon found his own hostess in the person of Mary Stead, the daughter of Benjamin Stead and Mary Johnson. Benjamin, a wealthy Charleston merchant, had taken his family to London to live some years before the War for Independence had begun. Mary, who had been educated in France, was cultivated, charming, spoke fluent French and loved to read. The couple were married on July 23, 1786—Mary was thirty-four years old and Charles was forty.

Apparently Charles and Mary took Charles's youngest daughter Eliza into their home to raise leaving the twelve-year-old Maria and the ten-year-old Harriott with their grandmother. Maria and Harriott were close in age to their eight-year-old cousin Harriott Horry and the three girls were good friends and extremely close to their grandmother. Evidently Charles did not want to disrupt this satisfactory arrangement.

In 1786 Eliza was sixty-three years old and was, by the standards of her day, well into that period of life known as "old age." She had outlived many of her friends and acquaintances—a source of great sorrow to her. "How conducive to the enjoyment of life are those we have long known," she wrote to her old friend Mr. Keate in England. "'A friend that has many years been ripening by our side' is a treasure indeed.... Out living those we loved is what gives the principal gloom to long protracted life," she told him. She then continued:

> There was never any thing very tremendous to me in the prospect of old age, the loss of friends excepted, but this loss I have keenly felt; This is all the terror that the Spectre with the Sithe [Scythe] and hour glass ever exhibited to my view, nor since the arrival of this formidable period have I had any thing else to deplore from it. I regret no pleasures that I cant enjoy, and I enjoy some that I could not have had at an early season. I now see my children grown up, and blessed be God! see them such as I hoped, and what is there in youthful enjoyments preferable to this, what is there in youthful enjoyments preferable to passions subdued, and ... to the tranquility of which the calm evening of life naturally produces; sincere is my gratitude to Heaven for the advantages of this period of life as well as for those that are past.

Mr. Keate, a poet, had sent Eliza an elegant edition of his all his poetical works for which she thanked him most gratefully. Eliza, of course, had read all of his works before and had copies of them but, "not," she told him, "in so rich a dress." In a reminiscent mood she confided to him that she had always received a great deal of pleasure in reading his poetry for in reading it "I think myself in company with you, I hear you speak [and] I recollect the happy hours we have passed together with my ever dear Mr. Pinckney whose virtues I still revere, whose memory I tenderly love and whose uncommon affection and partiallity to me will be gratefully remembered to my last hour."[12] It was one of her last surviving letters.

Eliza took great pleasure in her family and diligently followed the careers of her sons, of whom she was very proud. In 1787 it was time to elect a new governor for the state and Tom had been nominated for the office. On February 22 Charles wrote a short note to his mother: "Yesterday the Election of officers commenced in the Assembly; I have the pleasure to acquaint you my Brother was elected with the greatest Eclat to the office of Governor; there were 170 Voters, out of which he had 163 Votes, the others were Votes of a whimsical Nature."[13]

That same February the national congress finally agreed to hold a General Convention in Philadelphia in May to revise the Articles of Confederation which had proved unsatisfactory. On March 8 the South Carolina General Assembly elected John Rutledge, Charles Cotesworth Pinckney, Charles Pinckney III and Pierce Butler as delegates to the convention in Philadelphia. On April 19 Governor Thomas Pinckney signed their commissions. Taking little Eliza to Hampton to be looked after by her grandmother, Charles and Mary sailed to Philadelphia in the spring of 1787. While he was gone Charles left Harriott in charge of his property.

Eliza had not forgotten her grandson in England and was still following his progress very closely. In 1787 Daniel was eighteen years old and friends in England were indicating that he was more interested in enjoying himself than in attending to his lessons. His conduct was causing his mother a great deal of pain and Eliza was troubled by it. She wrote to him in February of 1787:

> You never expressed a greater truth My dear Child when you said that you knew I loved you, Heaven can witness how truly, how sincerely I love you! and my affection has so much of Instinct in it, that I feel that no improper conduct of yours can ever eradicate from my heart the tender impression which nature has placed there; misconduct in You or misfortunes happening to You, may grieve and afflict me, and imbitter the little of life that remains to me, but I can never cease to love You…. You are no less dear to others but 'tis your misfortune not to be acquainted with your own family. Your mother deserves all your affection, and is worthy your highest esteem, do not afflict her then, with seeming to doubt it, or write her any more such strange letters as the two last she received … but write her such as will relieve her distressed mind as full of affection for you as of grief.[14]

Eliza had given Daniel the same kind of advice she had given her sons when they were his age. Since they had turned out well and since she was of an optimistic nature, she believed that Daniel, too, would turn out well. Daniel had finished his studies at Westminster and then decided to go on to Cambridge University—however, his years of study at the university would, in the future, be liberally interspersed with pleasure trips to Europe.[15]

Soon Eliza's attention was claimed by the addition of two more grandchildren. In 1788 Tom and Betsey had a daughter named Rebecca Motte Pinckney and the next year Betsey gave birth to a son. Tom and Betsey named their second son Charles Cotesworth Pinckney II after his uncle. In 1789 Tom's term as governor of the state was over and he returned to his private law practice and to managing his plantations—all of which he had neglected during his term as governor.

Although Eliza and Harriott were busy with plantation affairs and raising children, they managed to find time to undertake some projects. For example, following Tom's advice, they instituted the new tidal method of rice cultivation on the Horry plantations and, like Tom, found that it greatly increased the yield of the rice fields. They also had another special project they wanted to undertake—the addition of a portico to the house at Hampton. It is thought that Eliza suggested the design for the portico since it was modeled after a portico constructed by the Adams brothers for Hampton-on-Thames, the villa of the famous British actor David Garrick. The portico was added to Garrick's villa in the 1750s when Eliza and Charles were living in England and was undoubtedly seen by them as Garrick was one of Eliza's favorite actors. Plans were drawn-up and work began on the project in 1790.

At the beginning of 1790 Eliza received a devastating blow—her very good friend Lady Mary Middleton died. Lady Mary had gone to visit family and friends in Great Britain and was due back in South Carolina in time for Christmas which she had promised to spend with Eliza and Harriott at Hampton. Eliza and Harriott knew she was sailing on *Britannia* and when they heard the ship had docked in Charleston, they waited at Hampton for a message from her. It never came. Lady Mary had died three weeks before the ship reached port and had been buried at sea.

Both Eliza and Harriott were grieved by her death, but Eliza was affected more deeply—for Lady Mary had been "a friend that had many years been ripening" by her side. She had met Lady Mary aboard ship when she, Charles and Harriott were sailing back to Charleston in 1758. Lady Mary, then married to Thomas Drayton, and her sister Lady Ann had been of great comfort to Eliza during the difficult months after the death of her husband. The relationship between Mary and Eliza had deepened in 1776 when the widowed Lady Mary had married Henry Middleton and become Charles Cotesworth's mother-in-law.

The beginning of the year 1790 found Eliza in low spirits—distressed by the loss of her good friend and suffering from the effects of ill health. In April Eliza was examined by a doctor from Charleston for an unidentified illness. The examination was probably done at the insistence of her children who were worried about her. "I enclose you a letter from Dr. Turnbull," wrote Charles to his sister, "on the complaint of our ever dear Mother, and am happy to find that he does not deem it of so dangerous a nature as we suspected. Do prevail on my Mother to attend to his advice, & in case the application [he prescribes] should not be altogether successful, do apprize him of it."[16]

Failing health or not there was one grand event left for Eliza to attend. In 1791 as George Washington was beginning his third year as president, he planned to tour the southern cities just as he had toured the northern ones the year before. Since he would be visiting the cities between Virginia and Savannah, Harriott knew the president would be stopping at Georgetown before making his way to Charleston. She wrote to him: "I heard with great pleasure that your Excellency purposed favoring this part of the Continent with a visit and as my house on Santee is in your rout to Charleston; If you will do me the honor of making it a stage [a stopping point] I shall be extremely happy."[17]

The president was pleased to accept and on April 28 John Rutledge, Jr., sent a note to Thomas Pinckney at Fairfield. According to Rutledge the president was currently at Clifton, the plantation of William Alston now married to Mary Motte Tom's sister-in-law, and was traveling on to Georgetown where he was to be entertained by the gentlemen of the town at a dinner after which he would take tea with the ladies. He "intends dining at Mrs. Horry's on Sunday," Rutledge wrote. "General Moultrie requests that you will have your boats at Santee to assist in carrying over the President's horses."[18]

At eleven o'clock in the morning on May 1, 1791, Harriott, Eliza, little Harriott Horry and Maria and Harriott Pinckney walked out the front door of the house at Hampton and stood proudly on the newly finished portico to watch as the president's carriage and the rest of his entourage made their way up the long driveway. There was a fine spring breeze blowing with just a hint of jessamine in the air as Thomas Pinckney escorted President Washington up the steps to the portico where he was greeted by his hostess and the other ladies—all wearing sashes painted with his likeness and printed with mottoes of welcome to him. Harriott then led the president into the house to the spacious ballroom where they were to dine.

The food served the president and the other guests would have been excellent—Harriott and Eliza would have seen to it that it was. Washington, always interested in agriculture, was impressed by Hampton and enjoyed talking with Harriott about the successes she had achieved on the plantation. He also enjoyed talking to Eliza about her indigo experiments—he had seen indigo growing on his journey into South Carolina and indeed had been entertained in Georgetown by the Winyah Indigo Society an agricultural and social organization of indigo planters. Later Washington would send Eliza a drill plow which he thought would be useful in the planting of indigo.

While he was there Harriott and Eliza asked the president to settle a dispute between them. The ideal for country houses at this time was for visitors to be able to obtain a sweeping vista of the house from the driveway leading up to it. In the large expanse of lawn in front of Hampton house there was a young oak tree. It spoiled the view of the house for no matter at what angle the house was viewed, the tree intruded. Harriott wanted to cut it down, but Eliza, the tree enthusiast, wanted to keep it. They asked the president to give his opinion—he thought the tree should remain. Consequently, the tree, known as "the Washington Oak" still stands today on the lawn of Hampton and intrudes into every picture taken of the house by visitors to the site.

After leaving Hampton Washington lodged at the Manigault house and went on to Charleston the next day where he was greeted by two more Pinckneys—Charles Pinckney III, the governor of South Carolina, and Charles Cotesworth Pinckney. Washington knew Charles Cotesworth from the early days of the war when Charles had been a member of his military family and had renewed his acquaintance with him more recently at the Constitutional Convention in Philadelphia. On this trip he had been able to meet the other Pinckney brother—Thomas. Washington was impressed with both of them.

When Washington returned to Philadelphia after his southern tour, he faced many pressing issues and problems, but there was one problem in particular that gave him a great deal of pleasure to resolve. The British had decided to exchange diplomatic representatives with the United States—a great step, in Washington's opinion, to gaining the prestige the new nation needed. Who, though, should he appoint to this important position? In November of 1791 he offered the post to Thomas Pinckney. Tom accepted and his nomination was confirmed by the Senate in mid–January 1792.

The entire Pinckney family was pleased by the honor the president had bestowed on Tom and the trust he placed in him to carry out such an important mission, but the appointment also filled some of them with a measure of sadness. It was especially difficult for Tom's wife as she was reluctant to leave her family and friends in South Carolina to go and live among people who had so recently been their enemies. And for Eliza there must have also been some regrets in spite of the pride she felt in the appointment. She had just turned sixty-nine in December of 1791 and at that time would have been considered quite an old woman. The chances were very good that she would not live to see Tom return. However, she put a good face on the matter as did the rest of the family and with the good wishes of their friends and family ringing in their ears, Tom, Betsey and the children left South Carolina for Philadelphia in the spring. After Tom had a chance to confer with government officials and prepare for his mission, they sailed for England on June 25 arriving in London on August 3.

Eliza's health was gradually deteriorating. For some time her hand had not been steady enough to allow her to write to her grandson who was her chief correspondent in her later years. Her last surviving letter dated 18 February 1787 was to him and any future letters that were sent from Eliza to Daniel, were most likely dictated to one of her granddaughters. The exact nature of Eliza's physical ailments, or "complaints" as they were often called, is not precisely known. All the information about her health comes from comments made by her children in their surviving letters.

In May of 1792 Charles reported to his brother in Philadelphia that Eliza "had had another slight attack of the Erysipelas, but was a good deal better."[19] Erysipelas, or St. Anthony's fire, is a disease caused by a streptococcus bacteria that enters the skin through a cut, abrasion or insect bite and produces a warm, red rash on the victim's face and arms. In addition to the rash it can cause high fever, shaking, chills, fatigue, headaches and vomiting—the lymph nodes may also be swollen. Today it is easily treated with antibiotics which, of course, would not have been available to Eliza. People in Eliza's time did die of the disease, in fact, Lord Botetourt, the Royal Governor of Virginia, died of Erysipelas in 1770.

Even today after treatment with antibiotics there is a 20 percent chance that the disease will return so it is not surprising that Eliza had a recurrence of it. However, when Charles wrote to his brother in May he was able to inform him that Eliza had recovered and was well enough to accompany Harriott and her granddaughters to Georgetown to visit a friend. However, there was another health issue in addition to the Erysipelas for in July Charles was writing to tell Tom that their mother's complaint was not worse and "excepting that complaint, she is very well."[20]

It was not until August that Charles identified Eliza's complaint as cancer. He wrote to Tom in London:

> We sent to the Northward for Leeches to apply to my Mothers Cancer, but Dr. Shippen [a prominent Philadelphia doctor] says there are none of the right sort there; they having the same defect that ours have, not sticking to the flesh—Could you not procure some, & send them by a careful Captain? as to preserve their lives, the water must be changed once a day at least so they say to the Northward; but we have had them live a week here in the same water without dying—you can enquire on this subject of some experienced Apothecary.[21]

The 18th-century medical theory which held that sickness and disease were the result of an imbalance in the humors or fluids in the body was based loosely on a theory developed by a Greek physician and philosopher named Galen who lived in the second century. According to Galen tumors or cancers in the breast were the result of too much black bile in the body and he advocated aggressive bloodletting at the sight of the tumor as a cure. Leeches were often employed for bloodletting in the 18th century—especially in areas where using a lancet to open a vein was not feasible. Evidently, Eliza's doctors subscribed to Galen's theory and thought leeches applied to her breast would help relieve the excess of black bile and restore her to health.

Besides supplying leeches Tom was able, now that he was in London, to provide news of Daniel to his anxious mother and grandmother. That young man, he wrote, had left off his studies in England to travel to Paris where according to reports, he was "doing what from time immemorial had been the principal business in Paris, amusing himself." Tom was expecting him to return to London soon and so had not yet told him of the state of his grandmother's health. He wrote to Harriott on January 27, 1793, to apprise her of Daniel's ignorance on the matter. "This," he wrote, "will account to my Mother for his not having written to her on the subject."[22]

By April Charles and Harriott were becoming more and more alarmed by their mother's condition. She was growing weaker "while the Cancers, particularly the one under the Arm, were continually increasing in size." For some months Charles and Harriott had been trying to persuade Dr. Tate, a Philadelphia surgeon known for his successful treatment of cancers in the breast, to come to South Carolina to minister to Eliza. Dr. Tate was reportedly able to effect his cures without resorting to either surgery, an acknowledged but disputed method of treatment, or the application of caustic poultices to erode the tumors. Unfortunately Dr. Tate was not able to leave his patients in Pennsylvania, but strongly recommended that Eliza come to Philadelphia as soon as possible and, as an added inducement "mentioned he had very lately cured a Lady of Seventy Years of age who had been in a most deplorable State."[23]

Charles, Harriott and Eliza's Charleston doctor all urged her to make the trip. Charles wrote to his brother on April 16: "I proposed to accompany her with my Sister and Children, and to stay the summer there—She was at first averse to going, but at length consented on the express stipulation that I should not go with her; but only my Sister, Maria & the two Harriotts; as she seemed positive on this point; and said she would not by any means [given the dangers of an ocean voyage] consent to risque us all at once, I acquiesced, and on last Wednesday the 10th of this Month they embarked on board the *Delaware*, commanded by Captain Art."[24]

Epilogue

On the morning of Wednesday April 10, 1793, the *Delaware* weighed anchor and, catching the tide, moved quickly through the choppy waters of the harbor to the sandbar that guarded its entrance. There was a brisk wind blowing that morning, but, unfortunately, as the ship approached the bar and prepared to cross over, the wind began to swirl from a contrary direction pushing the ship back into the harbor. After making several unsuccessful attempts, the captain turned the ship about and dropped anchor near Sullivan's Island to await a favorable wind. For the rest of the day and the following night the ship rode at anchor swaying from side to side and bobbing up and down.

Eliza had been suffering from a "sickness of the stomach" for many weeks before she embarked on the voyage and, as she was known to be seasick even on board a ship tied up at the wharf, Charles was much heartened when his sister informed him that their mother had not been sick all day Wednesday while the *Delaware* was at anchor. She had eaten dinner in the middle of the afternoon with a good appetite, Harriott wrote, and it was not until later that night that both of them succumbed to the motion of the ship and became sick. Charles was, therefore, encouraged to hope that his mother would find the voyage more comfortable than she had anticipated and since the weather had changed, he was also hopeful that the ladies would have a "fine passage."

The next day dawned with favorable winds and the *Delaware* was able to cross over the bar and begin her passage up the coast. Charles's hopes for an uneventful and pleasant voyage, however, were not to be realized. As soon as the *Delaware* entered the waters of the Atlantic Ocean the weather took a turn for the worse. Strong, swirling winds tumbled the ship about on heavy seas and once a water spout was spotted in the distance forcing the captain to change direction until it disappeared. The weather did not improve as the voyage continued. "Indeed," Harriott wrote in her journal, "from the time [of] crossing

the bar we have had a most dismal passage.... Capt. Art says he never had yet"
so continually a violent passage as this one.[1]

Eliza was sick during the entire voyage and consequently weak and
exhausted by the time they reached Philadelphia on April 20. Harriott recorded
their arrival:

> At about 8 O'Clock we arrived at our destined port, the weather miserably bad and the
> wind so high we could not get nearer than the stream, my Mother very sick and obliged to
> be lifted in a chair into the boat which danced extremely, but carried us safe on shore where
> Mrs. Izards Coach met us and conveyed us to our lodgings at the corner of Spruce and 3rd
> Streets.[2]

Eliza had come to Philadelphia to consult two of the most prominent
medical men in the city—Dr. William Shippen and Dr. James Tate. William
Shippen was a distinguished physician and one of the founders of the College
of Physicians in Philadelphia and James Tate was a highly-acclaimed surgeon
known for the success he had achieved in treating cancer. He had been recommended to Eliza's family by George Washington who claimed Dr. Tate had
cured him of "a cancerous complaint." Dr. Shippen's role was to examine Eliza,
diagnose her condition and prescribe medicines for her while Dr. Tate was to
be in charge of her treatment for cancer.

Dr. Shippen called on the ladies the first day they arrived simply to pay
his respects and to become acquainted with his patient. He returned the next
day to do a thorough examination of Eliza's breast. Dr. Tate visited Eliza on the
morning of April 23 and found her still violently sick to her stomach. Nevertheless, he seemed cautiously optimistic about her condition.

William Burrows, a fellow South Carolinian then living in Philadelphia
with his wife, had promised Tom that he would call on his mother, sister and
nieces when they came to town and offer them any assistance he could. After
he and his wife visited the ladies, William was able to pass along to Tom the
favorable comments made by Eliza's doctors. Dr. Shippen and Dr. Tate, he
wrote, both "feared nothing but your Mother's advanced Age," for the cancer,
in their opinion was treatable and if they had discovered it earlier they could
have quickly "eradicated" it.[3] Dr. Tate, however, wanted to delay his treatment
until Eliza was no longer sick at her stomach.

Philadelphia was the capital of the newly formed United States of America and was crowded with members of government as Congress was sitting at
the time. During the days that followed, while Eliza waited for her sick stomach
to improve, there was a steady procession of ladies and gentlemen who came
to call at the lodgings on Spruce Street. Among the well-known visitors were
Alexander Hamilton, General Benjamin Lincoln and President Washington.
"General Washington was extremely kind," wrote Harriott, "and said as Mrs.

Washington was sick he offered in her name as well as his own every thing in their power to serve and begged we [would use] no ceremony."[4]

Mrs. Izard, the wife of Ralph Izard, the senator from South Carolina, took Harriott and the young ladies to call upon Mrs. Washington and then to return the calls of the other ladies who had visited them. She arranged to take them for rides about the city and for walks in the gardens that were just starting to display the signs of spring. Dr. Tate was also very attentive and wanting to reassure Harriott of the efficacy of his treatment, invited her to visit some of his patients. She recorded the visit she made in her journal:

> Some time ago Doctor Tate begged I would walk with him to see some of his cancerous patients who were cured, and some who were then under care that I might ask them what questions I chose of the pains, etc. which they suffered. I saw Mrs. Duboyce who from the scars and seams on her breast must have been bad indeed, I saw another lady who was about half cured and in a fair way of doing well who also had a large Tumor in her breast and received much satisfaction from seeing them.[5]

Meanwhile Eliza's stomach was not improving. She was continually sick and vomiting daily. In great concern Harriott sent for Dr. Shippen. He ordered Eliza to take nothing but porter, a dark beer, and whey. He also gave her an anodyne, a soothing solution, to help ease the pain she was experiencing. The anodyne, Harriott recorded, "with the porter stoped the sickness of the stomach and tho' extremely weak she had a better day than since we landed."[6]

When Dr. Tate came to examine Eliza, he found his patient no longer sick at her stomach, but so frail and weak that he was reluctant to proceed with the treatment. However, Eliza begged him to attempt the cure anyway and was so insistent that Dr. Tate relented and started her on the medication. For a while, it appeared that his medicine was beginning to work on the cancer and then the sick stomach returned with increased severity. For almost two weeks Eliza endured bouts of incessant vomiting and grew steadily weaker and weaker. The end finally came on May 26. Harriott recorded in her journal: "my dear Mother continued to suffer extremely with the sick Stomach and vomiting, and for several hours was in great agony when it pleased Almighty God to take her to himself."[7] Her daughter and her three granddaughters were with her when she died.

Eliza Lucas Pinckney was buried in St. Peter's churchyard in Philadelphia on May 27, 1793. During the five weeks that Eliza had spent in Philadelphia before her death, she had been visited by a great many people, many of whom were important members of government. Her funeral was well-attended and no less a personage that our first president, George Washington, volunteered to be one of her pall-bearers.

Thomas learned of his mother's death from William Burrows who wrote to him, at Harriott's request, on the day Eliza was buried. "A few weeks ago, your Mother came here for her Health," he wrote, "and particularly to get cured of a Cancer, which would have been effected had it not been for her Age & other Infirmities.... The Family received every Attention from the most respectable Part of the City, and no Attention was wanting, yet nothing could avert the Stroke of Death, which happened on Saturday night last."[8]

Charles, other family members and friends in Charleston did not learn of Eliza's death until sometime in July. Southwesterly winds had prevented the arrival of any ships from the north for well over a month after her death. By July 17 Charles had heard the sad news. He wrote to his brother: "I too easily construed the not hearing any news by the post into a confirmation that my Mother's recovery was happily advancing; when the fatal account at last came and met me unprepared to receive it."[9] He sent his brother a copy of Eliza's obituary which was printed in the Charleston *City Gazette* on July 17, 1793. The unknown author gave this account of her:

> This all accomplished lady, possessed, in a most eminent degree, all the amiable and engaging qualities, united to all the virtues and graces, which embellish and exalt the female character.—Her manners had been so refined, by a long and intimate acquaintance with the polite world, her countenance was so dignified by serious contemplation and devout reflection, and so replete with all the mildness and complacency which are the natural results of a regular uninterrupted habit and practice of virtue and benevolence that it was scarcely to behold her without emotions of the highest veneration and respect. Her understanding, aided by an uncommon strength of memory, had been so highly cultivated and improved by travel and extensive reading, and was so richly furnished, as well with scientific, as practical knowledge, that her talent for conversation was unrivalled, and her company was sedulously sought after by all, without distinction of age or sex, who could be so happy as to gain admission into it. Her religion was rational, liberal, and pure. The source of it was seated in the judgement and the heart, and from thence issued a life, regular, placid, and uniform.

Chapter Notes

Introduction

1. Harriott Pinckney, 1793 Journal, 10 April 1793, in *The Papers of Eliza Lucas Pinckney and Harriott Horry Pinckney Digital Edition*, ed. Schulz.
2. Dr. Ananya Mandal, M.D., "History of Breast Cancer," http://www.news-medical.net/health/History-of-Breast-Cancer.aspx.
3. Eliza Lucas Pinckney (ELP) to Thomas Talbot, 2 October 1758, in Pinckney, *The Letterbook of Eliza Lucas Pinckney*, 102–103.
4. *Ibid.*, 6–7, ELP to Mrs. Richard Boddicott, 2 May 1740.

Chapter One

1. Parker, *The Sugar Barons, Family, Corruption, Empire and War in the West Indies*, 11.
2. Taylor, *American Colonies*, 205.
3. Pinckney, *The Letterbook of Eliza Lucas Pinckney*, xv note.
4. Williams, "Eliza Lucas and Her Family: Before the Letterbook," *South Carolina Historical Magazine (SCHM)*, 99, 262 note 5.
5. ELP to George Lucas, 4 June 1741, in Pinckney, *The Letterbook of Eliza Lucas Pinckney*, 16. Eliza mentions that Mrs. Lucas was shocked by the news of the death of her mother.
6. *Ibid.*, 7, ELP to Mrs. Richard Boddicott, 2 May 1740.
7. Anne Mildrum Lucas to Charles Pinckney (1699–1758), 30 January 1746, in *The Papers of Eliza Lucas Pinckney and Harriott Pinckney Horry Digital Edition*, ed. Schulz.
8. Oliver, *The History of the Island of Antigua*, II, 403.
9. *Ibid.*, 404.
10. *Ibid.*, 401.
11. *Ibid.*, 403.
12. *Ibid.*, 401.
13. *Ibid.*, 400. There is no mention of the year of George Lucas's birth, but he had to have been born by 1689 as he would have had to have been at least twenty-one years of age in 1710 when he was elected to the Assembly.
14. *Ibid.*, 401.
15. *Ibid.*, 404.
16. *Ibid.*, 205.
17. Headlam, "Calendar of State Papers, Colonial Series, America and West Indies, 1726–1727," 78, as cited in Ramagosa, "Eliza Lucas Pinckney's Family in Antigua, 1668–1747," *SCHM*, 99, 242.
18. Oliver, *The History of the Island of Antigua*, II, 404.
19. Pares, *A West-India Fortune*, 30–31.
20. *Ibid.*, 119.

21. ELP memorandum dated 11 November 1741, in Pinckney, *The Letterbook of Eliza Lucas Pinckney*, 24.

22. *Ibid.*, memorandum dated January 1742.

23. ELP to Harriott Pinckney Horry, 12 February 1775, in *The Papers of Eliza Lucas Pinckney and Harriott Pinckney Horry Digital Edition*, ed. Schulz.

24. Ravenel, *Eliza Pinckney*, 307.

25. ELP to unidentified person, 10 September 1785, in *The Papers of Eliza Lucas Pinckney and Harriott Pinckney Horry Digital Edition*, ed. Schulz.

26. Ravenel, *Eliza Pinckney*, 11.

27. ELP to Mary Bartlett in Pinckney, *The Letterbook of Eliza Lucas Pinckney*, 35.

28. *Ibid.*, 13–14, ELP to Mrs. Richard Boddicott, 2 May 1741.

29. Williams, "Eliza Lucas and Her Family: Before the Letterbook," *SCHM*, 99, 266, note 8.

30. Bryant, *The London Experience of Secondary Education*, 72.

31. ELP to Mary (Polly) Lucas, December 1747, in *The Papers of Eliza Lucas Pinckney and Harriott Pinckney Horry Digital Edition*, ed. Schulz.

32. Williams, "Eliza Lucas and Her Family: Before the Letterbook," *SCHM*, 99, 266.

33. Wulf, *The Brother Gardeners*, 43.

34. *Ibid.*, 18–19.

35. Earle, *The Making of the English Middleclass*, 158 and 199.

36. Williams, "Eliza Lucas and Her Family: Before the Letterbook," *SCHM*, 99, 266.

37. ELP to George Lucas in Pinckney, *The Letterbook of Eliza Lucas Pinckney*, 5.

38. *Ibid.*, 23.

39. Fryer, "The Mind of Eliza Lucas Pinckney: An 18th Century Woman's Construction of Herself," *SCHM*, 99, 229.

40. *Ibid.*, 236.

41. Pares, *A West-India Fortune*, 6.

42. Ravenel, *Eliza Pinckney*, 116–118.

43. Williams, *Plantation Patriot*, viii.

44. Eliza mentioned in a letter to Mrs. Boddicott (see *Letterbook*, p. 23) that Mr. Boddicott was hardly forty when she left England and since Richard Boddicott was baptized March 7, 1697, he would have been forty in March of 1737.

45. Land indenture, 1729, National Archives of Antigua and Barbuda, St. John's, Antigua, West Indies, as cited in Ramagosa, "Eliza Lucas Pinckney's Family in Antigua, 1668–1747," *SCHM*, 99, 245.

46. Gaspar, *Bondsmen and Rebels*, 223–224.

47. Oliver, *The History of the Island of Antigua*, III, 315.

48. Gaspar, *Bondsmen and Rebels*, 32.

49. Edgar, *The Letterbook of Robert Pringle*, I, 11. George Lucas carried a letter from Robert Pringle to a correspondent in Antigua.

50. ELP memorandum dated 3 February 1744, in Pinckney, *The Letterbook of Eliza Lucas Pinckney*, 58.

51. Smith, *Caribbean Rum*, 43.

52. Mortgage in *South Carolina Deed Abstracts 1719–1722, Vol. I*, 339.

53. Oliver, *The History of the Island of Antigua*, I, 189.

54. Lucas to Beale mortgage, Public Register, Conveyances Vol. V, 81, as cited in Williams, "Eliza Lucas and Her Family: Before the Letterbook," *SCHM*, 99, 276.

Chapter Two

1. Rogers, *Charleston in the Age of the Pinckneys*, 55.

2. ELP to Thomas Lucas, 22 May 1742, in Pinckney, *The Letterbook of Eliza Lucas Pinckney*, 39–40.

3. Advertisement in *South Carolina Gazette*, Aug. 25–Sept. 1, 1739, and Dec. 29–Jan. 5, 1740, as cited in Pinckney, *The Letterbook of Eliza Lucas Pinckney*, 7 note 4.

4. Public Register, Conveyances, Vol. T, 609, SCDAH, as cited in Williams, "Eliza Lucas and Her Family: Before the Letterbook," *SCHM*, 99, 273.

5. *Ibid.*, 274, Colonial Land Grants, Copy Series, Vol. 42, 109, 120, SCDAH.
6. ELP memorandum dated 25 July 1740, in Pinckney, *The Letterbook of Eliza Pinckney*, 10. Ravenel, *Eliza Pinckney*, 59.
7. Account, George Lucas to William Murray, 24 March 1753, in *The Papers of Eliza Lucas Pinckney and Harriott Pinckney Horry Digital Edition*, ed. Schulz.
8. ELP memorandum dated 7 January 1743, in Pinckney, *The Letterbook of Eliza Lucas Pinckney*, 57.
9. Manumission, John (Quash) Williams, 12 May 1750, in *The Papers of Eliza Lucas Pinckney and Harriott Pinckney Horry Digital Edition*, ed. Schulz.
10. ELP to Mrs. Richard Boddicott, 2 May 1740, in Pinckney, *The Letterbook of Eliza Lucas Pinckney*, 6.
11. *Ibid.*, ELP to George Lucas, 5–6.
12. ELP to unidentified person, 10 September 1785, in *The Papers of Eliza Lucas Pinckney and Harriott Pinckney Horry Digital Edition*, ed. Schulz.
13. ELP memorandum dated 25 July 1740, in Pinckney, *The Letterbook of Eliza Lucas Pinckney*, 10.
14. *Pennsylvania Gazette*, Jan. 29, 1741.
15. While there is no mention of the fire in the notes and letters copied into the Letterbook, it is difficult to believe that Eliza did not write to her father about such a momentous event. The most likely explanation can be found in a note Eliza made in the Letterbook of March 1741: "Wrote an answer to my Papa's 2 last letters 24th of March and finished my last Coppy book with a letter to him dated the 20th of April." The letter describing the "Great Fire" must have been in that earlier "Coppy book," which unfortunately has not survived.
16. ELP to Mrs. Richard Boddicott, 2 May 1741, in Pinckney, *The Letterbook of Eliza Lucas Pinckney*, 13–14.
17. *Ibid.*, ELP to George Lucas, 1 June 1742, 51.
18. *Ibid.*, 36, ELP to Mary Bartlett.
19. *Ibid.*, 12, ELP to Charles Pinckney, 6 February 1741.
20. Rogers, *Charleston in the Age of the Pinckneys*, 91.
21. ELP to George Lucas, 1 June 1742, in Pinckney, *The Letterbook of Eliza Lucas Pinckney*, 51.
22. Charles Pinckney had learned shorthand when he was studying law in London and had taught it to Eliza.
23. ELP to Mary Bartlett, in Pinckney, *The Letterbook of Eliza Lucas Pinckney*, 34–35.
24. *Ibid.*, 33.
25. *Ibid.*, 15–16, ELP to George Lucas, 4 June 1741.
26. Ibid., 50, ELP to George Lucas, 1 June 1742.
27. The court-martial of General James Oglethorpe was held in June of 1744. He was completely exonerated of all charges and Col. Cook was consequently dismissed from service.
28. ELP to Mrs. Richard Boddicott, 29 June 1742, in Pinckney, *The Letterbook of Eliza Lucas Pinckney*, 42.
29. *Ibid.*, 68, ELP to Mrs. Chardon.
30. *Ibid.*, 44–45, ELP to George Lucas, Jr.
31. *Ibid.*, 41.
32. *Ibid.*, 51–52, ELP to George Lucas, Jr.
33. *Ibid.*, 54.
34. *Ibid.*, 56–57, ELP to George Lucas, 11 November 1742.
35. *Ibid,,* 27, ELP to Mary Bartlett, January 1742.
36. *Ibid.*, 59, ELP to George Lucas, 10 February 1742.
37. *Ibid.*, 59.
38. *Ibid.*, 16, ELP to George Lucas, 4 June 1741.
39. *Ibid.*, 8, ELP to George Lucas, July 1740.
40. *Ibid.*, 16, ELP to George Lucas, 4 June 1741.
41. *Ibid.*, 56, ELP memorandum dated 8 September 1742.
42. ELP to an unidentified person, 10 September 1785, in *The Papers of Eliza Lucas Pinckney and Harriott Pinckney Horry Digital Edition*, ed. Schulz.
43. For more information about the manufacture of indigo see Ravenel 102–105; www.unf.edu, Florida History on Line: Indigo Cultivation: Life at Governor James Grant's Villa Plantation;

Map of the Parish of St. Stephens in Craven County by Henry Mouzon, Jr., in the Collections of the South Carolina Historical Society as see in the Letterbook between pp. 108–109.

44. ELP to George Lucas, 1 June 1741, in Pinckney, *The Letterbook of Eliza Lucas Pinckney*, 50.

45. George Lucas to Charles Pinckney, 24 December 1744, in *The Papers of Eliza Lucas Pinckney and Harriott Pinckney Horry Digital Edition*, ed. Schulz.

46. *Ibid.*, ELP to an unidentified person, 10 September 1785.

47. *Ibid.*

48. ELP to Mrs. King, 27 February 1762, in Pinckney, *The Letterbook of Eliza Lucas Pinckney*, 175.

49. *Ibid.*, 26. ELP to Mary Bartlett 14 January 1742.

50. *Ibid.*, 36.

51. *Ibid.*, 31.

52. *Ibid.*, 27.

53. *Ibid.*, 38.

54. *Ibid.*, 35.

55. *Ibid.*, 36.

56. *Ibid.*, 41.

57. *Ibid.*, 37.

58. ELP memorandum 1742, in *The Papers of Eliza Lucas Pinckney and Harriott Pinckney Horry Digital Edition*, ed. Schulz.

59. *Ibid.*

60. ELP to Mary Bartlett, in Pinckney, *The Letterbook of Eliza Lucas Pinckney*, 35.

61. *Ibid.*, 60, ELP to Miss Dunbar, 11 April 1743.

62. Ranks above major were not purchased. George Lucas was promoted to Lt. Colonel to replace Lt. Colonel Morris of the 38th Regiment who had died.

63. ELP to Mary Bartlett, May 1743, in Pinckney, *The Letterbook of Eliza Lucas Pinckney*, 60–64. The letter to Mary Bartlett contains a detailed description of Crowfield, one of the most beautiful estates in colonial South Carolina. It, unfortunately, is no longer in existence. A drawing of the grounds, based on Eliza's description, and the remains can be found in Samuel G. Stoney, *Plantations of the Carolina Low Country* (Charleston, SC, 1938) 54–55 and 119.

64. *Ibid.*, 61–62.

65. Oliver, *The History of the Island of Antigua*, I, 255.

Chapter Three

1. The exact year of Charles Pinckney's birth is unknown. The family's papers were destroyed during the American Revolution; therefore, it cannot be proved whether he was born in 1699 or 1700.

2. Williams, *A Founding Family the Pinckneys of South Carolina*, 24.

3. The information on Charles Pinckney and his family comes from Frances Leigh Williams, *A Founding Family the Pinckneys of South Carolina*, 3–18.

4. Ravenel, *Eliza Pinckney*, 87.

5. Eliza Lucas Pinckney Marriage Settlement, May 1744, in *The Papers of Eliza Lucas Pinckney and Harriott Pinckney Horry Digital Edition*, ed. Schulz. The manuscript itself is badly damaged and many of the words are unreadable.

6. Ravenel, *Eliza Pinckney*, 69–70.

7. *Ibid.*, 91–92.

8. ELP to Mrs. Richard Boddicott, [July] (1744), in *The Papers of Eliza Lucas Pinckney and Harriott Pinckney Horry Digital Edition*, ed. Schulz.

9. *Ibid.*, ELP to Charles Pinckney, [1744].

10. *Ibid.*, ELP to Fanny Fayerweather, [1744].

11. Ravenel, *Eliza Pinckney*, 101.

12. *Ibid.*

13. ELP to George Lucas, [1744], in *The Papers of Eliza Lucas Pinckney and Harriott Pinckney Horry Digital Edition*, ed. Schulz.

14. Ravenel, *Eliza Pinckney*, 90.

15. ELP to Sarah Lamb Bartlett, 7 March 1745, in *The Papers of Eliza Lucas Pinckney and Harriott Pinckney Horry Digital Edition*, ed. Schulz.

16. *Ibid.*, ELP to Mary Bartlett, [1745].

17. *Ibid.*, ELP to George Lucas, [1744].

18. *Ibid.*, ELP to George Lucas, [July] [1744].

19. *Ibid.*, George Lucas, Articles of Agreement, 6 July 1744.

20. *Ibid.*, ELP to George Lucas, [1744].

21. Letter from London dated December 3, 1744, and printed in the *South Carolina Gazette*, April 1, 1745, as cited in Pinckney, *The Letterbook of Eliza Lucas Pinckney*, xviii.

22. ELP to unidentified person, 10 September 1785, in *The Papers of Eliza Lucas Pinckney and Harriott Pinckney Horry Digital Edition*, ed. Schulz.

23. Earle, *The Making of the English Middle Class*, 159.

24. James Glen, "Description to the Board of Trade, 1749," in Milling, ed., *Colonial South Carolina: Two Contemporary Descriptions*, 60.

25. Account, George Lucas to William Murray, 24 March 1753, in *The Papers of Eliza Lucas Pinckney and Harriott Pinckney Horry Digital Edition*, ed. Schulz.

26. *Ibid.*, ELP to unidentified person, 10 September 1785.

27. *Ibid.*, ELP to George Lucas, [1744].

28. *Ibid.*, ELP to Mary Bartlett, [June] [1745].

29. *Ibid.*, George Lucas to Charles Pinckney, 22 May 1745.

30. *Ibid.*, George Lucas, Jr. to Charles Pinckney, 21 October 1745.

31. *Ibid.*

32. *Ibid.*, Charles Pinckney to George Lucas, 28 August 1745.

33. *Ibid.*, ELP to Mary Bartlett, [20] May [1746].

34. Ravenel, *Eliza Pinckney*, 111–112.

35. Smith and Smith, *Dwelling Houses of Charleston, South Carolina*, 336–372.

36. Anne Mildrum Lucas to Charles Pinckney, 30 January 1746, in *The Papers of Eliza Lucas Pinckney and Harriott Pinckney Horry Digital Edition*, ed. Schulz.

37. Cotesworth was the maiden name of Charles Pinckney's mother.

38. ELP to Mary Bartlett, [20] May [1746] in *The Papers of Eliza Lucas Pinckney and Harriott Pinckney Horry Digital Edition*, ed. Schulz.

39. *Ibid.*, ELP to Mrs. Richard Boddicott, 20 May [1746].

40. Ravenel, *Eliza Pinckney*, 114.

41. *Ibid.*, 114–115.

42. George Lucas to Charles Pinckney, 12 April 1746, in *The Papers of Eliza Lucas Pinckney and Harriott Pinckney Horry Digital Edition*, ed. Schulz.

43. *Ibid.*, ELP to Mary Bartlett, 2 December 1747.

44. The wrap is in the possession of Tom Drake, a descendant of Eliza's, and an illustration of it can be seen in Feeser, *Red, White, & Black Make Blue*, illustration 9.

45. ELP to Mrs. Evance, 19 June 1760, in *The Letterbook of Eliza Lucas Pinckney*, 152.

46. Ravenel, *Eliza Pinckney*, 138–140.

47. ELP, "Days sett apart to be remember'd," 24 August 1758, in *The Papers of Eliza Lucas Pinckney and Harriott Pinckney Horry Digital Edition*, ed. Schulz.

48. For more information about Peter Leigh see Letter of Peter Manigault to his father Gabriel Manigault, 25 August 1753 in *SCHGM*, 32, 187–188.

49. Charles Pinckney, Rent Roll, 24 January 1753, in *The Papers of Eliza Lucas Pinckney and Harriott Pinckney Horry Digital Edition*, ed. Schulz.

50. ELP to [Mary Wragg?] in Pinckney, *The Letterbook of Eliza Lucas Pinckney*, 76.

51. Peter Manigault to Mrs. Manigault, 16 May 1753 in *SCHGM*, 32, 176.

52. *Ibid.*, 179.

53. *Ibid.*, 192.

54. Ravenel, *Eliza Pinckney*, 145.

55. *Ibid.*, 144–146.

56. *Ibid.*, 146–147. The entire surviving parts of the letter can be found on pages 144–158.

57. *Ibid.*, 149.

58. *Ibid.*, 131.

59. ELP to Mrs. Gabriel Manigault, December–January 1753–54, in Pinckney, *The Letterbook of Eliza Lucas Pinckney*, 79–81.

60. Williams, *A Founding Family the Pinckneys of South Carolina*, 14.

61. Charles Pinckney, Account, 1 July 1754, in *The Papers of Eliza Lucas Pinckney and Harriott Pinckney Horry Digital Edition*, ed. Schulz.
62. *Ibid.*
63. Pinckney, *The Letterbook of Eliza Lucas Pinckney*, 74.
64. Peter Manigault to Mrs. Gabriel Manigault, 29 March 1754, in *The Papers of Eliza Lucas Pinckney and Harriott Pinckney Horry Digital Edition*, ed. Schulz.
65. Letter, Peter Manigault to Gabriel Manigault, *SCHGM*, 32, 178.
66. ELP to Lady Carew, in Pinckney, *The Letterbook of Eliza Lucas Pinckney*, 84.
67. *Ibid.*, 87–88, ELP to Lady Carew, 7 February 1757.
68. *Ibid.*, 93, ELP to Lady Mary Drayton, June-July 1758.
69. Williams, *A Founding Family the Pinckneys of South Carolina*, 16.

Chapter Four

1. ELP to Mr. Keate, in Pinckney, *The Letterbook of Eliza Lucas Pinckney*, 129.
2. *Ibid.*, 99, ELP to Mrs. Evance, August 1758.
3. *Ibid.*, 99–100.
4. *Ibid.*, 97–98, ELP to Mr. Morley, August 1758.
5. In the 18th century the word "infant" meant a child who had not reached the age of 21—a minor.
6. ELP to Mr. Gerrard, in Pinckney, *The Letterbook of Eliza Lucas Pinckney*, 96–97.
7. *Ibid.*, 94–95, ELP to Charles and Thomas Pinckney, August 1758.
8. *Ibid.*, 101–102, ELP to Mrs. Lucas, 25 September 1758.
9. *Ibid.*, 129, ELP to Mr. Keate.
10. *Ibid.*, 116, ELP to Lady Carew, May 1759.
11. Charles Cotesworth Pinckney (CCP) to Harriott Pinckney, 6 April 1759, in *The Papers of Eliza Lucas Pinckney and Harriott Pinckney Horry Digital Edition*, ed. Schulz.
12. Lady Ann Mackenzie was one of the seven daughters of George Mackenzie, Earl of Cromartie, and his wife Elizabeth Gordon. The Earl, a Scotsman, had backed the losing side in the uprising of 1745 when followers of Bonny Prince Charlie tried to put him on the throne of England in place of George II. The Earl managed to keep his head, but his estates were forfeited. When Lady Mary, Ann's sister, married Thomas Drayton in England and came to South Carolina, Ann decided to accompany her. It is probable that their brother George also came with them and that they came to South Carolina on board the same ship that carried Charles, Eliza and Harriott.
13. ELP to Lady Carew, May 1759, in Pinckney, *The Letterbook of Eliza Lucas Pinckney*, 116.
14. Will of Charles Pinckney, Public Record Office, London, England, folios 41–55 11/947.
15. ELP to Mr. Morley, 14 March 1760, in Pinckney, *The Letterbook of Eliza Lucas Pinckney*, 144.
16. *Ibid.*, 185, ELP to Mrs. Onslow, 27 February 1762.
17. *Ibid.*, 134, ELP to Dr. Kirkpatrick, February 1760.
18. ELP to Mrs. Evance, 15 March 1760, in *The Letterbook of Eliza Lucas Pinckney*, 147–148.
19. *Ibid.*, 153, ELP to Mrs. Evance.
20. *Ibid.*, 160, ELP to Mr. Morley, 8 February 1761.
21. For the Cherokee viewpoint of the war see David H. Corkran, *The Cherokee Frontier: Conflict and Survival 1740–1762.*
22. ELP to Mrs. King, 27 February 1762, in Pinckney, *The Letterbook of Eliza Lucas Pinckney*, 175.
23. *Ibid.*, 176.
24. *Ibid.*, 133, ELP to Dr. Kirkpatrick, February 1760.
25. *Ibid.*, 119, ELP to Mrs. King, May 1759.
26. *Ibid.*, 175–176, ELP to Mrs. King, February 1762.
27. *Ibid.*, 162, ELP to Mrs. King.
28. *Ibid.*, 179, ELP to Lady Carew, July 1760.
29. *Ibid.*, 180–181, ELP to Mr. Keate, February 1762.
30. *Ibid.*
31. Harriott Pinckney to Miss R., April 1766, in *The Papers of Eliza Lucas Pinckney and Harriott Pinckney Horry Digital Edition*, ed. Schulz.

32. ELP to Mrs. King, 19 July 1760, in Pinckney, *The Letterbook of Eliza Lucas Pinckney*, 155.
33. Ravenel, *Eliza Pinckney*, 217.
34. ELP to Charles and Thomas Pinckney, February 1759, in Pinckney, *The Letterbook of Eliza Lucas Pinckney*, 110.
35. *Ibid.*, 123, ELP to CCP, 16 July 1759.
36. *Ibid.*, 145, ELP to Mr. Morley, 14 March 1760.
37. *Ibid.*, 142, ELP to Charles and Thomas Pinckney, March 1760.
38. Ravenel, *Eliza Pinckney*, 209.
39. ELP to CCP, 15 April 1761, in Pinckney, *The Letterbook of Eliza Lucas Pinckney*, 167–168.
40. ELP to unidentified person, [1760] in *The Papers of Eliza Lucas Pinckney and Harriott Pinckney Horry Digital Edition*, ed. Schulz.
41. ELP to CCP, 15 April 1761, in Pinckney, *The Letterbook of Eliza Lucas Pinckney*, 168.
42. *Ibid.*, 169–170, ELP to William Henry Drayton, 6 April 1761.
43. Ravenel, *Eliza Pinckney*, 231.
44. *Ibid.*, 230.
45. *Ibid.*, 239.
46. Harriott Pinckney to Miss R., April 1766, in *The Papers of Eliza Lucas Pinckney and Harriott Pinckney Horry Digital Edition*, ed. Schulz.
47. Ravenel, *Eliza Pinckney*, 239–240.
48. *Ibid.*, 241.
49. ELP to Daniel Horry, 9 March 1768, in *The Papers of Eliza Lucas Pinckney and Harriott Pinckney Horry Digital Edition*, ed. Schulz.
50. *Ibid.*, ELP to CCP, [1768].
51. Harriott Pinckney Horry (HPH) to Elizabeth Izard, 27 November 1769, in *The Papers of Eliza Lucas Pinckney and Harriott Pinckney Horry Digital Edition*, ed. Schulz.
52. Mackesy, *The War for America 1775–1783*, 1.
53. HPH to Thomas Pinckney (TP), 12 March 1773, in *The Papers of Eliza Lucas Pinckney and Harriott Pinckney Horry Digital Edition*, ed. Schulz.
54. *Ibid.*, ELP to HPH, May [1774].
55. Ravenel, *Eliza Pinckney*, 253.
56. Wallace, *South Carolina: A Short History*, 251–252.
57. Franklin, *The Writings of Benjamin Franklin, vol. VI*, 179.
58. TP to CCP, 16 April 1774, in *The Papers of Eliza Lucas Pinckney and Harriott Pinckney Horry Digital Edition*, ed. Schulz.
59. Garden, *Anecdotes of the American Revolution Vol. 2*, 3.
60. TP to CCP, 16 April 1774, in *The Papers of Eliza Lucas Pinckney and Harriott Pinckney Horry Digital Edition*, ed. Schulz.
61. *Ibid.*, ELP to HPH, 12 February 1775.
62. *Ibid.*, ELP to HPH, February 1775.
63. Parker, *Parker's Guide*, 103.
64. HPH to Elizabeth Trapier, 28 November 1775, in *The Papers of Eliza Lucas Pinckney and Harriott Pinckney Horry Digital Edition*, ed. Schulz.
65. Journal of the Second Provincial Congress, 265.
66. TP to HPH, 11 June 1776, in *The Papers of Eliza Lucas Pinckney and Harriott Pinckney Horry Digital Edition*, ed. Schulz.
67. *Ibid.*, CCP to ELP, 5 June 1776.
68. *Ibid.*, CCP to ELP, 7 July 1776.

Chapter Five

1. Henry Laurens to a friend quoted in Wallace, *The Life of Henry Laurens*, 224.
2. TP to HPH, 9 May 1776, in *The Papers of Eliza Lucas Pinckney and Harriott Pinckney Horry Digital Edition*, ed. Schulz.
3. Ravenel, *Eliza Pinckney*, 270.
4. Fryer, "The Mind of Eliza Pinckney: An Eighteenth Century Woman's Construction of Herself," *SCHM*, 99, 237.

5. Quincy, *Memoir of the Life of Josiah Quincy Jun. of Massachusetts By His Son*, 115–116.

6. Edgar, *Partisans and Redcoats*, 28–29.

7. ELP to HPH, 28 May 1778, in *The Papers of Eliza Lucas Pinckney and Harriott Pinckney Horry Digital Edition*, ed. Schulz.

8. *Ibid.*, ELP to HPH, 8 June 1776.

9. *Ibid.*

10. *Ibid.*, TP to HPH, 23 May 1778.

11. *Ibid.*, TP to HPH, 7 April 1778.

12. *Ibid.*, TP to HPH, 21 November 1778. The date of the birth of Harriott Horry was entered into the Horry family bible and later transcribed as October 4, 1770. However, this excerpt from Thomas Pinckney's letter to his sister proves that the year was misinterpreted and she was in fact born in 1778.

13. *Ibid.*, HPH to ELP, 30 December 1778.

14. *Ibid.*, TP to HPH, 7 January 1779.

15. *Ibid.*, Charles Pinckney II to ELP, 24 February 1779.

16. *Ibid.*

17. *Ibid.*, TP to ELP, 17 May 1779.

18. *Ibid.*, ELP to TP, 17 May 1779.

19. Higgins, "The South Carolina Rev. War Debt & Its Holders, 1779–1780," *SCHM*, 72, 15–29.

20. Accounts Audited of Claims Growing Out of the Revolution, Eliza Lucas Pinckney, 8 October 1779, in *The Papers of Eliza Lucas Pinckney and Harriott Pinckney Horry Digital Edition*, ed. Schulz.

21. Williams, *A Founding Family the Pinckneys of South Carolina*, 139, footnote 97.

22. Garden, *Anecdotes*, II, 264.

23. Williams, *A Founding Family the Pinckneys of South Carolina*, 141, footnote 106.

24. *Ibid.*, 143, footnote 115.

25. CCP to ELP, 15 October 1779, in *The Papers of Eliza Lucas Pinckney and Harriott Pinckney Horry Digital Edition*, ed. Schulz.

26. *Ibid.*

27. *Ibid.*

28. Moultrie, *Memoirs of the American Revolution So Far as It Related to the States of North and South Carolina*, II, 60.

29. TP to HPH, 30 March 1780, in *The Papers of Eliza Lucas Pinckney and Harriott Pinckney Horry Digital Edition*, ed. Schulz.

30. *Ibid.*, TP to HPH, 12 April 1780.

31. *Ibid.*, TP to ELP, 10 April 1780.

32. Moultrie, *Memoirs of the American Revolution So Far as It Related to the States of North And South Carolina*, II, 86.

33. *Ibid.*, 86–97.

34. *Ibid.*, 104–105. The British put the number of men captured at 5,683. The number is high because it included not only Continental soldiers and militia, but also a number of noncombatants who were asked to bring in their arms, but who never participated in the defense of Charleston. According to Rivington's *Royal Gazette* the British force numbered 13,572.

35. Tarleton, *A History of the Campaigns of 1780 and 1781 in the Southern Provinces of North America*, 27.

36. This episode was taken from *Eliza Pinckney*, a biography of Eliza, written by her great-great-granddaughter, Harriot Horry Ravenel, in 1896. It is reported to be one of the earliest memories of Harriott Pinckney, Charles Cotesworth's daughter, then aged four. Ms. Ravenel explains in the preface to her work: "When 'tradition' is given [as the source], I mean the stories and accounts of Mrs. Pinckney's grandchildren; the old people to whose conversations I listened in childhood and youth, drinking in their endless tales of the old time and of the part which their relations and friends had borne in it. For these traditions I have been careful not to trust my own memory alone, and have written only such things as are corroborated by the recollections of the other surviving members of the same generation." It can be found on pp. 286–287.

37. For more information on the Battle at Waxhaws see the following websites: www.allthingsliberty.com/2013/08debating-waxhaws-was-there-a-massacre/ and www.carolana.com/sc/revolutionbattleofwaxhaws.html.

38. Tarleton, *A History of the Campaigns of 1780 and 1781 in the Southern Provinces of North America*, 75.
39. CCP to TP, 9 June 1780, in *The Papers of Eliza Lucas Pinckney and Harriott Pinckney Horry Digital Edition*, ed. Schulz.
40. *Ibid.*, TP to ELP, 11 June 1780.
41. *Ibid.*, ELP to Elizabeth Motte Pinckney, 18 June 1780.
42. *Ibid.*
43. *Ibid.*, Elizabeth Motte Pinckney to ELP, 17 July 1780.
44. *Ibid.*, TP to ELP, July [1780].
45. Tarleton, *A History of the Campaigns of 1780 and 1781 in the Southern Provinces of North America*, 75.
46. ELP to TP, August 1780, in *The Papers of Eliza Lucas Pinckney and Harriott Pinckney Horry Digital Edition*, ed. Schulz.
47. *Ibid.*
48. *Ibid.*, ELP to Elizabeth Motte Pinckney, 12 September 1780.
49. *Ibid.*, CCP to ELP, 7 September 1780.
50. *Ibid.*, ELP to TP, September 1780.
51. *Ibid.*, ELP to Elizabeth Motte Pinckney, 12 September 1780.
52. *Ibid.*, TP to HPH, 7 September 1780.
53. Pinckney, *Life of General Thomas Pinckney by his grandson Rev. Charles Cotesworth Pinckney.* 77.
54. *Ibid.*, CCP to ELP, 29 December 1780.
55. *Ibid.*, HPH to ELP 25 December 1780.
56. *Ibid.*, TP to Daniel (Charles Lucas Pinckney—CLP) Horry, 26 October 1780.
57. *Ibid.*, ELP to TP, 6 December 1780.
58. *Ibid.*, ELP to Mrs. Evance 25 September 1780.
59. *Ibid.*, ELP to TP, 6 December 1780.
60. Greene, *The Papers of Nathanael Greene*, 6, 589.
61. Itemized bill in Pinckney Papers, Red Box, "1744–1832 and 1857," Library of Congress.
62. ELP to Daniel (CLP) Horry, 6 July 1783, in *The Papers of Eliza Lucas Pinckney and Harriott Pinckney Horry Digital Edition*, ed. Schulz.
63. *Ibid.*, ELP to Daniel (CLP) Horry, 16 April 1782.
64. *Ibid.*, CCP to ELP, 25 July 1781.
65. *Ibid.*, Daniel Huger Horry, Jr., Accounts Audited of Claims Growing out of the Revolution, 25 June 1783.

Chapter Six

1. "Correspondence of Hon. Arthur Middleton," *SCHGM*, 3, 106–107.
2. CCP to HPH, 22 September 1782, in *The Papers of Eliza Lucas Pinckney and Harriott Pinckney Horry Digital Edition*, ed. Schulz.
3. *Ibid.*, Edward Rutledge to Arthur Middleton, 16 March 1782.
4. *Ibid.*, HPH to unidentified person, [1782].
5. *Ibid.*, Daniel Huger Horry, Jr., Accounts Audited of Claims Growing out of the Revolution, 25 June 1783 and Petitions to the South Carolina General Assembly, 1785, #5, South Carolina Department of Archives and History.
6. *Ibid.*, ELP to Daniel (CLP) Horry, 7 August 1783.
7. *Ibid.*
8. *Ibid.*, ELP to Dr. Alexander Garden, May 1782.
9. *Ibid.*
10. ELP to Mrs. Onslow in Pinckney, *The Letterbook of Eliza Lucas Pinckney*, 185.
11. HPH to ELP, 7 and 8 November 1785, in *The Papers of Eliza Lucas Pinckney and Harriott Pinckney Horry Digital Edition*, ed. Schulz.
12. *Ibid.*, ELP to George Keate, 2 April 1786.
13. *Ibid.*, CCP to ELP, 22 February 1787.
14. *Ibid.*, ELP to Daniel (CLP) Horry, 6 February 1787.

15. Daniel Huger Horry changed his name to Daniel Charles Lucas Pinckney Horry sometime after he finished his education. He returned to South Carolina for a brief time in 1798 but then returned to France where he married the great-niece of Lafayette. He spent the rest of his life in France and died there in 1828.

16. CCP to HPH, 17 April 1790, in *The Papers of Eliza Lucas Pinckney and Harriott Pinckney Horry Digital Edition*, ed. Schulz.

17. *Ibid.*, HPH to George Washington, 14 April 1791.

18. John Rutledge, Jr., to TP, April 28 [29], Pinckney Papers, Red Box F in Library of Congress.

19. CCP to TP, 25 May 1792, in *The Papers of Eliza Lucas Pinckney and Harriott Pinckney Horry Digital Edition*, ed. Schulz.

20. *Ibid.*, CCP to TP, 14 July, 1792.

21. *Ibid.*, CCP to TP, 27 August 1792.

22. *Ibid.*, TP to HPH, 27 January 1793.

23. *Ibid.*, CCP to TP, 16 April 1793.

24. *Ibid.*

Epilogue

1. HPH, 1793 Journal, 16 April 1793, in *The Papers of Eliza Lucas Pinckney and Harriott Pinckney Horry Digital Edition*, ed. Schulz.

2. *Ibid.*, Journal, 20 April 1793.

3. *Ibid.*, William Ward Burrows to TP, 27 April 1793.

4. *Ibid.*, Journal, 7 May 1793.

5. *Ibid.*, Journal, 9 May 1793.

6. *Ibid.*, Journal, 7 May 1793.

7. *Ibid.*, Journal, 10 to 26 June 1793.

8. *Ibid.*, William Ward Burrows to TP, 27 May 1793.

9. *Ibid.*, CCP to TP, 17 July 1793.

Bibliography

Borick, Carl P. *A Gallant Defense the Siege of Charleston, 1780.* Columbia: University of South Carolina Press, 2003.

Bryant, Margaret. *The London Experience of Secondary Education.* London: Athlone, 1986.

Buchanan, John. *The Road to Guilford Courthouse the American Revolution in the Carolinas.* New York: John Wiley & Sons, 1997.

Corkran, David H. *The Cherokee Frontier: Conflict and Survival, 1740–1762.* Norman: University of Oklahoma Press, 1962.

"Correspondence of Hon. Arthur Middleton." *South Carolina Historical and Genealogical Magazine* 27, Third Series.

Coulter, E. Merton, *Georgia: A Short History.* Chapel Hill: University of North Carolina Press, 1947.

Earle, Peter. *The Making of the English Middle Class: Business, Society and Family Life in London, 1660–1730.* Berkeley: University of California Press, 1989.

Edgar, Walter. *The Letterbook of Robert Pringle,* 2 vols. Columbia: University of Carolina Press, 1972.

_____. *Partisans and Redcoats.* New York: HarperCollins, 2001.

Feeser, Andrea. *Red, White & Black Make Blue: Indigo in the Fabric of Colonial South Carolina Life.* Athens: University of Georgia Press, 2013.

Franklin, Benjamin. *The Writings of Benjamin Franklin.* Albert Henry Smyth, ed. 10 vols. New York, 1905–1907.

Fryer, Darcy R. "The Mind of Eliza Pinckney: An Eighteenth-Century Woman's Construction of Herself." *South Carolina Historical Magazine* 99, Third Series.

Garden, Alexander. *Anecdotes of the American Revolution Illustrative of the Talents and Virtues of the Heroes and Patriots Who Acted the Most Conspicuous Parts Therein, Volume II.* Charleston: A. E. Miller, 1828.

Gaspar, David Barry. *Bondsmen and Rebels.* Baltimore: Johns Hopkins University Press, 1985

Glen, James. "Description to the Board of Trade, 1749." Chapman J. Milling, ed. *Colonial South Carolina: Two Contemporary Descriptions.* Columbia: University of South Carolina Press, 1951.

Greene, Nathanael. *The Papers of General Nathanael Greene, 10 Volumes.* Providence: Rhode Island Historical Society, 1989.

Higgins, Robert W. "The South Carolina Rev. War Debt & Its Holders, 1776–1780." *South Carolina Historical Magazine* 72, First Series.

Journal of the Second Provincial Congress. Charles-Town, 1776.

Langley, Clara A. Abstractor. *South Carolina Deed Abstracts 1719–1772.* Easley, SC: Southern Historical Press, Inc., 1983.

Mackesy, Piers. *The War for America 1775–1783.* Cambridge: Harvard University Press, 1964.

Merriman, John. *Modern Europe, Volume One, From the Renaissance to the Age of Napoleon.* New York: W. W. Norton, 1996

Mandal, Dr. Ananya, MD. "History of Breast Cancer." http://www.news-medical.net/health/History-of-Breast-Cancer.aspx.

Manigault, Peter. Letters of Peter Manigault in *South Carolina Historical and Genealogical Magazine* 32, First Series.

Moultrie, William. *Memoirs of the American Revolution So Far as It Related to the States of North and South Carolina.* New York, 1802.

Nicholson, Desmond V. *Antigua, Barbuda and Redonda: A Historical Sketch* Antigua: The Museum of Antigua and Barbuda, n.d.

Oliver, Vere Langford. *The History of the Island of Antigua, 3 vols.* London: Mitchell and Hughes, 1894–1899.

Pares, Richard. *A West-India Fortune.* London: Longmans, Green, 1950.

Parker, John C., Jr. *Parker's Guide to the Revolutionary War in South Carolina,* 2d ed. Conshohocken, PA: Infinity Publishing, 2013.

Parker, Matthew. *The Sugar Barons, Family, Corruption, Empire and War in the West Indies.* New York: Walker & Company, 2011.

Pennsylvania Gazette, Jan. 29, 1741

Pinckney, the Rev. Charles Cotesworth. *Life of General Thomas Pinckney/By His Grandson Rev. Charles Cotesworth Pinckney.* Boston: Houghton Mifflin, 1895.

Pinckney, Elise, ed. *The Letterbook of Eliza Lucas Pinckney, 1739–1762.* Columbia: University of South Carolina Press, 1997.

Pinckney Papers, Red Box. "1744–1832 and 1857." Library of Congress, Washington, D.C.

Pinckney Papers, Red Box F, Library of Congress, Washington, D.C.

Quincy, Josiah. *Memoir of the Life of Josiah Quincy Jun. of Massachusetts: By His Son.* Boston: Cummings, Hilliard, 1825.

Ravenel, Harriott Horry. *Eliza Pinckney.* New York: Charles Scribner's Sons, 1896.

Ramagosa, Carol Walter. "Eliza Lucas Pinckney's Family in Antigua, 1668–1747." *South Carolina Historical Magazine* 99, Third Series.

Rogers, George C., Jr. *Charleston in the Age of the Pinckneys.* Columbia: University of South Carolina Press, 1980.

Rogoziński, Jan. *A Brief History of the Caribbean, From the Arawak and the Carib to the Present.* New York: Facts on File, 1992.

Schulz, Constance, ed. *The Papers of Eliza Lucas Pinckney and Harriott Pinckney Horry Digital Edition* (American Founding Era Collection). Charlottesville: University of Virginia Press Rotunda, 2012.

Salley, A. S., Jr. "Col. Miles Brewton and Some of His Descendants," *South Carolina Historical and Genealogical Magazine* 2.

Sirmans, M. Eugene. *Colonial South Carolina, A Political History, 1663–1763.* Chapel Hill: University of North Carolina Press, 1966.

Spruill, Julia Cherry. *Women's Life & Work in the Southern Colonies.* New York: W. W. Norton, 1972.

Stedman, Charles. *The History of the Origin, Progress and Termination of the American War, 2 Vols.* London, 1794.

Smith, Alice R. Huger, and D.E. Huger Smith. *Dwelling Houses of Charleston, South Carolina,* Charleston: History Press, 2007.

Tarleton, Banastre. *A History of the Campaigns of 1780 and 1781 in the Southern Provinces of North America.* London: 1787.

Taylor, Alan. *American Colonies.* New York: Viking Press, 2001.

Wallace, David D. *The Life of Henry Laurens.* New York, 1915.

———. *South Carolina: A Short History, 1520–1944.* Columbia: University of South Carolina Press, 1961.

Webber, Mabel L. "The Thomas Pinckney Family of South Carolina." *South Carolina Historical and Genealogical Magazine* 39, First Series.

Weir, Robert. *Colonial South Carolina, a History.* Columbia: University of South Carolina Press, 1997.

Will of Charles Pinckney, Public Record Office, London, England, folios 41–55 11/947.

Williams, Frances Leigh. *A Founding Family: The Pinckneys of South Carolina,* New York: Harcourt, Brace, Jovanovich, 1978.

———. *Plantation Patriot: A Biography of Eliza Lucas Pinckney,* New York: Harcourt, Brace & World, 1967.

Williams, Harriet Simons. "Eliza Lucas and Her Family: Before the Letterbook." *South Carolina Historical Magazine* 99, Third Series.

Wulf, Andrea. *The Brother Gardeners.* New York: Alfred A. Knopf, 2009.

Index

215

Quash, Mulatto (John Williams) 30, 64
Quincy, Joshua, Jr. 101, 127

Ravenel, Harriott Horry 63
Rawdon, Lord 167, 181
Rice 21, 26–27, 29–30, 34, 40, 60, 62, 67, 98,
  102, 127–128, 136, 156, 175, 181, 188, 190,
  193–194
Ripley 74–75, 78, 85, 88, 93
Rugeley, Col. Henry 161
Rutledge, Edward 133, 180–182, 184, 189
Rutledge, John 120, 125, 143, 148, 154, 156,
  158–160, 182, 185

St. Andrew's Church 6, 55, 185
St. Augustine 30, 33, 38, 132–135, 137
St. Kitts (St. Christopher's) 8–9, 11
St. Peter's Church 201
St. Philip's Church 6, 105, 185
Santee region 101–102, 112, 119, 134–135,
  156, 158, 160, 166, 174, 180–182, 186, 190;
  river 102, 150–152, 154, 156, 159–160, 181,
  195
Savannah: city 37, 132, 137, 139, 141–144,
  146–147, 149, 152, 194; river 33, 87, 137–
  139
Seven Years' War 77, 81, 92; see also French
  and Indian War
Shippen, Dr. William 197, 200–201
silk 67, 73, 101–102, 106, 111
smallpox 37, 70–71, 91, 93, 151–152, 165,
  174; inoculation 70–71, 90, 93, 165

Snee Plantation 158, 170–171, 173–174
Starrat, George 23, 30, 62
Stead, Mary 191; see also Pinckney, Mary
  (Mrs. Charles Cotesworth)
sugar 8–13, 15, 20–23, 62, 99, 116, 136, 156,
  172
Sullivan's Island 119, 121–123, 151, 199
Sumter, Col. Thomas 165–166, 174

Tarleton, Lt. Col. Banastre 152, 154–155,
  158–162, 165, 173, 177
Tate, Dr. James 5, 200–201
Thompson, Lt. Col. William 122–123

Vernon, Adm. Edward 28, 33

Wappoo: creek 6, 13, 22, 27, 149, 152; planta-
  tion 29–30, 34, 36, 42, 45–51, 54–56, 59,
  62, 64
War of the Austrian Succession 39, 56, 62,
  69, 76–77
War of the Spanish Succession 23
Washington, George 77, 118, 131, 159, 163,
  166, 174, 180–181, 194–196, 200–201
Washington, William 154–155, 158
Waxhaws 161–162
West Indies 5–8, 10–13, 19, 24–25, 27–28,
  32, 34, 36, 39–43, 52, 60, 116, 136, 139,
  143, 145, 147, 188, 190; see also the Indies
Windward Islands 7
Woad 41
Woodward, Mrs. 28–29, 36, 64